T5-BQA-770

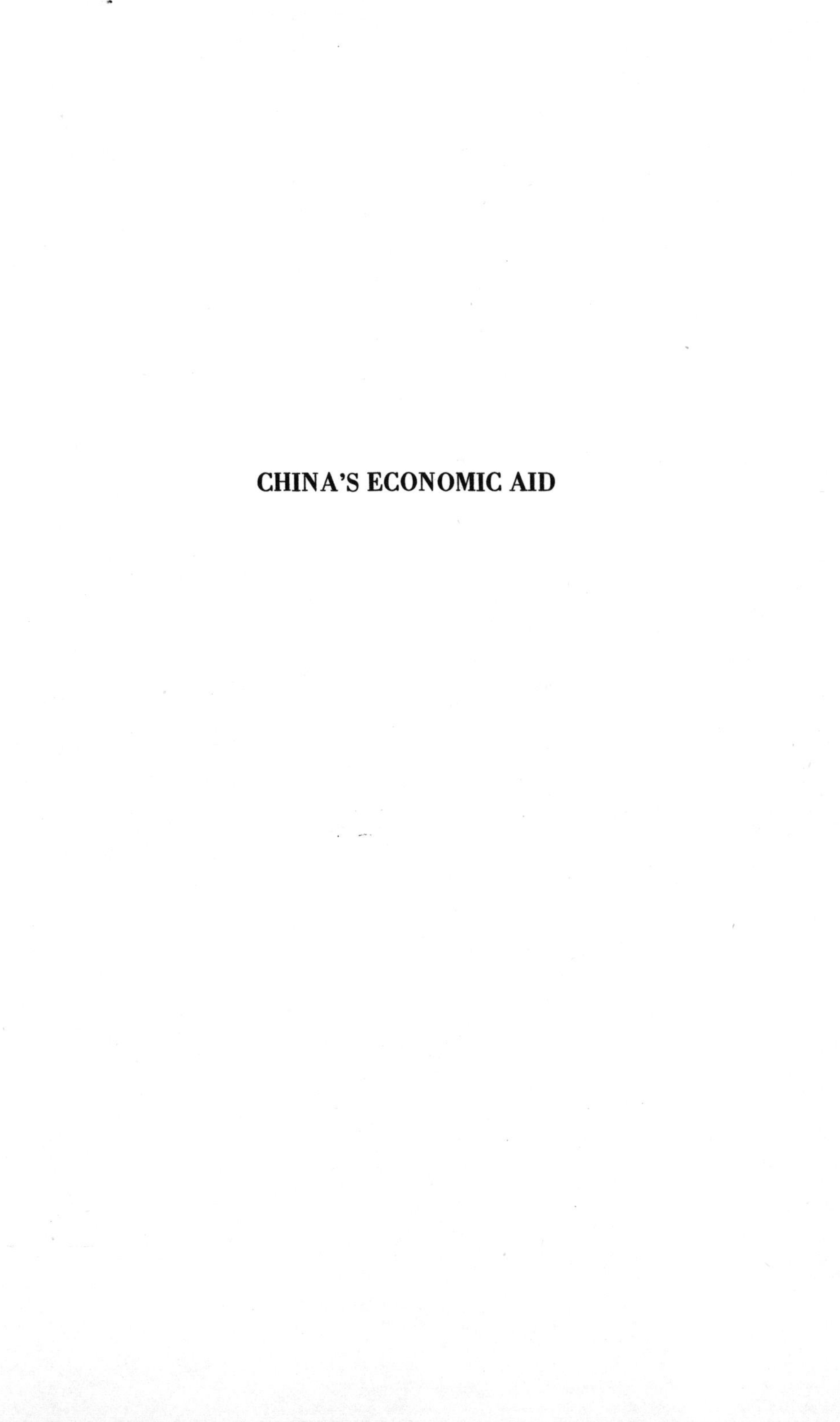

CHINA'S ECONOMIC AID

China's Economic Aid

by WOLFGANG BARTKE

A Publication of the Institute of Asian Affairs, Hamburg

HM Holmes & Meier Publishers • New York

Published in the United States of America 1975
by Holmes & Meier Publishers, Inc.
101 Fifth Avenue
New York, N.Y. 10003

Library of Congress Catalog Card No. 74-78315

ISBN 0-8419-0179-1

Printed in Great Britain

CONTENTS

NOTE

This paper covers China´s economic aid only, leaving out all reference to military aid. The information available on the economic aid she has granted to socialist countries is scanty. We know few details of Chinese aid to Albania and the People´s Republic of Mongolia and hardly any of the aid granted to North Korea, North Vietnam and Romania. The reason why the author has all the same decided to include in Part II (China´s Economic Aid Projects) even the few details known to him is that he wanted to give the reader a certain idea of the range of such aid, which may enable him to draw his own conclusions.

In order to render the picture as clear as possible, the countries receiving economic aid from China have been listed in alphabetical order in both Parts I and II, instead of making a subdivision by regions.

The paper covers China´s economic aid from its beginning up to and including December 1973.

An earlier study on the subject, covering the period from the beginning of Chinese economic aid until June 1971, appeared in German in January 1972 as No. 44 of "Mitteilungen des Instituts für Asienkunde Hamburg".

The translation of this paper from the German text was made by Mrs. Waldtraut Jarke, Hamburg.

SOURCES (with abbreviations)

AE	Afrique Express, Brussels
AN	Afrique Nouvelle, Dakar
ANA	Aden News Agency
Antara	Indonesian News Agency
ATA	Albanian News Agency
ATP	Agence Tschadienne de Presse
AW	Arab World
BfA	Bundesstelle für Aussenhandelsinformationen,
C.a.	CHINA aktuell, a monthly review of the Institut fuer Asienkunde Hamburg
CCA	Chinese Communist Affairs, Taipei
CDN	Ceylon Daily News
ChR	China-Report, Vienna
CN	China Notes
CT	China Topics
Dawn	"Dawn", Karachi
EAS	East African Standard, Nairobi
dpa	Deutsche Presseagentur, Hamburg
DT	Daily Telegraph, London
DW	Die Welt, Hamburg
EG	Evergreen Peking
ENA	Ethiopian News Agency
EpAkL	Entwicklungspolitische Aktivitäten der kommunistischen Länder, a monthly review of "Forschungsinstitut der Friedrich-Ebert-Stiftung", Bonn
FAZ	Frankfurter Allgemeine Zeitung
FCW	Free China Weekly, Taipei
FEER	Far Eastern Economic Review, Hong Kong
FML	Farouk M.Luqman, "Yemen 1970", Aden (?) 1970
FT	Foreign Trade, Peking
HB	Handelsblatt
HdE	Handbuch der Entwicklungshilfe, Nomos, Baden-Baden, ed. Dr.Krug
INA	Iraqi News Agency
JMJP	Jen-min Jih-pao (Volkszeitung), Peking
JT	Japan Times
KTA	The Kabul Times Annual, Kabul
MAPA	Maghrib Arab Press Agency, Rabat
NCNA	New China News Agency, Peking
NfA	Nachrichten für Aussenhandel, Cologne
NR	News Release, US Bureau of Public Affairs, Department of State, "Aid and Trade in 1972"
NT	The Nationalist, Dares Salam
NYHT	New York Herald Tribune
NZZ	Neue Zürcher Zeitung
OEL	Der Ostblock und die Entwicklungsländer, quarterly reports of "Forschungsinstitut der Friedrich-Ebert-Stiftung
OP	Ost-Probleme, Verlag Wissenschaft und Politik, Cologne
OR	Orient, Deutsches Orient-Institut, Hamburg
PCh	People's China
PR	Peking Rundschau, Peking
R	Reuter
RA(DMS)	Aden Radio, according to "Daily Monitoring Service", Aden
... Radio	relates to information taken from "Summary of World Broadcasts", Part 3, as edited by The Monitoring Service of the British Broadcasting Corporation, Caversham Park, Reading, Berks.
RM	Roter Morgen, Central Organ of the Communist Party of Germany, Marxist-Leninist, Hamburg
SANA	Syrian Arab News Agency
Ta	Tanyug, (Yugoslav News Agency)
TKP	Ta Kung Pao, Hong Kong
TT	The Times, London
UNDP	United Nations Development Program, Afghanistan Branch: Status of all Projects Financed Through Foreign Aid for Afghanistan's Development
UPI	United Press International
VVRCh	Verträge der Volksrepublik China, Schriften des Instituts für Asienkunde, Alfred Metzner Verlag, Frankfurt-Berlin und Otto Harrassowitz, Wiesbaden
WhChM	What is Happening in China Mainland, Taipei

CHINA'S ECONOMIC AID

There are two reasons why Chinese economic aid deserves our special attention. First, it is offered by a country which will itself continue to be a developing country for years to come, and secondly, the conditions under which this aid is offered have the character of a model.

It would be unfair to belittle the significance of Chinese aid by arguing that China sought to attain political aims by offering such aid. This is more or less true of all donors of economic aid. However, what distinguishes China from other donor countries is her guiding principle that economic aid must not bring economic profit to the donor. Of course, with Western industrial nations the motive of profitability is known to be inherent in the system, but it is difficult to understand that socialist countries, among them the Soviet Union, should also aim at making a profit out of their economic aid.

In an epoch when the rich countries were getting richer and richer, while the poor ones were sinking deeper and deeper into poverty, it was China, of all countries, that became a model donor of economic aid. China set new standards in this field, thereby causing other countries to reflect on the situation and blush at the thought that the term "aid" had been misused in such a shameless way.

Communist China has been demonstrating to the Western industrial nations (and it is only they we can consider here, because they keep asserting that their politics are founded on Christian traditions) what she understands by true aid which, in normal usage, can only be so called if it is substantially selfless.

We live in a time when the energy crisis has deprived the less developed countries of any chance of further development, because the costs of oil imports have risen to such an extent that they now exceed what those countries receive in the way of economic aid loans. Even before the crisis, the burden of the interest to be paid on the aid loans granted by capitalist and socialist donors lay heavily upon the recipients of economic aid but now this burden has become all but intolerable. No great imaginative power is needed to foresee that only China, who does not demand interest on her economic aid loans, will remain acceptable to the developing countries.

China is outstanding not only because she offers economic aid loans without interest, but also because her terms of repayment are more favourable than those granted by any other country, capitalist or communist. In the case of relatively large loans, China has made it a habit to offer the recipients a period of grace of 10 years, beginning on completion of the economic aid project in question. Only after the lapse of this period does repayment begin, the instalments usually being distributed over 20 years.

Table 1

THE FOREIGN AID OF THE PR CHINA TO LESS DEVELOPED COUNTRIES (in million US $)

	1956	1957	1958	1959	1960	1961	1962	1963	1964	1965	1966	
Asia	35.1	25.6	35.5		32.6	128	20.5		4.2	260	20	
1 Birma		4.2				88.2						
2 Cambodia	22.4	5.6			11.4							
3 Indonesia			25			30				200		
4 Laos							10					
5 Nepal	12.7				21.2	9.8					20	
6 Pakistan										60		
7 Sri Lanka		15.8	10.5				10.5		4.2			
Africa			4.9		25	39.2		74	119.2	21.1	15	
1 Algeria			4.9					51		2		
2 Burundi												
3 Cameroon												
4 Central Africa										4.1		
5 Chad												
6 Congo (Brazz.)									25.4			
7 Dahomey												
8 Equatorial Guinea												
9 Ethiopia												
10 Ghana						19.6			22.4			
11 Guinea					25							
12 Kenya									18			
13 Malagasy												
14 Mali						19.6			7.9		3	
15 Mauritania												
16 Mauritius												
17 Nigeria												
18 Ruanda												
19 Senegal												
20 Sierra Leone												
21 Somalia								23				
22 Sudan												
23 Tanzania									45.5		12	
24 Togo												
25 Tunisia												
26 Uganda										15		
27 Upper Volta												
28 Zaire												
29 Zambia												
Near Middle East	4		16	0.1			4.8	16.4	108.2	27.5		
1 Afghanistan										27.5		
2 Egypt	4								80			
3 Iraq												
4 South Yemen												
5 Syria								16.4				
6 Yemen			16	0.1			4.8		28.2			
Latin America												
1 Chile												
2 Guyana												
3 Peru												
Europe												
1 Malta												
Total	39.1	25.6	56.4	0.1	57.6	167.2	25.3	90.4	231.6	308.6	35	7

1)Estimate

68	1969	1970	1971	1972	1973	Total	at an interest of 2,5%	free of interest	Donation	still unused in Dec '73 (estimate)
2		219.3	128.2	68.2	30	1,089.2	69.7	711.9	257.6	
						92.4	4.2	84	4.2	25
					30[1)]	69.4			69.4	25
						255	55	150		229
						10		6[1)]	4	
				35[1)]		98.7		55	43.7	15
.2		210	93.7			445.7		335.7	110	110
		9.3	34.5	33.2		118	10.5	81.2	26.3	20
6	45	460	323.5	282	199	1,643.7	0.5	1,612.6	30.6	
			40			99.9		93	6.9	20
				20		20		20		15
				20[1)]	10[1)]	30		30		20
						4.1		4.1		
					12	12		12		10
1				30[1)]		56.4		56.4		20
				46		46		46		35
			10[1)]			10		10		5
			80			80		80		40
						42		42		15
	45			30[1)]		100		100		25
						18		15	3	12
					12	12		12		11
5[1)]		20			10[1)]	65.5		53.4	8.1	15
			23.5			27.5		27.5		15
				32		32		32		25
				3		3		3		1
				20		20		20		15
					20[1)]	20		20		18
			20[1)]			20		20		15
			110			133		130	3	70
		35	40			75		75		25
		270				327.5	0.5	320.4	6.6	80
				45		45		45		35
				36		36		36		25
						15		12	3	10
					10[1)]	10		10		8
					115	115		115		110
		135			10	168.8		168.8		60
.6		43.2	72	138.1		449.9		428.9	21	
				49		76.5		69.5	7	35
						94		80	14	80
			36			36		36		25
9.6		43.2		20[1)]		72.8		72.8		35
			36	47		99.4		99.4		45
				22.1		71.2		71.2		25
			42	117		159		159		
				65		65		65		65
				52		52		52		45
			42			42		42		30
						42.6				
				42.6		42.6		42.6		35
,6	45	722.5	565.7	647.9	229	3,384.4	70.2	2,993,4	309.2	1589

Another unique feature consists of the conditions China has made for the remuneration of Chinese aid personnel working in foreign countries. All Chinese economic aid agreements contain a clause that Chinese technicians and workers shall be paid in accordance with the standards of the receiving country. As the standard of living in most developing countries is low, the cost factor is thus reduced considerably. It is therefore fairly safe to assume that the expenses on salaries and wages in a Chinese economic aid project will amount to far less than half the costs arising for the recipient countries when comparable economic aid is offered by capitalist countries or communist countries other than China. Since about half the costs in any economic aid project are, as a rule, wages and salaries, this fact must be taken into consideration when Chinese aid is compared with aid offered by capitalist or other communist countries, if we want the comparison to be correct.

Thus China's economic aid contribution, which totalled US$ 3,384 million up to and including 1973, is certainly worth more than the same nominal sum when granted by any of the capitalist countries or the Soviet Union, because the reduction in personnel costs effected by the Chinese results in an increase in the actual "body" of economic aid.

A just appreciation of this situation therefore leads us to assume that the aid the People's Republic of China has offered over the years is in effect at least 25 % higher than the nominal loans would suggest. Hence we are justified in thinking that the Chinese economic aid loans totalling US$ 3,384m. are actually worth about US$ 4,200m.

This situation should be borne in mind by all those who peruse the statements, tables and analysis which follow: these can, of course, give nothing but the naked figures. The picture they reveal, however, is somewhat distorted and should be mentally revised so as to take into account the more favourable relation between personal and non-personal costs in Chinese aid.

The total amount of economic aid offered by China between 1956 and 1973

Table 1 shows all Chinese economic aid from the beginning up to and including 1973. As may be seen from the table, China has offered economic aid loans totalling US$ 3,384m., more than half of which had been used by the recipients by the end of 1973.

The greater part of the loans, viz. US$ 1,643m. (or 48,8 %), went to 29 countries in Africa. Second comes Asia where seven countries received a total of US$ 1,089m. (32 %). This order is of fairly recent date. Until 1972 Asia had occupied the first place, but the Cultural Revolution and the recognition of the People's Republic by the USA changed this. From 1971, when Henry Kissinger made his first visit to China, until the end of 1973, 30 states had entered into diplomatic relations with the People's Republic of China, including eight countries in Africa, and -even more important - the reluctance on the part of many of the non-aligned countries to accept Chinese economic aid disappeared. This applied especially to Africa. Whereas no more than 13 African countries had received Chinese economic aid before June 1971, this number had risen to no less than 29 by the end of 1973, in a matter of 30 months !

Table 2

CHINESE ECONOMIC LOANS TO LESS DEVELOPED COUNTRIES, 1956-1973

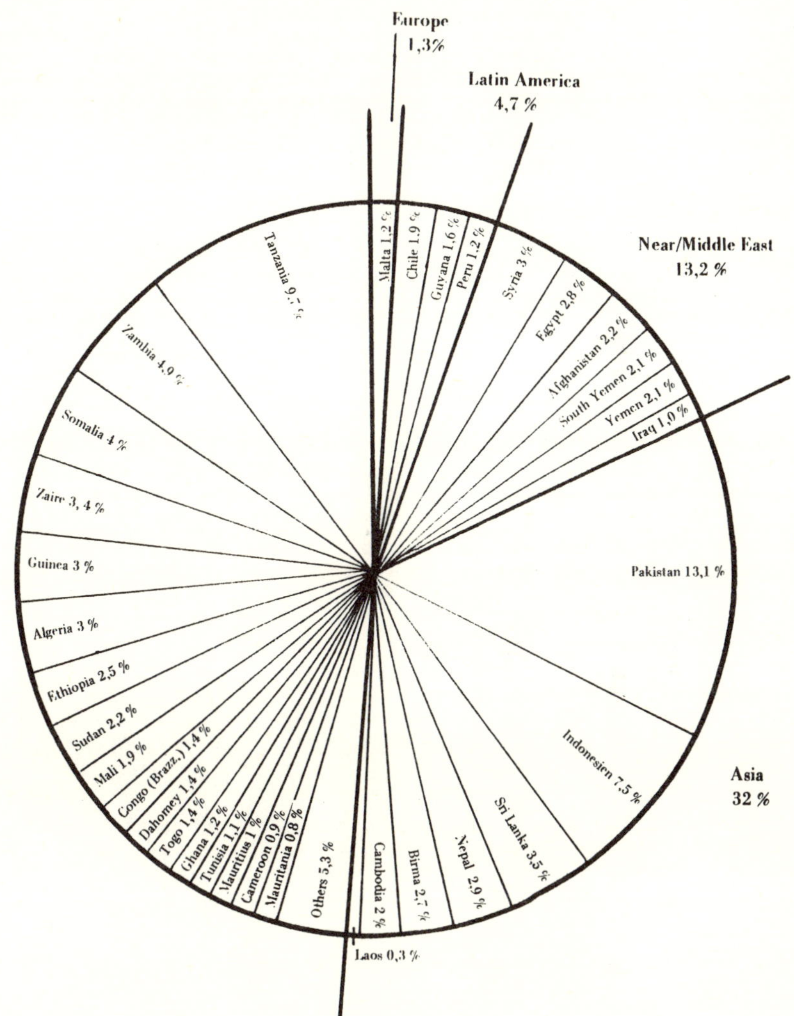

The political dividend China gained from her reconciliation with the USA was immense, because it enabled her to bring into full play her intentions of becoming the protector of the Third World nations. The scare of Communist infiltration, which had given China the reputation of being the political villain in the US-influenced parts of the world ever since the Dulles era, was now lifted.

In the list of recipients of Chinese economic aid loans, Africa and Asia are followed by the Near and Middle East, as represented by six countries which have received Chinese loans totalling US$ 450m. (13.2 %). In this region the change in foreign policy since 1971 has not had any effect on China's economic aid situation, and no new country was added to the list of recipients until the end of 1973.

In Latin America, however, China succeeded in making some headway following its reconciliation with the USA in 1971 and 4.7 % of her economic aid loans went to three countries, among them Chile, to which no economic aid was given after President Allende's fall.

The only European country receiving economic aid from China since 1972 is Malta. It may be assumed that Peking's satisfaction in offering this aid is particularly great. From China's point of view, the necessity of aiding Malta shows the inability of the European countries, which five decades ago still kept China in a semi-colonial state, adequately to support one of their poorer relations.

Table 2 illustrates the distribution, per cent, of Chinese economic aid over regions and countries. The idea is to help the reader recognize the centres of gravity.

Precedence of the recipients

Table 3, on the other hand, shows the precedence of the individual recipients of Chinese economic aid throughout the world, regardless of regions. It also indicates the extent to which the loans offered had actually been used by the recipients by the end of 1973.

Pakistan, with US$ 445m., ranks first. This is all the more remarkable, as the Chinese aid to this country did not begin until 1965 when Pakistan and India went to war over the Rann of Kutch, in which China clearly took Pakistan's side, because she was disappointed at India's refusal to come to a reasonable understanding with her Asian sister-country over bilateral problems, though the countries of the Third World had been strongly urged to do so at the Bandung Conference where Chou En-lai and Nehru had cooperated as speakers for the Third World. China's economic involvement in Pakistan must therefore be seen primarily under its political aspect. Of course, India's rapprochement with the Soviet Union has played a great part in this, as it has been one of the guiding principles of Chinese foreign policy since 1964 (or even earlier) to regard the Soviet Union's friends as China's enemies. Nowhere does the rivalry between the two big communist powers in the countries of the Third World come out more clearly than in Pakistan, where economic aid loans amounting to US$ 474m. from the Soviets vie with Chinese loans worth US$ 445. In 1971 the Soviet Union still offered Pakistan

Table 3

LOANS GRANTED BY THE PEOPLE'S REPUBLIC OF CHINA AND THE EXTENT TO WHICH THEY HAD BEEN USED BY 1973
(in million US - $)

	Country	Amount
1	Pakistan	445,7
2	Tanzania	327,5
3	Indonesia	255
4	Zambia	168,8
5	Somalia	133
6	Sri Lanka	118
7	Zaire	115
8	Guinea	100
9	Algeria	99,9
10	Syria	99,4
11	Nepal	98,7
12	Egypt	94
13	Birma	92,4
14	Ethiopia	80
15	Afghanistan	76,5
16	Sudan	75
17	South Yemen	72,8
18	Yemen	71,2
19	Cambodia	69,4
20	Mali	65,5
21	Chile	65
22	Congo (Brazz.)	56,4
23	Guyana	52
24	Dahomey	46
25	Togo	45
26	Malta	42,6
27	Ghana	42
28	Peru	42
29	Iraq	36
30	Tunisia	36
31	Mauritius	32
32	Cameroon	30
33	Mauritania	27,5
34	Burundi	20
35	Ruanda	20
36	Senegal	20
37	Sierra Leone	20
38	Kenya	18
39	Uganda	15
40	Chad	12
41	Malagasy	12
42	Laos	10
43	Equatorial Guinea	10
44	Upper Volta	10
45	Central Africa	4,1
46	Nigeria	3

Legend

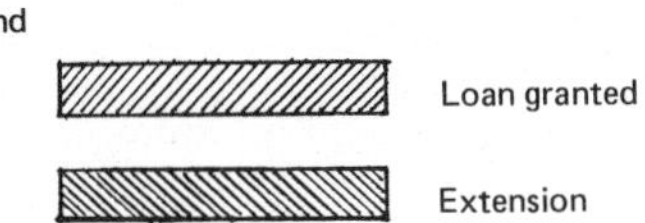

US$ 209m., which was a serious provocation to China, whose loan offers in that year totalled no more than US$ 94m. The Chinese press has neither mentioned the Soviet economic aid to Pakistan nor reproached the latter country for having accepted Soviet help. This shows, on the one hand, that the Sino-Soviet struggle for Pakistan's leaders have exercised great skill in playing off the two rivals against one another for Pakistan's benefit. It may safely be assumed that the reconciliation between Pakistan and India early in 1974 has been brought about by Moscow in an effort to push China into a secondary position. We must wait and see in how far China will succeed in making up for this temporary disadvantage - possibly by recognizing or even supporting Bangladesh.

The second place on the list of recipients of Chinese economic aid is occupied by Tanzania, with loans totalling US$ 327m. She owes this high rank to the fact that China offered the highest loan ever for the construction of the Tan-Zam railway. China's ambitions to make this project a success are due to the fact that the World Bank had declared the project unprofitable, while a mixed Canadian and French consortium arrived at the opposite conclusion but did not find anybody to provide the funds. China wants to prove that she is capable of carrying out large projects for the benefit of non-aligned countries within a shorter time and on more favourable terms than any other country. Occasional difficulties arising from the supply of poor-quality products, by the sale of which the project is partly financed, may be neglected, as China offered Tanzania a new loan amounting to US$ 71m. in March 1974, when President Kaunda visited Peking.

The third country on the list of economic aid recipients is Indonesia, with loans worth US$ 255m. The table clearly shows that only a minor portion of this sum had been used when China discontinued her aid. Zambia ranks fourth and this is chiefly due to the Tan-Zam railway. There are still four more countries receiving loans of US$ 100 million or more, viz. Somalia (133m.), Sri Lanka (118m.), Zaire (115m.) and Guinea (100m.).

It should be noted that almost half of the Chinese loans have gone to the above-indicated eight states (with loans worth US$ 1,163m.), while 38 other recipients had to be content with the remainder. Since Indonesia no longer receives any aid, seven countries must therefore now be considered centres of gravity for Chinese economic aid.

Chinese loans as distributed over the years

Table 4 is a list of the loans offered during the various years. After a modest beginning of economic aid in 1956-1958, a recession followed in 1959, when China's loans totalled a mere US$ 0.1m. In 1960 they passed the 100 million dollar limit but fell again in the following two years. By the end of 1963, i.e. during the first eight years, China had granted economic aid to 21 countries. The first peak was reached in 1964 (US$ 231.6m.) and another one in 1965 (US$ 308.6m.). During the years of the Cultural Revolution (1966-1969) there was another recession. The absolute maximum so far was reached in 1970, when loans totalled US$ 722.5m.; this was mainly due to the enormous loan for the Tan-Zam railway (US$ 405m.) and the then highest sum offered to Pakistan (US$ 210m.). 1970 must therefore be

Table 4

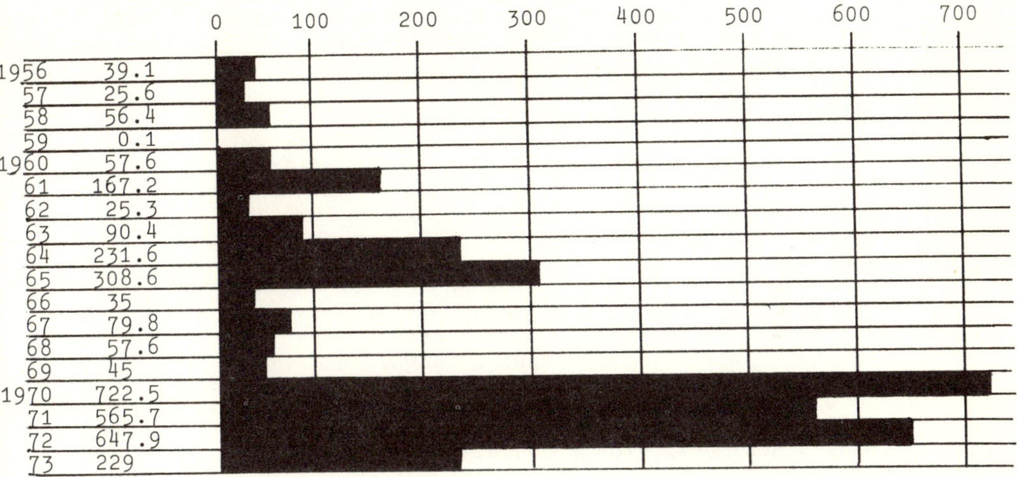

Table 6

LOANS AT AN INTEREST OF 2.5 %, in million US$

	1958	1961	1964	Total
Burma	4.2[1]			4.2
Sri Lanka	10.5			10.5
Indonesia	25	30[2]		55
Tanzania			0.5	0.5
	39.7	30	0.5	70.2

1) declared interest-free on June 15, 1964
2) 2 %

regarded as an exceptionally good year for loans. Very high loans were also offered in 1971 (US$ 565.7m.) and in 1972 (US$ 647m.), when China's foreign policy departed from its isolationist course after the Cultural Revolution, thereby opening up a great variety of new possibilities for economic aid loans. The fact that in 1973 the total fell to US$ 229m. merely underlines the exceptional character of the three preceding years. It may therefore be assumed that in future the loans offered by China will range between US$ 300m. and 500m. per annum.

The recessions apparent in Table 4 had internal causes. There were certain periods when China was so thoroughly absorbed by her own problems that she had no time for international involvement. However, it should be noted that the implementation of economic aid on the whole has at no time suffered from the domestic situation, and even during the Cultural Revolution the projects already begun were continued.

Chinese donations

An item of particular interest in Chinese economic aid are the donations (Table 5), officially referred to as "non-repayable loans". Between 1956 and 1973 China gave a total of US$ 309m. as a donation to six countries each in Africa and Asia and to two countries in the Near and Middle East. The African countries received US$ 30.6m., the Asian countries, US$ 257.6m., the Near and Middle Eastern countries, US$ 21m. Asia takes precedence, owing to China's desire to create goodwill on her own doorstep. In any case it should be noted that no less than US$ 257m., i.e. 23.6 % of all loans offered to the seven Asian countries (US$ 1,089m.) consists of donations. The country profiting most is Cambodia all of whose loans are non-repayable. (The 1973 loan, the sum of which has been estimated by us, has not officially been declared a donation, but under the existing circumstances, we can safely assume that a government which has never received anything but donations in the past will not have to pay back its loans while it is in exile).

The second country benefited by donations is Nepal, 44 % of whose Chinese loans (totalling US$ 98.7m.) were donations. Pakistan, too, profited from China's generosity, when China declared that two earlier loans totalling US$ 110m. would be converted to donations. Sri Lanka received 22 % of all loans, totalling US$ 118m., as donations. This shows that among the countries benefited by Chinese donations are three direct neighbours of India - an indication of their political significance.

Loans with interest

Next to the donations, the Chinese loans, for which interest has to be paid, call for our attention (Table 6). When China began to offer economic aid, she still recognized the primacy of the Soviet Union, which has made it a rule never to grant economic aid loans without interest. However, China soon endeavoured to gain a certain independence from the Soviet model. While pursuing this policy, she did not adopt the Soviet principle with regard to interest on loans. The fact that China did demand interest on loans in five cases was probably due to her initial doubts as to the worthiness of the recipients to receive interest-free loans. In the case of Indonesia, China's suspicions were

Table 5

CHINESE DONATIONS

	1956	1957	1958	1959	1960	1961	1962	1963	1964	1965	1966	1967	1968	1969	1970	1971	1972	1973	TOTAL	Proportion of total loans (in %)
AFRICA			4.9		0.2			3	13.9	5	3.6								30.6	1.8
Algeria			4.9							2									6.9	7
Kenya									3										3	16
Mali					0.2				7.9										8.1	12
Somalia								3											3	2
Tanzania									3		3.6								6.6	2
Uganda										3									3	17
ASIA	35.1	15.8	5.6		32.6	14	14.5										110		257.6	23.6
Burma						4.2													4.2	5
Cambodia	22.4		5.6		11.4													30[1)]	69.4	100
Laos							4												4	40
Nepal	12.7				21.2	9.8													43.7	44
Pakistan																	110		110	25
Sri Lanka		15.8					10.5												26.3	22
NEAR MIDDLE EAST	4											10					7		21	4.7
Afghanistan																	7		7	9
Egypt	4											10							14	17
	39.1	15.8	10.5		32.6	14.2	14.5	3	13.9	5	3.6	10					117		309.2	

1) Estimate

justified, while Sri Lanka was found deserving of better treatment, so that the loan was later declared to be free of interest. Apart from a very small loan to Tanzania in 1964 (US$ 0.5m.), it may be said that, after the Sino-Soviet breach, China has definitely found her own way of offering all economic aid loans without interest, which certainly sets an example for other donors.

China´s aid as compared with aid offered by the Soviet Union and the East European countries

A comparison between economic aid granted by China and aid granted by the Soviet Union and other socialist countries in Eastern Europe during the period between 1954 and 1972 permits us to draw the following conclusions :

The economic aid offered by all communist countries together totalled US$ 15,477m., of which the Soviet Union alone provided US$ 8,229m. (or 53%), the socialist countries in Eastern Europe US$ 4,110m. (27 %), and China US$ 3,128m. (20 %). It is true that China ranks last here, but we must not forget that she herself is one of the less developed countries. For example, when China began to offer economic aid in 1956, the steel production of Czechoslovakia, a comparatively small country, exceeded that of China. Even in 1972 the amount of steel produced by China was a mere 13 % of the amount produced by the Soviet Union and the other socialist countries in Eastern Europe. These few indications relating to one of the key industries should suffice to throw into relief China´s special achievements in the field of economic aid.

Table 7 also shows that 1972 was the first year in which China surpassed the Soviet Union as a donor of economic aid. Even granting that, as stated above, the years from 1970 till 1972 were exceptional, this fact remains significant. It clearly indicates the growing rivalry between China and the other communist donors of economic aid and makes us wonder if China may not generally have succeeded already in outdoing her rivals, including in particular the Soviet Union.

The rivalry between China and the Soviet Union

Table 8 shows where China´s economic aid was greater than that of the Soviet Union and vice versa. It may be seen at a glance that China predominates in Africa, where her aid surpasses that of the Soviet Union in 22 countries, as against 8 where the Soviet Union is predominant. Among the 22 countries where Chinese exceeds Soviet aid are 10 to which Moscow does not give any aid at all. Again we clearly see China´s endeavours to befriend the non-aligned countries, whose advocate she aspires to be. That she is pursuing this course with great effect may be seen, inter alia, from the fact that the establishment of diplomatic relations was in many cases promptly followed by agreements on economic and technical cooperation, involving aid loans. It is not mere chance that China has meanwhile ousted the Soviet Union as a donor of economic aid in Africa,- not only as far as the sums offered are concerned but also as regards the number of countries to which such aid has been offered.

Things are different in Asia where the Soviet Union has given more than twice as much economic aid as China, the lion´s share falling to India (US$ 1,593m.) and Afghanistan (US$ 826m.). Even

Table 7

LOANS OF THE COMMUNIST COUNTRIES TO LESS DEVELOPED COUNTRIES (in million US-$)[3]

	1954-1972				1971				1972				1973
	Total	USSR	Eastern Europe	China	Total	USSR	Eastern Europe	China	Total	USSR	Eastern Europe	China	China
Total	15.477	8229	4110	3128	1804	865	468	471	1871	581	645	648	219
Africa	3480	1252	800	1418	614	192	99	323	491		209	282	189
Algeria	767	421	246	100	229	189		40	150		150		
Burundi	20								20			20	
Cameroon	28	8		20[1]					20			20[1]	10[1]
Central Africa	6	2		4	2	2							
Chad													12
Congo (Brazz.)	66	10		56					30			30[1]	
Dahomey	46			46					46			46	
Equatorial Guinea	1	1		10[1]	11	1		10[1]					
Ethiopia	199	102	17	80	80			80					
Ghana	237	93	102	42									
Guinea	293	168	25	100					30			30[1]	
Kenya	66	48		18									
Malagasy													12
Mali	138	60	23	55									10[1]
Mauritania	30	3		27	23			23					
Mauritius	32			32					32			32	
Morocco	128	88	40										
Nigeria	48	7	38	3	24		24		3			3	
Ruanda	20			20					20			20	
Senegal	7	7											20[1]
Sierra Leone	48	28		20[1]	20			20[1]					
Somalia	204	66	5	133	110			110	2		2		
Sudan	292	64	153	75	115		75	40					
Tanzania	360	20	13	327					7		7		
Togo	45			45					45			45	
Tunisia	143	34	73	36					36			36	
Uganda	31	16	15										
Upper Volta													10[1]
Zaire													115
Zambia	225	6	50	169					50		50		10
Asia	4261	2353	849	1059	243	209		34	177	74	35	68	30
Bangla Desh	99	74	25						99	74	25		
Birma	133	15	26	92									
Cambodia	81	25	17	39									30[1]
India	1,975	1,593	382										
Indonesia	632	114	263	255									
Laos	10			10									
Nepal	119	20		99					35			35[1]	
Pakistan (2)	994	474	74	446	303	209		94					
Sri Lanka	218	38	62	118	34			34	43		10	33	
Near/Middle East	6412	4092	1871	449	690	423	195	72	804	363	303	138	
Afghanistan	914	826	12	76	5	5			170	121		49	
Egypt	1,963	1,198	671	94	338	196	142						
Iran	997	562	435						10		10		
Iraq	1,004	549	419	36	295	222	37	36	200		200		
South Yemen	103	14	16	73	16		16		20			20[1]	
Syria	703	317	287	99	36			36	224	84	93	47	
Turkey	548	534	14						158	158			
Yemen	180	92	17	71					22			22	
Latin America	1197	448	590	159	257	41	174	42	359	144	98	117	
Argentina	54	45	9										
Bolivia	56	30	26		27	2	25						
Brazil	312	85	227										
Chile	423	238	120	65	134	39	95		229	144	20	65	
Colombia	7	2	5		5		5						
Ecuador	15		15		5		5						
Guyana	52			52					52			52	
Peru	223	28	153	42	86		44	42	78		78		
Uruguay	45	20	25										
Venezuela	10		10										
Europe	127	84		43					43			43	
Greece	84	84											
Malta	43			43					43			43	

(1) Estimate

(2) Including Bangladesh

(3) The figures for the USSR and Eastern Europe have been taken from NR 8/1973, Appendix Table 1

in Pakistan, whose friendship China has been trying hard to gain since 1965, the Soviet Union still takes precedence (with economic aid worth US$ 474m.) over China (with US$ 445m.). This close competition may also be seen from the last loans offered to Pakistan by the two rivals in 1971, when the Soviet Union again took the lead with US$ 209m., as compared with a mere US$ 94m. from China.

In the Near and Middle East, Soviet preponderance is also marked, Chinese aid amounting to no more than about one-tenth of the aid granted by the Soviet Union. China will hardly have a chance of seriously endangering Soviet predominance there. The relationship between Egypt and the Soviet Union demonstrates, however, that the balance of forces in this region is more than unstable.

In Latin America where, apart from Cuba, she did not gain a foothold until 1970, China is also inferior to the Soviet Union.

A comparison between the Soviet Union and China makes it quite clear where the Soviet centres of gravity are: in India (US$ 1,593m.), Egypt (1,198m.), Afghanistan (826m.), Iran (562m.), Iraq (549m.), Turkey (534m.), Pakistan (474m.) and Algeria (421m.). These countries have received a total of US$ 6,157m., i.e. 75 of all economic aid loans offered by the Soviet Union. This shows, on the one hand, the political involvement of the Soviet Union and on the other, the great political importance of economic aid in general. In comparison to the Soviet Union, China's tendency to give the bulk of her economic aid to few countries is less marked. Both donors give economic aid to 46 countries. While China has a wider influence in Africa, the Soviet Union ranks first in Latin America.

In Africa the rivalry between China and the Soviet Union has been decided for the time being in China's favour. On that continent the Soviet Union retains undisputed positions only in Algeria, Ghana and Morocco, while China has taken the lead in the other countries.

Centres of gravity in Chinese economic aid

Part III contains a specification of all Chinese economic aid projects. In the analysis below, two groups of projects will be singled out to demonstrate where China's special abilities lie and what is her most original contribution.

Textile mills

The experience which enables China to carry out large-scale projects in the textile industry dates back to the pre-communist, semi-colonial era when huge textile factories were erected in Chinese cities, in particular Shanghai, some of them with foreign capital. These factories are still the backbone of China's textile industry. From its beginning the People's Republic therefore had a relatively large potential of skilled labour in this field, of which it did not hesitate to make use when it started to give economic aid.

Table 9 is a list of the textile factories completed with Chinese economic aid in less developed countries as well as those under construction or planned. This type of aid has benefited 18 countries, where a total of 18 textile mills were completed or

Table 8

THE RIVALRY BETWEEN THE PR CHINA AND THE SOVIET UNION IN ECONOMIC AID

China spent more in	PRCh	USSR	USSR spent more in	USSR	PRCh
Africa	1284	286		943	358
Burundi	20		Algeria	421	100
Cameroon	30	8	Ethiopia	102	80
Central African Rep.	4	2	Ghana	93	42
Chad	12		Guinea	168	100
Congo (Brazz.)	56	10	Kenya	48	18
Dahomey	46		Morocco	88	
Equat. Guinea	10	1	Nigeria	7	3
Malagasy	12		Uganda	16	15
Mali	65	60			
Mauritania	27	3			
Mauritius	32				
Ruanda	20				
Senegal	20	7			
Sierra Leone	20				
Somalia	133	71			
Sudan	75	64			
Tansania	327	20			
Togo	45				
Tunisia	36	34			
Upper Volta	10				
Zaire	115				
Zambia	169	6			
Asia	643	212		2967	521
Birma	92	15	Bangladesh	74	
Cambodia	69	25	India	1593	
Indonesia	255	114	Pakistan	474	445
Laos	10		Afghanistan	826	76
Nepal	99	20			
Sri Lanka	118	38			
Near Middle East	72	14		3252	300
South Yemen	72	14	Egypt	1198	94
			Iran	562	
			Iraq	549	36
			Syria	317	99
			Turkey	534	
			Yemen	92	71
Latin America	94	28		420	65
Guyana	52		Argentina	45	
Peru	42	28	Bolivia	30	
			Brazil	85	
			Chile	238	65
			Colombia	2	
			Uruguay	20	
Europe	43			84	
Malta	43		Greece	84	

Table 9

TEXTILE MILLS BUILT WITH CHINESE AID

Country	Location	Technical data		Annual production		Costs in million US dollars	Number of workers	Time of construction	Remarks
		spindles	looms	cloth million m.	yarn tons				
Afghanistan	Bagrami	20 000	600	12	800			3/1969-3/1070	
Albania	Berat district	35 000	600					3/1966-11/1969	
Burma	Merktila	40 000	600					-1967	almost completed when econ.aid was discontinued
	Thamaing	21 600	196					-1965	
	unknown								planned for 1973
Cambodia	Kompong Cham	11 788	210	1.5	1450		613	-1960	
	Battambang	10 400	92	4.3	726			-1967	
Congo (Brazz.)	Kinsoundi							1966-1969	The factory substantially meets the country's needs.
Ghana	Juapong							10/1965-	not completed when econ.aid was discontinued
Indonesia	Bandjaran							-10/1965	70% completed when econ. aid was discontinued.
	Bandung	30 000						-10/1965	not completed when econ. aid was discontinued
									six more mills not completed
Iraq									
Mali	Ségou	24 500	400			16	3200	2/1966-5/1968	
Mongolia, PR	Ulan Bator							1958-1960	
Nepal				10					planned in 1973
Pakistan	Tarbela	25 000				6.5			planned in 1973
	Mirpur	25 000				9			planned in 1973
South Yemen	Aden ?								under construction since 1971
Sri Lanka	Pugoda			9	500	11	1100	5/1969- ?	
	Minneriya	25 000	600						planned in 1973
	several locations								50 small textile mills
Sudan	Hasahisa								planned in 1973
Syria	Hama					4		2/1969-3/1971	Annual production: 6,000 or 4,500 tons of textiles
	Idlib					4			
	Deir ez-Zor					4			
Tanzania	Ubungo	40 000	978	20	900	7 or 9	2000	1966-1968	
	Ruvu							-1972	
Yemen	Sana	12 000	300					1964-1967	

under construction in 1973. Another six mills were at the planning stage. Each of these factories has between 10,000 and 40,000 spindles and between 100 and 1,000 power looms. The construction cost between US$ 11m. and 16m. per mill. Textile mills were built in two communist countries, Albania and the People's Republic of Mongolia. Four mills were completed in the African states of Mali, Congo-Brazzaville, and Tanzania, respectively, while one mill was planned in 1973. One mill was under construction in Ghana when diplomatic relations were severed in 1966. Although economic aid started again with the resumption of diplomatic relations in February 1972, there had been no indication by the end of 1973 that the construction of the mill was being continued. In Asia five textile mills were built in Burma, Cambodia, Indonesia and Sri Lanka respectively, and several others are planned in Nepal and Pakistan. In the Near and Middle East textile mills were built in Syria and Yemen. Others are under construction or at the planning stage in Iraq, South Yemen and Syria.

Medical groups

A unique feature of Chinese economic aid are the mobile medical groups (Table 10), whose propaganda effect is enormous. While all the other Chinese economic aid groups working in foreign countries have no contact with the local population other than through their work, the mobile medical groups come into contact with a great number of people from all walks of life.

Table 10

CHINESE MEDICAL GROUPS

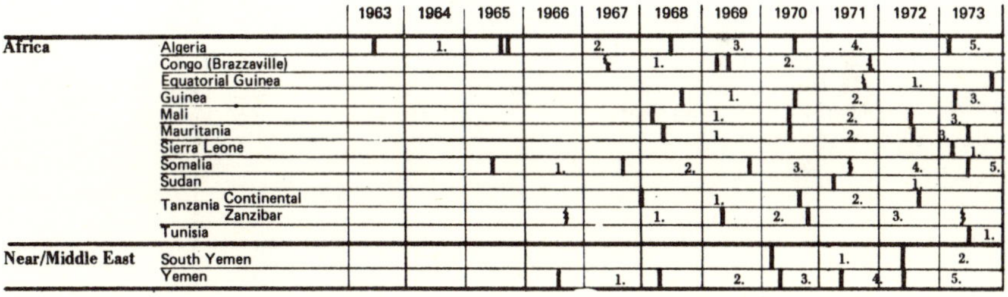

		1963	1964	1965	1966	1967	1968	1969	1970	1971	1972	1973
Africa	Algeria		1.			2.		3.		4.		5.
	Congo (Brazzaville)						1.		2.			
	Equatorial Guinea										1.	
	Guinea							1.		2.		3.
	Mali							1.		2.		3.
	Mauritania							1.		2.		3.
	Sierra Leone											1.
	Somalia				1.		2.		3.		4.	5.
	Sudan										1.	
	Tanzania Continental							1.		2.		
	Tanzania Zanzibar						1.		2.		3.	
	Tunisia											1.
Near/Middle East	South Yemen									1.		2.
	Yemen					1.		2.	3.	4.		5.

Legend: The figure denotes the number of group concerned
estimated time of arrival/departure

Each medical group consists of between 20 and 50 persons, including doctors and medical workers. Every year each group treats about 50,000 out-patients and carries out an average of 3,000 surgical operations. The first such group started work in Algeria in 1963, and Chinese medical activities have since been going on in eleven African countries and two countries in the Near and Middle East. By the end of 1973, a total of 70 working years had been accomplished by the medical groups, which are as a rule replaced by new groups from China every two years. The number of out-patients treated by the Chinese groups had risen to a total of about 3 million, and the number of surgical operations to about 20,000.

Other tasks to be solved by the medical groups include the establishment of hospitals and factories producing pharmaceutical products. These installations are usually Chinese donations.

A point deserving attention is that Equatorial Guinea, Mauritania, Congo-Brazzaville and Tanzania have caused this form of Chinese economic aid to be discontinued.

It has already been stated above that the salaries and wages of Chinese economic aid personnel in the devleoping countries are very much lower than those paid to the staff sent by Western countries and the Soviet Union. The practical effect of this on the medical groups will now be explained.

By the end of 1973 each of the Chinese medical groups - which average 35 persons, i.e. 5 doctors and 30 medical workers - had accomplished a total of about 70 working years. In the case of comparable groups from capitalist countries, the monthly salary of one doctor would be US$ 2,000 and of one medical worker US$ 1,200. The salaries of 5 doctors in each group for 70 working years would total about US$ 8m. and of 30 medical workers about US$ 30m. In addition, non personal costs, as for the maintenance of mobile stations and the establishment of hospitals and pharmaceutical factories, must be estimated at another US$ 10m. This would mean a total expenditure of about US$ 50m. The Chinese, on the other hand, have generally agreed to adapt the level of salaries and wages to be paid to their economic aid personnel to the wage level in the recipient countries. It would probably be justified to assume that the cost of China's project may be estimated at about a quarter of that of comparable projects undertaken by capitalist countries.

On the whole, China's way of offering economic aid can be regarded as exceptionally effective. It is to be hoped that the other donor countries will follow the Chinese example so that what is now misleadingly called "aid" will eventually come truly to deserve that name.

LEADING CHINESE PERSONNEL ENGAGED IN ECONOMIC AID

Ministry of Economic Relations with Foreign Countries

Originally formed as a staff office of the State Council, raised to a Commission of the State Council in June 1964, transformed to a Ministry in April 1971.

Before the Cultural Revolution, the following cadres worked in what was then the Commission of Economic Relations with Foreign Countries (as of 1966):

Chairman:	Fang Yi	方　毅
Vice-Chairmen:	Hsieh Huai-te	谢怀德
	Li Ch'iang	李　強
	Li Ying-chi	李应吉
	Wang Tao-han	汪道涵
	Yang Lin	杨　琳

Fang Yi, since January 1961 Director of the Staff Office of Economic Relations with Foreign Countries, remained head when the office was transformed to become a Commission of the State Council in 1964 and also after transformation to a Ministry in 1971. Fang has thus been the top Chinese cadre in economic aid for 14 years. In April 1969 Fang was elected alternate member of the 9th Central Committee of the CCP and in August 1973, member of the 10th Central Committee.

Hsieh Huai-te was appointed Vice-Chairman of the Commission in December 1964 and remained on this post until January 1971 when he disappeared. The reasons for his disappearance are unknown.

Li Ch'iang, who had become Deputy Director of the Staff Office of Economic Relations with Foreign Countries in 1961, became Vice-Chairman of the Commission after transformation. After the Cultural Revolution he was one of the Vice Ministers of Foreign Trade, became Acting Minister in January 1973, and has been Minister since October 1973.

Since the Cultural Revolution the following team has been responsible, first in the Commission of Economic Relations with Foreign Countries and, after transformation, in the Ministry (as of December 1973):-

Minister:	Fang Yi	方　毅
Vice Ministers:	Ch'en Mo-hua (f)	陈慕华
	Han Tsung-cheng	韓宗正
	Hsieh Huai-te	谢怀德
	Li K'e	李　克
	Shih Lin	石　林
Responsible persons:	Chang Yün-chih	張韵之
	Ch'en Chin-lung	陳晋龙
	Ch'eng Fei	程　飞
	Chiang P'ing	江　平
	Chou P'ing	周　平
	Chung Yü-yi	钟羽仪
	Lü Hsüeh-chien	吕学俭
	Yang Jung-chieh	杨荣杰

Personal data of leading personnel (unless stated on the previous page)

Ch´en Mo-hua (f) appeared for the first time in 1962 when she was Deputy Director in the Bureau of Complete Industrial Sets in the Staff Office of Economic Relations with Foreign Countries. After the Cultural Revolution, she reappeared in 1970 and was seen in the company of an industrial development delegation from Pakistan. Since April 1971 she has been Vice Minister in the new Ministry of Economic Relations with Foreign Countries. In January 1972 she was deputy leader of a Chinese government delegation visiting Zambia. In August 1973 she was elected member of the Central Committee of the CCP by the 10th Party Congress.

Han Tsung-cheng was Deputy Director of a Bureau in the Commission of Economic Relations with Foreign Countries in 1970, and has been Vice Minister since the transformation of this Commission in April 1971. In July 1971, Han was in the Chinese party and government delegation, which visited North Korea. In August 1973 he led an economic delegation to Malta.

Li K´e was Director of the Fifth Department of the Commission of Economic Relations with Foreign Countries in 1965 and disappeared one year later. He reappeared in May 1973 as a Vice Minister after the transformation of the Commission.

Shih Lin had been appointed adviser to the Chinese delegation for the Second Afro-Asian Conference scheduled to take place in Algiers in 1965 which never took place. After the Cultural Revolution he reappeared in 1970 and has been a Vice Minister of the transformed Commission since May 1973.

Chang Yün-chih was Deputy Director in the Office of International Cooperation in the Scientific and Technological Commission in 1961. After the Cultural Revolution he reappeared in December 1970 as a responsible person in the Commission of Economic Relations with Foreign Countries. Chang was not seen after February 16, 1972.

Ch´en Chin-lung was a responsible person in the Second Bureau of the Ministry in November 1971 when he visited Guinea as a member of the Chinese government delegation. This remained his only appearance.

Ch´eng Fei has been Director of a Bureau in the Ministry since July 1972. In May 1973 he was a member of the Chinese government delegation to Sri Lanka.

Chung Yü-yi acted as a responsible person of the Commission, or Ministry, respectively, between September 1970 and April 1972, when he was seen for the last time.

Lü Hsüeh-chien was a responsible person in a department of the Ministry between July 1970 and April 1972. He led an economic and technical study group to Sierra Leone in April 1972 and has not been seen since that time.

Yang Jung-chieh appeared as Deputy Director of a department of the Ministry in October 1973.

PART I

THE AGREEMENTS ON ECONOMIC AID

1965, Mar 24: Agreement on economic and technical cooperation (1). China grants an interest-freeloan of US-$ 27.5m (2). One quarter of this sum is to be given as a consumer goods loan (3).

Oct 13: Protocol relating to the agreement on economic a and technical cooperation (4). Afghanistan is to receive one quarter of the loan in the form of consumer goods, the proceeds from the sale of which will be used for the construction of the Chinese aid projects (4).

1966, Jul 29: Protocol relating to the agreement on economic and technical cooperation (5).

Sep 25: Protocol relating to the agreement on economic and technical cooperation.
Subject: Construction of a station for the cultivation of silkworms (6).

1967, Apr 1: Protocol relating to the agreement on economic and technical cooperation.
Subject: Construction of an experimental fishbreeding centre (7).

4: Protocol relating to the agreement on economic and technical cooperation.
Subject: Construction of a poultry farm (8).

Dec 6: Protocol relating to the agreement on economic and technical cooperation.
Subject: Construction of an experimental tea plantation (9).

1968, Mar 17: Agreement on the delegation of Chinese experts and the supply of building material (10).

Nov 19: Supplement to the agreement on economic and technical cooperation (10).

1969, Mar 8: Protocol relating to the agreement on economic and technical cooperation.
Subject: Experimental fishbreeding centre (11).

12: Protocol relating to the agreement on economic and technical cooperation.
Subject: Experimental tea plantation (12).

1970, Nov 14: Protocol relating to the agreement on economic and technical cooperation.
Subject: Use of the remainder of the loan. US-$ 2m. to be used for the purchase of Chinese consumer goods (13).

---

(1) NCNA Mar 24, 1965 (2) HdE II D 21 p.15 (3) BfA/NfA Sep 2, 1966 (4) Kabul Radio Oct 13, 1965 (5) NCNA Jul 29, 1966 (6) NCNA Sep 28, 1966 (7) NCNA Apr 2, 1967 (8) NCNA May 28, 1967 (9) NCNA Dec 14, 1967 (10) EpAkL 2/69 p.71 (11) NCNA Mar 9, 1969 (12) NCNA Dec 23, 1969 (13) NCNA Nov 17, 1970 and Kabul Radio Nov 14, 1970

1971, Jan 2: Protocol relating to the agreement on economic and technical cooperation.
Subject: Parwan irrigation project (1).

1972, Jul 25: Chinese donation of hospital (2) estimated at US-$ 7m.

May (?) US-$ 25m. credit allocation for the expansion of the Bagrami textile mill (3).

1973, Feb : Notes for the expansion of the Bagrami textile mill (4)

Nov 21: Protocol on hospital construction (5).

---

(1) Kabul Radio Jan 2, 1971 (2) NCNA Jul 25, 1972 (3) FEER Sep 30, 1972 (4) NCNA Mar 1, 1973 (5) NCNA Nov 21, 1973

1958, Nov : Donation of US-$ 4.9m. (1).

1963, Oct 28: Agreement on economic and technical cooperation (2). China grants an interest-free loan of NF 250m. = US-$ 51m. (3).

1964, Sep 19: Protocol relating to the agreement on economic and technical cooperation (4). (No details).

1965, Feb : Donation of a cargo-ship of 13,000 t (5) (estimated value: US-$ 2m).

Mar : Chou En-lai offers Ben Bella a loan of US-$ 25m. (at an interest of 1 %, term: 20 years). No agreement. Ben Bella rejects the Chinese offer to send 5,000 experts to Algeria (1).

Dec 8: Protocol on medical aid.
Subject: Delegation of a new Chinese medical group (6). (The protocol on the sending to Algeria of the first Chinese medical group in 1963 was not published).

1966, Jun 20: Protocol relating to the agreement on economic and technical cooperation.
Subject: Construction of exhibition and fair buildings (7).

Sep 26: Protocol relating to the agreement on economic and technical cooperation.
Subject: Construction of a ceramics plant 8).

1970, Mar 17: Protocol on medical aid (9).
Subject: the forth Chinese medical group
(The protocol on the sending of the third medical group was not published).

1971, Jul 27: Agreement on economic and technical cooperation (10). (no details).

1972, Apr : Protocol on China's medical aid (11).

Nov 6: Agreement on economic and technical cooperation (12). Chinese loan estimated at US-$ 25m.
Protocol relating to the agreement for undertaking certain agricultural and industrial projects (12)

---

(1) HdE II D 21 p.3 (2) JMJP Oct 31, 1963 (3) NCNA Oct 11, 1963 (4) JMJP Sep 20, 1964 (5) NCNA Feb 24, 1965 (6) NCNA Dec 8, 1965 (7) NCNA Jun 20, 1966 (8) NCNA Sep 26, 1966 (9) NCNA Mar 17, 1970 (10) NCNA Jul 27, 1971 (11) NZZ Apr 12, 1972 (12) NCNA Nov 6, 1972

1958, Nov 1: Agreement on economic and technical cooperation. China grants a loan of Kyat 20m. = US-$ 4.2m. at an interest of 2.5 %. The loan is intended for the construction of a cotton mill (1)

1961, Jan 9: Agreement on economic and technical cooperation. China grants an interest-free loan of £ 30m. = US-$ 84m.., payable between Oct 1, 1961 and Sep 30, 1967. Repayment between 1971 and 1980 (2). With this agreement China undertakes to give technical aid to Burma by sending experts and technicians, to deliver complete plants, sets of machines, material, and technical know-how, to help in the training of Burmese technicians, to supply other materials for sale in Burma so that the Chinese aid can be paid for (3).
Donation of US-$ 4.2 m. (?) for the construction of another cotton mill (4).

Dec 21: Protocol relating to the agreement on economic and technical cooperation.
Subject: Specification of 13 industrial and infrastructural projects to be built with the loan granted in 1961, viz. three hydroelectric stations at Kentung, Kunlong, Machambaw, one cotton mill at Merktila, one paper factory at Sittang, one tire factory at Rangoon, two sugar factories at Bilin and Paungde, two plywood factories at Moulmein and Rangoon, expansion of the steel works at Ywana built by the German firm of DEMAG, two bridges crossing the Salween River (5).

1962, Feb : Protocol relating to the agreement on economic and technical cooperation (6). (No details given).

1964, Jul 13: In a joint communiqué China and Burma decide to speed up the projects covered by the agreement of January 1962 (6).

1967, Nov : As a result of the discontinuance of Chinese aid (July 1967), 412 Chinese experts are called back (7).

1971, Oct 7: Supplement relating to the agreement on economic and technical cooperation of Jan 9, 1961: The governments of China and Burma agree to resume their programme of cooperation. According to letters exchanged, the unused funds of Kyats 270m. (=US-$ 55m.) will be spent on projects to be determined by the Union of Burma Government. Meanwhile the time-limit by which the loans were to be spent according to earlier agreements, has been extended until Sep 1975. The loans, which are free of interest, are to be repaid between Oct 1980 and Sep 1990 (8).

---

(1) HdE II D 21 p.16 (2) JMJP Jan 10, 1961 (3) HdE II D 21 p.17 (4) FEER Feb 15, 1962 (5) HdE II D 21 p.17 (6) HdE II D 21 p.18 (7) NCNA Nov 6, 1967 (8) Rangoon Radio Oct 7, 1971 and NCNA Oct 8, 1971

1972, Jan 6: Agreement on economic and technical cooperation (1)
China grants a loan of US-$ 20m.(2).

---

(1) NCNA Jan 6, 1972 (2) NZZ Jan 6, 1973

1956, Jun 21: Agreement on economic aid.
China makes a donation of Riel 800m. (=US-$ 22.4 m.), and promises to supply the following aid:
(1) Supply of equipment and building material
(2) Supply of products and goods
(3) Sending of experts in the fields of agriculture, and irrigation, light industry, communications and transport, social institutions, and power industry (1)
Protocol relating to the agreement on economic aid. This protocol stipulates that deliveries may be made from 1958 onward. Joint commissions will be set up. The commission in Phnom Penh is to specify the aid projects, arrange the preliminaries, and deal with further problems. The commission in Peking is to arrange substantially the preconditions for the deliveries.
A joint communiqué covers the following projects: a textile mill, paper and plywood plants, development of irrigation projects, power supply in agricultural regions, construction of schools, hospitals, athletic grounds and halls, roads, and bridges (1).

1958, Mar 26: Exchange of notes on the prolongation of the agreement on economic aid (1).

Aug 24: China makes a donation of US-$ 5.6m. for the construction of a small foundry and other plants (1).

1960, Dec 19: Agreement on economic and technical aid.
China makes a donation of Riel 400m. (=US-$ 11.2 m.) to be used for the following projects:
(1) Completion or extension of the above-mentioned textile, paper, plywood, and cement plants
(2) Construction of a small foundry and a small machine factory.
(3) Planning of a railway-line between Phnom Penh and Sihanoukville.
(4) Development of rice, tea, and fruit plantations (2).

1966, Jun 5: Protocol relating to the agreement on economic and technical aid of 1960 (?).
Subject: Construction of 12 laboratories and one factory for the Royal University of Kompong Cham (3).

1973, Jan 13: Agreement on China's economic aid in 1973 (4).

---

(1) HdE II D 21 p.26 (2) FEER Jan 12, 1961 (3) NCNA Jun 5, 1966
(4) NCNA Jan 13, 1973

CAMEROON

1972, Aug 17: Agreement on economic and technical cooperation (1). Chinese loan estimated at US-$ 20m.

1973, Mar 28: Agreement on economic and technical cooperation (2). Chinese loan estimated at US-$ 10m.

(1) NCNA Aug 17, 1972 (2) NCNA Mar 28, 1973

CHAD

1973, Sep 20: Agreement on economic and technical cooperation (1). Chinese loan of US-$ 11m.(2).

(1) NCNA Sep 20, 1973 (2) NZZ May 23, 1973

1964, Sep 29: (1) Agreement on economic and technical cooperation (2).

1965, Jan 15: Protocol relating to the agreement on economic and technical cooperation (3). China grants an interest-free (4) loan of £ 1m. (5) (=US$ 4.1m.) (2).

1966, Jan 7: Severance of diplomatic relations (6) and discontinuance of Chinese aid.

---

(1) NCNA Sep 29, 1964 (2) HdE II D 21 p.13 (3) NCNA Jan 16, 1965 (4) EpAkL 2/69 p.70 (5) GT Jan 18, 1965 (6) NCNA Jan 7, 1966

CHILE

1972, Jun 8: Agreement on economic cooperation (1). China grants an interest-free loan of US$ 65m. (2). Protocol (?) on economic cooperation (1).

---

(1) NCNA Jun 8, 1972 (2) NZZ Jun 14, 1972

1964, Jul 1: China grants an interest-free loan of US-$ 5m., half of it in cash. Repayment, starting in 1977, to be made in goods or free currency (1)

Feb 10: Agreement on economic and technical cooperation (2). China grants an interest-free loan of NF 100m. (=US-$ 20.4 m.). The agreement covers a period of 25 years, expiring in 1989. The loan will be used for the supply of complete sets of equipment, spare parts, and the local costs of Chinese aid. Repayment between 1980 and 1989 in equal yearly instalments (1).

1965, Feb 6 : Protocol relating to the agreement on economic and technical aid (3). (No details given).

Jun 13: Protocol relating to the agreement on economic and technical cooperation (4).
The following aid projects are specified in the protocol:
- a hosiery plant for stockings in Brazzaville
- a model cotton farm in Niari
- amplification of Congo R.´s transmitting power to 100 kilowatts
- a palm oil refinery in the northern part of the country
- improvement of river fisheries
- plants for the pickling of fish in Mossaka and Pointe Noire
- paddy rice fields in the Congo Basin (5).

Sep 13: Protocol relating to the agreement on economic and technical cooperation
Subject: textile mill in Kinsoundi (6).

1966, Jan 17: Protocol relating to the agreement on economic and technical cooperation
Subject: Amplification of Brazzaville Radio´s transmitting power (7)

1967, Jan 24: Protocol on medical aid (8)

1968, Feb 7: Protocol relating to the agreement on economic and technical cooperation
Subject: Construction of a dockyard for small boats (9)

Aug 12: Protocol relating to the agreement on economic and technical cooperation
Subject: State-farm (10). China grants a loan of US-$ 1 m. (11).

1969, Sep 6: Protocol relating to the agreement of economic and technical cooperation.
Subject: Construction of a dockyard for small boats (12).(Perhaps a supplement to the prot.of Feb 2,1968).

---

1) HdE II D 21 p.7 (2) NCNA Oct 2, 1964 (3) NCNA Feb 6, 1965 (4) NCNA Jun 14, 1965 (5) ATP Jun 15, 1965 (6) NCNA Sep 14, 1965 (7) Peking Radio Jan 20, 1966 (8) NCNA Jan 25, 1967 (9) NCNA Feb 8, 1969 (10) NCNA Aug 13, 1968 (11) EpAkL 2/69 p.67 (12) NCNA Sep 7, 1969

1969, Oct 10: Agreement on economic and technical cooperation (1)

1970, Jul 9: Protocol on medical aid (2)

1971, Jan 30: Protocol on the construction of a hospital at Fort Rousset (3)

1972, Feb 3: Protocol on the supply of building material for the Combe state-farm (4)

Oct 19: Agreement on economic and technical cooperation (5). Chinese loan estimated at US-$ 30m..

1973, May : Protocol on economic and technical cooperation (6)

Jul 30: Loan agreement (7) (loan estimated at US-$ 10m.).

---

(1) NCNA Oct 10, 1969 (2) NCNA Jul 9, 1970 (3) NCNA Jan 30, 1971
(4) EpAkL 3/72 (5) NCNA Oct 20, 1972 (6) NCNA May 25, 1973
(7) NCNA Jul 30, 1973

CUBA

No agreements on China´s economic aid have ever been published.

DAHOMEY

1972, Dec 29: Agreement on economic and technical cooperation (1) China grants an interest-free loan of US-$ 46m. to be repaid within 15 to 45 years, starting in 1988 (2)

---

(1) NCNA Dec 29, 1972 (2) NZZ Jan 19, 1973

1956, Nov 10: China makes a donation of sfr 20m. (1) (=US-$ 4.7m.)

1964, Dec 21: Agreement on economic and technical cooperation (2). China grants a loan of US-$ 80m. to be used in payment for the importation of Chinese goods during the period between 1965 and 1968. Repayment to start in 1972 and to cover a period of 10 years (3).

1967, Jun : China offers Egypt a gift of 150 000 t of wheat (4) worth US-$ 10m. (5).

1972, Sep : China grants an interest-free loan of US-$ 80.5m. for a duration of 20 years to be used in the construction of 15 plants (6). (As Egypt had not made any use of the 1964 loan, the 1972 loan may be assumed to be a repetition of China´s offer for that loan).

1973, Jun 26: Protocol on the building of a sand brick factory (7).

(1) HdE II D 21 p.12 (2) JMJP Dec 22, 1964 (3) HdE II D 21 p.13 (4) dpa Jun 11, 1967 (5) CN Jun 15, 1967 (6) NZZ Oct 4, 1972 (7) NCNA Jun 27, 1973

1971, Jan 22: Agreement on economic and technical cooperation (1) estimated at US-$ 10 m.

1972, Oct 24: Supplementary protocol on economic and technical cooperation (2)

1973, May 29: Protocol on sending a Chinese medical team (3)

---

(1) NCNA Jan 22, 1971 (2) NCNA Oct 26, 1972 (3) NCNA May 31, 1973

ETHIOPIA

1971, Oct 9: Agreement on economic and technical cooperation (1). China grants an interest-free loan of US-$ 80 m. to be repaid in goods or hard currency (2)

1973, Feb 20: Protocol on economic and technical cooperation (3).

---

(1) NCNA Oct 9, 1971 (2) Ethiopian News Agency Oct 10, 1971 (3) NCNA Feb 20, 1973

1961, Aug 18: Agreement on economic and technical cooperation. China gives an interest-free loan of Ghana-£ 7m. (= US-$ 19.6m.), payable between Jul 1, 1962 and Jun 30, 1967. Repayment between Jul 1, 1967 and Jun 30, 1981, in export goods or in a currency acceptable to China. The Chinese aid will cover the following items:

(1) technical aid by sending Chinese experts
(2) supply of complete sets of equipment, machinery, and material, technical know-how, and other goods
(3) training of Ghanaian technicians and skilled workers (1).

1962, Oct 18: Protocol relating to the agreement on economic and technical cooperation
Subject: Construction of a textile mill, a knitwear factory, a pencil factory, and a plant for making porcelain and enamelled goods (2).

1964, Jul 15: Supplement to the agreement on economic and technical cooperation. China grants an interest-free loan to be used for the first Ghanaian 7 Year Plan (1963/64-1969/70) of £ 8m. (=US-$ 22.4m.) Repayment over a period of 10 years (3).
(It has not been clearly stated whether, or not, this new loan is to be used for aiding projects that had been planned but not carried out, viz. the establishment of a soap factory, a plywood mill, a drug factory, and a fishbreeding experimental station).

1966 : With the severance of diplomatic relations by Ghana on Oct 20, 1966 (4), the Chinese economic aid was temporarily discontinued.

1972, Sep 14: Protocol on the agreement on economic and technical cooperation (5) of August 1961.

---

(1) JMJP Aug 22, 1961 (2) JMJP Oct 20, 1962, HdE II D 21 p.5, EpAkL 2/69 p.78 (3) JMJP Jul 17, 1964, Accra Radio Jul 17, 1964, HdE II D 21 p.5, EpAkL 2/69 p.66 (4) NCNA Oct 29, 1966 (5) NCNA Sep 14, 1972

1960, Sep 13: Agreement on economic and technical cooperation. China grants an interest-free loan of Rub 100m. (=US-$ 25m.) , payable by Jun 30, 1963. Repayment between 1970 and 1979, either in export goods or in a currency acceptable to China.
The aid covers the following items:
(1) technical aid by sending Chinese experts, technicians, and skilled workers
(2) Supply of complete sets of industrial equipment, machinery, material, and other goods.
(3) training of Guinean technicians and skilled workers (1).

1961, Sep 18: Protocol relating to the agreement on economic and technical cooperation (2). (No details given).

1963, May 2: Protocol relating to the agreement on economic and technical cooperation (3). (No details given).

1965, Feb : Protocol relating to the agreement on economic and technical cooperation.
Subject: Construction of a conference building (4).

1966, Jun 2: Protocol relating to the agreement on economic and technical cooperation.
Subject: Construction of a cinema (5).

Nov 16: Agreement on economic and technical cooperation(6). Protocol relating to this agreement.(No details given).

1967, Dec 30: Protocol on medical aid (7).

1968, May 24: Agreement between the PR China, Guinea and Mali on the construction of the Guinea-Mali Railway (8).

1969, Feb 28: Chinese loan (9) of approx. US-$ 45m. (10).

Oct 9: Agreement on economic and technical cooperation (11). Subject: Repair of the Conakry-Kankan railway-line. Repair of Conakry harbour. Development of an extensive agrotechnical programme. Construction of a cement plant having a capacity of 200 000t a year (12).

1970, Mar 10: Protocol on medical aid (13).

Nov 2: Protocol relating to the agreement on economic and technical cooperation (14).(No details given).

1972, Dec 13: Agreement on China providing a financial loan (15) estimated at US-$ 30m.

---

(1) JMJP Sep 14, 1960, and HdE II D 21 p.6 (2) JMJP Sep 20, 1961 (3) JMJP May 3, 1963 (4) NCNA Sep 26, 1967 (5) NCNA Jun 2, 1966 (6) NCNA Nov 16, 1966 (7) NCNA Jan 1, 1968 (8) NCNA May 25, 1968 (9) NCNA Feb 28, 1969 (10) FEER Nov 7, 1970 (11) NCNA Oct 9, 1969 (12) Conakry Radio Oct 31, 1969 (13) NCNA Mar 13, 1970 (14) NCNA Nov 2, 1970 (15) NCNA Dec 13, 1972

1972, Apr 9: Agreement on economic and technical cooperation (1). China offers aid in the amount of US-$ 52m. (2).

Nov 8: Protocol to economic and technical cooperation agreement (3).

---

(1) NCNA Apr 13, 1972 (2) JT Jun 30, 1972 (3) NCNA Nov 8, 1972

1956, Nov 3: Exchange of notes on economic and technical co-operation in the field of light industry. China will send experts and supply equipment (1).

1958, Apr 17: China grants a loan of SF 48m. (=US-$ 11.5m.) at an interest of 2.5 %. The payment will be made in the form of goods delivered. Repayment, starting in 1959, will be made either in £ or in the currency of another country acceptable to China, within 10 years (1).

Oct 8: China grants a loan of US-$ 13.5m., at an interest of 2.5 %.(1).

1961, Oct 11: Agreement on economic and technical cooperation (2). China grants a loan of SF 129.6m. (=US-$ 30m.), at an interest of 2 % (3). Originally this loan was to be used in the construction of six spinning mills. In August 1963 the contract was revised so as to cover the erection of eight spinning mills (at Makassar, Tapanuli, Madjalaja, Padang, Lombok, and Bandjermasin). Besides a plant for the production of spare parts was earmarked. The construction of weaving mills, as originally planned, was cancelled (4).

1963, Oct 16: Protocol relating to the agreement on economic and technical cooperation (5). (No details given).

1964, Jan 28: Protocol relating to the agreement on economic and technical cooperation (6). (No details given).

1965, Jan 25: Agreement on economic and technical cooperation. China grants an interest-free loan of US-$ 50m.(7).

Mar 31: Protocol relating to the agreement on economic and technical cooperation.
Subject: Minutes of the agreement on economic and technical cooperation (8). (No details given).

Apr 6: Protocol relating to the agreement on economic and technical cooperation of Oct 11, 1961.
Subject: Construction of a paper mill (9).

Sep 14: Protocol relating to the agreement on economic and technical cooperation of Oct 11, 1961.
Subject: Construction of a conference building (10).

Sep 30: Agreement on economic and technical cooperation(11). China grants a new loan. According to Russian sources, China's two loans, granted on May 31 and Sep 30, 1965, respectively, were worth US-$ 150 (12).

---

(1) HdE II D 21 p.22 (2) JMJP Oct 12, 1961 (3) Djakarta Radio Oct 20, 1961 (4) HdE II D 21 p.22 f. (5) JMJP Oct 17, 1963 (6) JMJP Jan 30, 1964 (7) HdE D 21 p.23 (8) NCNA Mar 31, 1965 (9) NCNA Apr 6, 1965 (10) NCNA Sep 14, 1965 (11) NCNA Sep 30, 1965 (12) HdE II D p.23

1966, Apr 18: China announces the discontinuance of her economic aid to Indonesia (1)

(1) NCNA May 18, 1966

IRAQ

1971, Jun 21: Agreement on economic and technical cooperation (1). China grants an interest-free loan of Yüan 100m.=Iraqi Dinar 1m.=US-$ 36m. Repayment, nt, after ten years of grace, commencing in 1984, by supplying goods, in annual instalments over 10 years (2).

1973, Nov 27: Protocol on economic and technical cooperation. Subject: Building of a bridge over the River Tigris at Mosul (3).

(1) NCNA Jun 21,1971(2)INA Jun 25, 1971 (3) NCNA Nov 27, 1973

KENYA

1964, May 10: Agreement on economic and technical cooperation (1). China makes a donation of £ 1.1m. (= US$ 3m.) and grants an interest-free loan of £ 6m. (=US$ 15m.). The loan is to be used for the Chinese aid projects covering the period between 1964 and 1969. Repayment to start in 1975 (2).

Dec 10: Protocol relating to the agreement on economic and technical cooperation.
Subject: Chinese experts to be sent to Kenya and other items (3).

(1) JMJP May 11, 1964, HdE II D 21 p.7 (3) NCNA Dec 10, 1964

LAOS

1962, Jan 13: Agreement on the construction of the Mong La - Phong Saly road (1). China makes a donation of US$ 4m. (2).

Dec 4: Communiqué on economic aid. China grants a long-term loan of unknown value, estimated at US$ 6m., to be used for
(1) the construction of some industrial projects
(2) the supply of complete sets of equipment
(3) the extension in length of the Mong La-Phong Saly road to Namtha in Honei Sai (3).

(1) JMJP Jan 14, 1962 (2) HdE II D 21 p.27 (3) JMJP Dec 5, 1962

MALAGASY

1973, Feb: China grants a loan of US$ 12m. (1)

(1) FAZ Feb 5, 1973

1961, Sep 22: Agreement on economic and technical cooperation (1). China grants an interest-free loan of Mali F 4.8 billion (=US-$ 19.4m.) and a donation of Mali F 50m. (=US-$ 0.2m.) (2).

1962, Nov 9: Protocol relating to the agreement on economic and technical cooperation.
Subject: Supply of complete sets of equipment and sending of experts and technicians (3).

1963, Dec 30: Supplementary protocol relating to the agreement on economic and technical cooperation (4). (No details given).

1964, Nov 3: Protocol (?) relating to the agreement on economic and technical cooperation (5). China grants a loan of Mali F 2 billion (=US-$ 7.9m.) (6).
Subject: Sets of industrial equipment (5).

1965, Mar 17: Protocol relating to the agreement on economic and technical cooperation.
Subject: Construction of a textile mill at Sêgou (7).

Sep 1: Protocol relating to the agreement on economic and technical cooperation.
Subject: Construction of a broadcasting station, a cinema and 2 hotels (8).

1966, Jun 9: Loan agreement (9). China grants a loan of US-$ 3m. (10). (Terms unknown).

1967, Aug 14: Agreement on economic and technical cooperation (11). (No details).

Dec 14: Protocol on medical aid (12).

1968, May 24: Agreement between the PR China, Mali and Guinea on the construction of the Guinea-Mali railway line (13).

1970, Dec 21: Agreement on economic and technical cooperation (14). (No details given). Chinese loan estimated at US-$ 20 m.

1973, Apr 4: Protocol on China's sending of a medical team (15).

Jun 24: Agreement on economic and technical cooperation (16). Loan estimated at US-$ 10 m.

---

(1) JMJP Sep 23, 1961 (2) HdE II D 21 p.8 (3) JMJP Nov 11, 1962 (4) NCNA Dec 30, 1963 (5) NCNA Nov 3, 1964 (6) HdE II D 21 p.8 (7) NCNA Mar 18, 1965 (8) NCNA Sep 2, 1965 and EpAkL 2/69 p.80 (9) NCNA Jun 9, 1966 (10) EpAkL 2/69 p.68 (11) NCNA Aug 14, 1967 (12) NCNA Dec 15, 1967 (13) NCNA May 25, 1968 (14) NCNA Dec 21, 197o (15) NCNA Apr 4, 1973 (16) NCNA Jun 24, 1973

1972, Apr 8: Agreement on a long-term and interest-free loan (1). China grants a loan of US-$ 42.6m. - 10 % to be paid forthwith, the remainder in the form of development projects. Repayment to start in 1984, over 10 years (2).

Nov 16: Protocol on development projects and technical assistance (3)

1973, Sep 19: Protocol on development projects and technical assistance (4).

---

(1) NCNA Apr 27, 1972 (2) NZZ Apr 29, 1972 (3) NCNA Nov 17, 1972
(4) NCNA Sep 20, 1973

MAURITANIA

1967, Feb 16: Agreement on economic and technical cooperation (1). China grants a loan of US-$ 4m.(2).

Oct 14: Protocol relating to the agreement on economic and technical cooperation (3). (No details given).

Nov 8: Protocol on medical aid (4).

1969, Nov 27: Protocol relating to the agreement on economic and technical cooperation. Subject: Drilling of wells at Kiffa, Kankossa, Boumdeit, and in other districts (5).

1971, Apr 1: Agreement on economic and technical cooperation (6). China grants a loan of CFA 650 m.(7) (=US-$ 2.7m.) or CFA 5,650m. (8) (more reasonable!) (=US-$ 23.5m.) , or US-$ 20.5m. (9).

1972, Aug 21: Protocol on the dispatch of a new Chinese medical team (10).

---

(1) NCNA Feb 16, 1967 (2) FEER Apr 18, 1968 (3) NCNA Oct 15, 1967 (4) NCNA Nov 10, 1967 (5) NCNA Nov 29, 1969 (6) NCNA Apr 1, 1971 (7) MAPA Apr 19, 1971 (8) BfA/NfA Jun 21, 1971 (9) NZZ Jan 6, 1973 (10) NCNA Aug 21, 1972

MAURITIUS

1972, Aug 9: Agreement on economic and technical cooperation (1). China grants a loan of Mauritian Rupees 175m. = £ 13.158m. (2) or US-$ 32m. (3).

---

(1) NCNA Aug 15, 1972 (2) Johannesburg Radio Jun 20, 1972 (3) NZZ Sep 9, 1972

1956, Oct 7: Agreement on economic aid. China makes a donation of India Rupees 60 m. (= US-$ 12.7m.) One third of the donation is in the form of financial aid, two thirds, in the form of goods (1).

1960, Mar 21: Agreement on economic aid covering three years China makes a donation of India Rupees 100 m. (= US-$ 21.2m.) Besides, China undertakes to pay the remainder (India Rupees 40m.) under the 1956 agreement. The aid is intended for equipment, machinery, and technical advice (2).

1961, Sep 5: Protocol relating to the agreement on economic and technical cooperation (2). (No details given).

Oct 15: Agreement on the construction of the Kodari-Kathmandu road. China makes a donation of £ 3.5m. (3) (=US-$ 9.8m.)

1963, Jan 13: Protocol relating to the agreement on economic aid of Mar 1960.
Subject: Construction of the Kathmandu - Kodari road (3).

1964, Apr 27: Supplementary protocol relating to the agreement on economic aid of March 1960 and to the protocol of September 1961 (3).
Subject: (1) Construction of the Dhalkewar-Ithari road,
(2) Construction of a brick factory at Kathmandu
(3) Construction of a warehouse at Birganj .
These projects take the place of those specified in the appendix to the protocol of September1961 (4).

May 25: Protocol relating to the economic aid agreement (really only a protocol) of September 1961.
Subject: Construction of a hydroelectric station (5).

Oct 4: Protocol relating to the agreement on economic aid.
Subject: Construction of irrigation projects (6).

1965, Apr 23: At the request of the Nepalese government, China suspended the preparations for two projects near the Indian border, viz. the Ithari-Dhalkewar road and the Kamala irrigation project (4).

Aug : Protocol relating to the agreement on economic aid.
Subject: Construction of the Kathmandu-Pokhara road (7).

1966, Oct 18: Exchange of documents on the conversion of the Chinese loans given in 1956 and 1960 from India Rupees 160m. to £ 12m. (8).

---

(1) NCNA Oct 7, 1956 (2) HdE II D 21 p.28 (3) EpAkL 2/69 p.74
(4) HdE II D 21 p.28 (5) NCNA May 28, 1964 (6) EpAkL 2/69 p.74
(7) NCNA Aug 7, 1965 (8) EpAkL 2/69 p.75

1966, Dec 21: Agreement on economic and technical cooperation. China grants an interest-free loan of NRp 150m. (= US-$ 20m.), for the period commencing on Dec 21, 1966, and ending on Dec 31, 1977 (1).

1967, Mar 14: Contract on the delivery of 20,000 t of rice (donation) (2).

May 25: Protocol relating to the agreement on economic and technical cooperation.
Subject: Hydroelectric station at Sunkosi (3).

1968, Mar 26: Protocol relating to the agreement on economic aid of 1960.
Subject: Prolongation of the agreement until 1975 (2).

Sep 27: Protocol relating to the agreement on economic and technical cooperation.
Subject: Construction of the Kathmandu-Bhaktapur road (4).

1970, Dec 24: Protocol relating to the agreement on economic and technical cooperation.
Subject: Long-distance transmission line from the hydroelectric station at Sunkosi to Chantara and to Barahbise (5).

1971, : Chinese loan of US-$ 35m. (6).

Mar 7: Protocol relating to the agreement on economic and technical cooperation.
Subject: Repairs to be made at the Kathmandu-Kodari road (7).

Jul 16: Exchange of letters regarding
(a) Chinese assistance in the construction of bitumen infiltration pavement for the Kathmandu-Pokhara highway
(b) cotton planting survey in Nepal (8).

Oct 27: Exchange of letters regarding the survey on mineral deposits (9).

1972, Mar 14: Exchange of letters regarding
(a) a trolley bus project along the Kathmandu-Bhaktapur highway
(b) extension of the Kathmandu brick and tile factory (10).

Nov 18: Agreement on economic and technical cooperation (11).

---

(1) HdE II D 21 p.29 and EpAkL 2/69 p.75 (2) EpAkL p.75 (3) NCNA Jun 9, 1967 (4) NCNA Sep 29, 1968 (5) NCNA Dec 24, 1970 (6) FEER Apr 1, 1972 (7) NCNA Mar 7, 1971 (8) NCNA Jul 17, 1971 (9) NCNA Oct 28, 1971 (10) NCNA Mar 15, 1972 (11) NCNA Nov 18, 1972

1973, Feb 26: Exchange of letters on operating the Sunkosi hydrostation (1)

Mar 20: Protocol on economic and technical cooperation Subject: Construction of a 30 km ringroad in Kathmandu (2).

26: Protocol on economic and technical cooperation Subject: Construction of the Kathmandu-Bhaktapur trolley bus service (3).

(1) Kathmandu Radio Feb 26, 1973 and NCNA Feb 27, 1973 (2) Kathmandu Radio Mar 20, 1973 (3) NCNA Mar 28, 1973

1972, Nov 3: Agreement on economic and technical cooperation (1). China grants a loan of US-$ 3m. (2).

(1) NCNA Nov 4, 1972 (2) NZZ Jan 6, 1973

1965, Feb 18: Agreement on economic and technical cooperation (1). China grants an interest-free loan of US-$ 60 m. (2), half of it in currency, the other half in goods (3).Term : 20 (?) years, repayment to commence after a grace period of 10 years in the form of goods (4).

Jun 15: Loan protocol relating to the agreement on economic and technical cooperation.
Subject: Mintes on the use of the loan of February 1965 (2).

Nov 14: Protocol relating to the agreement on economic and technical cooperation (5). (No details given).

1966, Jun 23: Protocol relating to the agreement on economic and technical cooperation.
Subject: Construction of the Taxila heavy machine project (6).

Jul 30: Agreement on economic and technical cooperation (7) (No details given).

1967, Aug 28: Protocol relating to the agreement on economic and technical cooperation of February 1965.
Subject: Taxila heavy machine project (8).

Dec 23: Agreement on economic and technical cooperation. China grants an interest-free loan of US-$ 40m. for a period of 20 years. Repayment to commence after a grace period of 10 years (9).

1968, Dec 26: Agreement on economic and technical cooperation(10). China grants an interest-free loan of Yüan 100m. (=PRp 200m.) (11) = US-$ 42m. (12)). Life: 20 years. Repayment to commence after a grace period of 10 years (11).
Repayment is to be effected by means of raw material exports. About two thirds of the loan are to serve for the development of Pakistan´s industry, the remainder is not bound to any special project (12).

1970, Apr 9: Protocol relating to the agreements on economic and technical cooperation of February 1965 and December 1968 (13).
Subject: Several industrial projects, among them a factory for refractory brick, a chemical fertilizer plant, and a sugar refinery (14).

Nov 14: Agreement on economic and technical cooperation (15) China grants an interest-free loan of Yüan 500m. (=US-$ 210m.). Repayment, after a grace period of 10 years, to be distributed over a period of 10 years(16).

---

(1) JMJP Feb 19, 1965 (2) Karachi Radio Jun 15, 1965 (3) Karachi R. Dec 24, 1967 (4) OEL 21, 9/65 p.217 f. (5) HdE II D 21 p.29 (6) NCNA Jun 23, 1966 (7) HdE D 21 p.30 (8) EpAkL 2/69 p.76 (9) Karachi R. Dec 28, 1967 (10) NCNA Dec 26, 1968 (11) Karachi R. Dec 26, 1968 (12) EpAkL 2/69 p.76 (13)NCNA Apr 9, 1970 (14) Karachi R. Apr 9, 1970 (15) NCNA Nov 14, 1970 (16) Karachi R.Nov 14, 1970

1971, Jan (?) China grants an interest-free loan of Yüan 7.1m. (=US-$ 3m.)(1).

Apr 28: Protocol relating to the agreements on economic and technical cooperation.
Subject: Construction of a sugar refinery (2).

May : China extends the US-$ 210m. loan of November 1970 to US-$ 300.7m. (3).

Dec 2: Protocol on the construction of a refractory factory (4).

1972, Jun : China writes off two project-cum-commodity loans of about US-$ 110m. (probably the loans of 1965 and 1968) and defers the repayment of the US-$ 210m. loan of 1970 for 20 years (5).

1973, May 22 Protocol on the construction of the Tarbela-Wah transmission line (6).

Sep 20: Protocol on the construction of the Tarbela cotton spinning mill (7).

---

(1) Karachi Radio Jan 8, 1971 (2) Karachi R. Apr 28, 1971 (3) NZZ May 18, 1971 (4) NCNA Dec 2, 1971 (5) FEER Jul 8, 1972 (6) Karachi R. May 22, 1973 (7) Karachi R. Sep 20, 1973

PERU

1971, Nov 28: Agreement on economic and technical cooperation (1). China grants an interest-free loan of Soles 1.841m. (2) (=US-$ 42m.). The loan is payable over 20 years, with the provision that Peru will not begin repayment until after 10 years (2).

---

(1) NCNA Nov 28, 1971 (2) Radio del Pacifico, Lima, Nov 29, 1971

1970, Nov 25: Agreement on economic and technical cooperation. China grants an interest-free long-term loan to be used for the supply of Chinese equipment for industrial projects (1). The loan is in the amount of US-$ 245m. (2).

1971, Mar 22: Protocol relating to the agreement on economic and technical cooperation.
Subject: Delivery of industrial equipment (3).

Protocol relating to the agreement on economic and technical cooperation
Subject: Conditions for the delivery of complete industrial equipments and material (3).

Protocol relating to the agreement of economic and technical cooperation.
Subject: Treatment and terms of work for the Chinese engineers and technicians sent to Romania (3).

Oct 16: Protocol on the supply of complete projects and technical assistance (4).

28: Agreement on a long-term interest-free loan (5).

1972, Mar 14: Protocol on economic and technical cooperation(6).

(1) NCNA Nov 25, 1970 (2) FAZ Nov 2, 1971 (3) NCNA Mar 22, 1971
(4) NCNA Oct 16, 1971 (5) NCNA Oct 29, 1971 (6) NCNA Mar 3, 1972

RUANDA

1972, May 13: Agreement on economic and technical cooperation (1). China grants a loan of US-$ 20 m. to be repaid within a period of 15 years, in the form of goods (2).

Oct 11: Protocol on the agreement of economic and technical cooperation (3).

1973, Jun 6: Minutes of talks on road building, sugar refinery, and rice cultivation (4).

(1) NCNA May 19, 1972 (2) NZZ Sep 9, 1972 (3) NCNA Oct 12, 1972
(4) NCNA Jun 8, 1973

SENEGAL

1973, Nov 23: Agreement on economic and technical cooperation (1). (Loan estimated at US-$ 20m.)

---

(1) NCNA Nov 23, 1973

SIERRA LEONE

1971, Jul 30: Agreement on economic and technical cooperation (1). Chinese loan estimated at US-$ 20m.

1972, Oct 6: Protocol on a Chinese medical team being sent to Sierra Leone (2).

Oct 9: Protocol relating to the agreement on economic and technical cooperation (3).

1973, Aug 3: Protocol on the construction of a national stadium (4).

Nov 10: Supplementary protocol to the agreement on economic and technical cooperation (5).

---

(1) NCNA Jul 30, 1971 (2) NCNA Oct 6, 1972 (3) NCNA Oct 9, 1972 (4) NCNA Aug 3, 1973 (5) NCNA Nov 10, 1973

1963, Aug 9: Agreement on economic and technical cooperation (1). China grants an interest-free loan of US-$ 20m. (2) for a term of 10 years (3). Repayment in 17 years (4). Besides, China makes a donation of US-$ 3m. (2).

1965, Dec 16: Protocol relating to the agreement on economic and technical cooperation.
Subject: Construction of a national theatre (5).

1966, Oct 23: Protocol relating to the agreement on economic and technical cooperation.
Subject: Terms of work for the Chinese experts working in Somalia (6).

1967, Aug 19: Protocol relating to the agreement on economic and technical cooperation.
Subject: Development of an experimental rice and tobacco station (7).

1969, Mar 18: Protocol relating to the agreement on economic and technical cooperation.
Subject: Projects of well-drilling in Beled Wen, Hargeisa, Baidaba, and Galkaayu (8).

1970, Jun 19: Protocol relating to the agreement on economic and technical cooperation (9).
China grants a loan (10) the amount of which is as yet unknown (estimated at US-$ 20m.).

1971, Mar 3: Protocol relating to the agreement on economic and technical cooperation.
Subject: Water supply projects in several towns of Somalia (11).

Mar 6: Protocol relating to the agreement on economic and technical cooperation.
Subject: Construction of a cigarette and match factory (12).

Jun 7: Agreement on economic and technical cooperation (13). Chinese loan estimated at US-$ 20m.

---

(1) JMJP Aug 10, 1963 (2) FEER Sep 19, 1963 (3) EpAkL 2/69 p.68 (4) CT YB 351 (5) NCNA Dec 16, 1965 (6) NCNA Oct 26, 1966 (7) EpAkL 2/69 (8) Mogadishu Radio Mar 18, 1969 (9) NCNA Jun 19, 1970 (10) EpAkL 8/70 (11) Mogadishu Radio Mar 3, 1971 (12) Mogadishu Radio Mar 6, 1971 (13) NCNA Jun 7, 1971

1973, Jul 19: Agreement on China providing emergency supplementary free economic aid (1), estimated at US-$ 40m.

---

(1) NCNA Jul 19, 1973

SOUTH YEMEN

1968, Sep 24: Agreement on economic and technical cooperation (1). China grants a loan of Denare 4m. (=US-$ 9.6m). (2).

1969, Dec 4: Protocol on medical aid (3).

1970, Jul 30: Protocol relating to the agreement on economic and technical cooperation.
Subject: China sending Chinese engineers and technicians (4).

Aug 7: Agreement on economic and technical cooperation (5). China grants an interest-free loan of Denare 28m. (=Yüan 100m.)(6) = US-$ 43.2m. (7).Term: 20 years, beginning with 1971 (6).

1971, Jul 7: Minutes of talks on the establishment of the Yemen cotton textile printing and dyeing combined enterprise (8).

Minutes of talks on the reconstruction of the Khormaksar salt works (8).

Aug 16: Minutes on talks of the construction of a road, the Zingibar bridge, and on the drilling of wells (9).

1972, Jul 12: Agreement on economic and technical cooperation(10). Chinese loan estimated at US-$ 20m.

1973, Mar 24: Protocol on the second stage of the road connecting the Fifth Governate with the First Governate (11).

---

(1) NCNA Sep 24, 1968 (2) Aden Radio Dec 9, 1970 (3) NCNA Dec 6, 1969 (4) NCNA Jul 31, 1970 (5) NCNA Aug 7, 1970 (6) OR 5/70 (7) FT Aug 18, 1970 (8) NCNA Jul 8, 1971 (9) NCNA Aug 16, 1971 (10) NCNA Jul 12, 1972 (11) Aden Radio Mar 24, 1973

1957, Sep 19: Agreement on economic aid for a five-year term. Chinese donation of CRp 75m. (=US-$ 15.8m. to be made in five equal instalments, beginning with January 1958 (1). In 1962 the duration of the donation was extended for another five years, i.e. until 1967 (2).

1958, Sep 17: Chinese loan of CRp 50m. (=US-$ 10.5m.), at an interest of 2.5 %. In 1958 the payment of the loan will be effected in the form of complete sets and material supplied to Sri Lanka. Beginning with 1961 the loan will be repaid in 10 equal yearly instalments in currencies of other countries or with Ceylonese export goods considered acceptable by China. In August 1962 the loan was prolonged for another three years (3). On Jun 15, 1964, it was converted into an interest-free loan (1).

1959, Jun : Protocol relating to the agreement on economic aid. Subject: Supply of a complete cotton mill (4).

1961, Aug 7: Protocol relating to the agreement on economic aid.
Subject: Supply of a complete cotton mill (1). (This protocol is probably a supplement to the 1959 one).

1962, Oct 3: Donation of CRp 50m. (=US-$ 10.5m. (5).

1964, Feb : Protocol relating to the agreement on economic aid.
Subject: Construction of a conference hall (6).

Jun 15: Protocol on the conversion of the loan of Sep 17, 1958, into an interest-free loan (7).

Jul 7: Protocol on the donation of 235 passenger coaches and freight-cars, as agreed in the economic aid agreement of 1957 (8).

Oct 21: Chinese loan of CRp 20m. (= US-$ 4.2m.) for 1965-1967, interest-free, repayable over 10 years, beginning with 1967 (9).

Nov 25: Protocol relating to the agreement on economic aid.
Subject: Supply, free of charge, of building material, machinery, and equipment for the Pugoda textile mill (7).

1965, Jul 13: Protocol relating to the agreement on economic aid.
Subject: Delivery of 162 railway carriages promised under the loan given on Oct 21, 1964 (10).

---

(1) HdE II D 21 p.19 (2) JMJP May 29, 1962 (3) JMJP Aug 3, 1962 (4) EpAkL 2/69 p.71 (5) JMJP Oct 4, 1962 and HdE II D 21 p.20 (6) Colombo Radio Apr 30, 1965, (7) HdE II D 21 p.20 (8) NCNA Jul 7, 1964 (9) NCNA Oct 26, 1964 (10) NCNA Jul 13, 1965

1970, Feb 8: Protocol relating to the agreement on economic aid.
Subject: Construction of a textile mill in Minneriya (1).

Sep 12: Chinese loan (2) worth US-$ 9.3m. (3).

1971, May 27: Chinese loan of CRp 150m. (=US-$ 31.5m.) (4), payable in two instalments during 1971.

Oct 8: Agreement on an interest-free loan in the form of 100,000 metric tons of rice (5) supplied by China, worth US-$ 13m. (estimated).

1972, Jun 29: Agreement on economic and technical cooperation.
Agreement on the construction of a cotton spinning, weaving, printing, and dyeing mill (6).
Chinese loan of CRp 307m. (=US-$ 33.26m.), of which CRp 260m. will be in hard currency, while 47 m. are intended for an integrated textile mill and the surveying work for a scheme to control the annual floods of the Mahaweli, Gin, and Kalu Gangas Rivers (7).

Sep 16: Loan agreement on providing a cargo ship (8), estimated at US-$ 2m. China purchased the ship for Sri Lanka, in view of the latter's foreign exchange difficulties (9).

---

(1) NCNA Feb 9, 1970 (2) NCNA Sep 12, 1970 (3) EpAkL 9/70 p.181 (4) Colombo Radio May 27, 1971 (5) NCNA Oct 8, 1971 (6) NCNA Jun 29, 1972 (7) FEER Jul 15, 1972 (8) NCNA Sep 16, 1972 (9) Colombo Radio Sep 2, 1972

1970, Aug 12: Agreement on economic and technical cooperation(1). China grants a loan of £ 14.5m. (2) (=US-$ 35m. The loan is interest-free and repayable within 16 years, in the form of agricultural products (3).

Dec 14: Protocol on medical aid (4).

1971, Dec 20: Agreement on economic and technical cooperation (5). China grants a loan of the same amount as in 1970 (6) (=US-$ 35m.)

1973, Jan 25: Notes on the construction of factories (7).

Apr : Protocol for fisheries development in the Lake Nuba (8).

---

(1) NCNA Aug 12, 1970 (2) Omdurman Radio Jun 30, 1970, and UPI Aug 24, 1970 (3) NZZ Jul 11, 1970 (4) NCNA Dec 14, 1970 (5) NCNA Dec 20, 1971 (6) NZZ Jul 23, 1972 (7) NCNA Jan 25, 1973 (8) Omdurman Radio Apr 4, 1973

SYRIA

1963, Feb 21: Agreement on economic and technical cooperation (1). China grants an interest-free loan of US-$ 16.4 m. Repayment between 1976 and 1985 in equal yearly instalments (2).

1967, Apr 13: Exchange of letters relating to the agreement on economic and technical cooperation. Subject: Construction of a cotton mill (3).

1968, Oct 20: Protocol relating to the agreement on economic and technical cooperation. Subject: Construction of a cotton mill (4).

1971, Jun : Chinese loan of US-$ 20m. (5).

Dec 14: Agreement on the construction of a spinning mill(6).

1972, May 24: Agreement on economic and technical cooperation(7). China grants a loan of US-$ 47 m. (8).

---

(1) JMJP Feb 22, 1963 (2) BfA/NfA (k) Mar 4, 1966 (3) NCNA Apr 16, 1967 (4) SANA Oct 20, 1968 (5) SANA Jun 6, 1971 (6) NCNA Dec 14, 1971 (7) NCNA May 24, 1972 (8) C.a. 7/72

Note:
On April 25, 1964, the two states of Tanganyika and Zanzibar were united to form Tanzania. The following agreements cover the two independent states as existing before union as well as the new state.

1964, Feb 21: China grants Zanzibar a loan of US-$ 0.5m., at an interest of 2.5 % (1).

Jun 6: China grants Zanzibar an interest-free long-term loan of £ 5m. (=US-$ 14m.) and a donation of £ 1m. (=US-$ 3m.) (2). China makes a donation of US-$ 2.8m. (1).

16: Agreement on economic and technical cooperation (3). China grants an interest-free loan of £ 10m. (2) (=US-$ 28m.) . Half of this loan will be in free currency (2). This loan includes the earlier loans to Zanzibar of US-$ 0.5m. (Feb 21, 1964) and 2.8 m. (Jun 8, 1964) (1).

1965, Jan 5: Protocol relating to the agreement on economic and technical cooperation.
Subject: Construction of a factory for agricultural machinery (4).
Exchange of letters concerning Chinese experts to be sent to Tanzania (5).

Agreement on medical aid by China (1).

May 11: Protocol relating to the agreement on economic and technical cooperation.
Subject: Extension of the State Broadcasting Station (6).

1966, Mar 22: China makes a donation of £ 30,000.
Subject: Extension of Dar es Salam University (7).

Jun 8: Agreement on economic and technical cooperation (8). China grants an interest-free loan of East African Shillings 40m.. (=US-$ 5.6m.) (1), and makes a donation of EA Shillings 20m. (7) (=US-$ 2.8m.) (1) to aid projects in the fields of agriculture, industry, and transport (7).

Jul 7: China places two cargo ships having a capacity of 21,000 RT at Tanzania's disposal (9)(estimated value: US-$ 3.5m.).

Oct 10: Protocol relating to the agreement on economic and technical cooperation.
Subject: Ubungo textile mill (1).

1967, Sep 5: Agreement of the Governments of the PR China, Tanzania, and Zambia on the construction of the Tanzania-Zambia Railway Line (10).

---

(1) EpAkL 2/69 (2) HdE II D 21 p.10 and NT Jun 1, 1965 (3) JMJP Jun 17, 1964 (4) NCNA Jun 6, 1970 (5) JMJP Jan 6, 1965 (6) NCNA May 11, 1965 (7) HdE II D 21 p.10 (8) NCNA Jun 8, 1966 (9) NCNA Jul 7, 1966 and FEER Jul 14, 1966 (10) NCNA Sep 5, 1967

1968, Apr 8: Loan protocol relating to the agreements on the construction of the Tanzania-Zambia Railway Line (1).
Protocol relating to the agreements on the construction of the Tanzania-Zambia Railway Line.
Subject: Chinese experts to be sent to Tanzania-treatment and working conditions (1).
Protocol relating to the agreement on the construction of the Tanzania-Zambia Railway Line.
Subject: Surveying and planning work (1).

Apr 27: Protocol relating to the agreement on the construction of the Tanzania-Zambia Railway Line.
Subject: Technical basis and practical handling of the loan (2).

May 6: Protocol relating to the agreement on medical aid by China (2).

1969, Jun 24: Protocol relating to the agreement on economic and technical cooperation.
Subject: Extension of the national stadium (3).

Nov 14: Supplement to the agreement on the construction of the Tanzania-Zambia Railway Line.
Subject: Starting point of the railway line shifted from Kidatu to Dar es Salaam (4).

Protocol relating to the agreement on the construction of the Tanzania-Zambia Railway Line.
Subject: Technical principles (4).

1970, May 8: Protocol relating to the agreement on economic and technical cooperation.
Subject: Development of a state-farm (5).

Jul 12: Protocol relating to the agreement on the construction of the Tanzania-Zambia Railway Line.
Subject: Amount of loan and terms of repayment (6).

Protocol relating to the agreement on the construction of the Tansania-Zambia Railway Line.
Subject: Report on the planning and surveying work (7).
Protocol relating to the agreement on the construction of the Tanzania-Zambia Railway Line.
Subject: Report on negotiations (6).
China grants an interest-free loan of Tanzania Shillings 2,866 m. (=US-$ 405 m.) . Repayment within a period of 30 years (7), commencing in 1983 (8) or 1976 (9). Two thirds of the loan (US-$ 270 m.) to be given to Tanzania.

31: Protocol relating to the agreement on economic and technical cooperation.
Subject: Construction of a sawmill in Zanzibar (10).

(1) NCNA Apr 9, 1968 (2) EpAkL 2/69 p.70 (3) NCNA Jun 24, 1969 (4) NCNA Nov 17, 1969 (5) NCNA May 10 and 11, 1970 (6) NCNA Jul 12, 1970 (7) Dar es Salaam Radio Jul 12, 1970, and NZZ Aug 22, 1970 (8) NZZ Nov 8, 1970 (9) NZZ Aug 22, 1970 (10) NCNA Aug 4,1970

TOGO

1972, Sep 19: Agreement on economic and technical cooperation (1). Chinese loan of US-$ 45m. (2).

(1) NCNA Sep 27, 1972 (2) NR Jun 15, 1973, p.4

TUNISIA

1972, Aug 27: Agreement on economic and technical cooperation (1). Chinese loan of US-$ 36m. (2).

1973, Jun 6: Protocol on dispatch of a Chinese medical team(3).

(1) NCNA Aug 27, 1972 (2) NR Jun 15, 1973 p.4 (3) NCNA Jun 6, 1973

1965, Apr 21: Agreement on economic and technical cooperation (1). China grants an interest-free loan of £ 4.3m. (2) (=US-$ 12m.) (2) and makes a donation of £ 1.07m. (2) (=US-$ 3m.) (3).

1970, Sep 5: Protocol relating to the agreement on economic and technical cooperation (4). (No details).

---

(1) JMJP Apr 22, 1965 (2) Kampala Radio May 3, 1965 (3) EpAkL 2/69 p.70 (4) NCNA Sep 6, 1970

UPPER VOLTA

1973, Sep 8: Agreement on economic and technical cooperation (1). (Chinese loan estimated at US-$ 10m.)

Dec 3: Agreement on economic and technical cooperation (2).

---

(1) NCNA Sep 15, 1973 (2) NCNA Dec 5, 1973

1958, Jan 12: Agreement on scientific, technical and cultural cooperation.
China grants an interest-free loan of SF 70m. (1) (=US-$ 16m.) (2). Repayment over a period of 10 years, commencing with the completion of the projects.
The Chinese aid includes the following items:
(1) technical aid by Chinese experts
(2) supply of complete sets of equipment for light industry
(3) construction of a highway
(4) training of Yemenite technicians and workers in China (1).
Other projects planned: Lamp and bulb factory, glass plant, tannery, factory for aluminium products, sugar factory, spinning mill, fish-canning factory, handicraft enterprises (3).

1959, Jan 23: Protocol relating to the agreement on scientific, technical and cultural cooperation.
Subject: Construction of the Hodeida-Sana highway, construction of a textile mill.
China grants a loan of US-$ 0.142m. over 10 years (2).

1962, Mar 13: Protocol relating to the agreement on scientific, technical and cultural cooperation.
Subject: 10 Chinese road-building experts and one interpreter to be sent to Yemen for one year to help maintain the Hodeida-Sana highway (4).

Nov 24: China grants an interest-free loan of US-$ 4.8m. (5)

1964, Jun 9: Agreement on economic and technical cooperation (6).
China grants an interest-free loan of £ 10m (5) (=US-$ 28.2m.) (7) for a term of 10 years (7). The loan is intended for the following items:
Construction of the Sana-Sada highway, a spinning mill, schools, and a hospital in Sana. Part of the loan shall be used for repair work on the Hodeida-Sana highway (5).

1965, Mar 23: Protocol relating to the agreement on scientific, technical, and cultural cooperation.
Subject: Construction of a textile mill (8).

1969, Jul 14: Protocol relating to the agreement on economic and technical cooperation.
Subject: Construction of a technical high-school (9).

1972, Mar 16: Minutes of talks on the building of the Taiz hospital (10).

Jul 21: Agreement on economic and technical cooperation (11).
China grants an interest-free loan of US-$ 22.1m. (12).

(1) NCNA Jan 13, 1958 (2) EpAkL 2/69 p.73 (3) HdE II D 21 p.25
(4) NCNA Mar 18, 1962 (5) HdE II D 21 p.25 (6) NCNA Jun 9, 1964
(7) EpAkL 2/69 p.73 (8) NCNA Mar 23, 1965 (9) NCNA Jul 14, 1969
(10) NCNA Mar 21, 1972 (11) NCNA Jul 21, 1972 (12) UPI Aug 7,1972

1973, Jan 14: Agreement on economic and technical cooperation (1).
China offers a loan of US-$ 115 m. (2).

---

(1) NCNA Jan 14, 1973 (2) NZZ Feb 1, 1973

1967, May 26: China grants a loan of US-$ 7m. (1).

Jun 23: Agreement on economic and technical cooperation (2). China grants an interest-free loan of US-$ 16.8m. (1).

Sep 5: Agreement between the PR China, Tanzania and Zambia on the construction of the Tanzania-Zambia-Railway Line (3).
For all other agreements relating to the Tan-Zam Railway cf. Tanzania !

1969, Feb 14: Protocol relating to the agreement on economic and technical cooperation.
Subject: Construction of the Lusaka-Mankoya highway (4). China grants a loan of Kwacha 12m. (5) (=US-$ 1.7m. (?)).

Dec 31: Protocol relating to the agreement on economic and technical cooperation.
Subject: Donation of a broadcasting station (6).

1970, Jan 31: Protocol relating to the agreement on economic and technical cooperation.
Subject: Construction of the Lusaka-Kaoma highway (7).

Jul 12: For the construction of the Tanzania-Zambia Railway Line China grants a loan of US-$ 405m. (8), one third of it (=US-$ 135m.) to Zambia.

1973, May : Chinese financial aid of US-$ 10m. to overcome the difficulties in transportation caused by the barring of the frontier between Zambia and Rhodesia (9).

---

(1) EpAkL 2/69 p.68 (2) NCNA Jun 23, 1967 (3) NCNA Sep 5, 1967 (4) NCNA Feb 15, 1969 (5) Lusaka Radio Jan 24, 1969 (6) NCNA Jan 5, 1970, and Mar 26, 1970 (7) NCNA Jan 31, 1970 (8) Dar es Salaam Radio Jul 12, 1970 (9) NZZ May 30, 1973

PART II

THE AID PROJECTS

General remarks

Afghanistan, one of the countries bordering on China, is regarded by Peking as a country it wishes to include in the "cordon sanitaire" rendering China's frontiers safe. The fact that Afghanistan occupies the 15th place in the list of recipients of Chinese economic aid is an indication of Peking's endeavours to make that country its friend. Afghanistan's common frontier with China is a mere 80 km. long, while the frontier with the Soviet Union has a length of more than 1,000 km. Afghanistan's primary interests therefore lie with Moscow. In the list of countries receiving economic aid from the Soviets, Afghanistan ranks third (with an amount of US$ 826m.) after India and Egypt. As compared with this amount, the Chinese aid totalling US$ 76.5m. seems modest. All the same, it is by no means unimportant, because the Soviet aid is tainted by visible mistakes in planning. Not only have the Soviets improved Afghanistan's infrastructure before encouraging agriculture but they also installed a huge irrigation system at Nangarhar at a cost originally estimated at US$ 8m., which eventually rose to as much as US$ 55m., the worst thing being that the annual maintenance cost of US$ 25m. was to be paid by Afghanistan herself.

A. Chinese loans

1965, Mar 24:	US$ 27.5m., free of interest (1)
1972, May :	Yuan 100m. =US$ 42m. (2), 25m. of which are to be used for the extension of the Bagrami textile mill (3).
Jul 25:	Chinese gift of a hospital (4), estimated at US$ 7m.

B. Aid projects completed

1. Irrigation project I (5)

Location:	?
Other details:	The project was being built late in 1967, and visited by Mohamed Zahir Shah on Nov 22, 1967 (5).

2. Irrigation project II

Location:	Parwan province (6), north of Kabul, on the Pandschir river (7).
Commencement:	October 1968 (8)
Completion:	Planned for 1971 (9).
Technical data:	On completion of the project, an area of 24,800 hectares (ha) will be irrigated (8). Among the products produced by means of this project will be the country's famous grapes which are exported fresh to India and Pakistan, or dried for raisins (10). The project will be developed in two phases, viz. Phase 1: Irrigation of 19.000 ha Phase 2: Irrigation of 24,000 ha. The project includes a hydroelectric station and a canal, 50 km long (9).

(1) NCNA Mar 24, 1965; Kabul Radio Oct 13, 1965; HdE II D 21 p.15 (2) Kabul R. May 22, 1972 (3) FEER Sep 30, 1972 (4) NCNA Jul 25, 1972 (5) NCNA Nov 23, 1967 (6) NCNA Aug 28, 1970 (7) BfA May 10, 1968 (8) NCNA Jun 26, 1969 (9) UNDP (10) FEER Sep 30, 1972

Other details: Mohamed Zahir Shah visited the project on Jun 23, 1969 (1).
In a protocol signed on Jan 2, 1971, it was stipulated that China will aid in the construction of a hydroelectric and pumping station (2). (We are probably right in assuming that this protocol relates to Irrigation Project II).

3. Fish-breeding experimental station

Protocol: Apr 1, 1967 (3)
Location: Darunta reservoir (4), Nangarhar province (5).
Commencement: April 1967 (6)
Completion: February 1968 (7), final protocol Mar 8, 1969 (8).
Technical data: The project covers an area of 3 ha. In 1968 China supplied 450,000 bits of fish-breed (9). The yield of the first catching season was 50,000 kg of fish (10). In spring and summer, a stock of 1.5 million fry of the carp family was hatched at the station. Some 1.2 million survived natural selection. About 800,000 of the fry were later transferred to the nearby Darunta, Naghlu, and Sarobi reservoirs. The remaining 320,000 fry are still in the ponds of the fish-breeding centre, and will be released into the reservoirs in winter 1972/73 and spring 1973. Big seasonal catches have been regularly made since the winter of 1969 (11).
Other details: Mohamed Zahir Shah visited the station on Feb 22, 1968 (12).
A supplementary protocol dated Mar 8, 1969, provides for further Chinese aid to the Darunta station (13) (not specified).

4. Poultry farm

Protocol: Apr 28, 1967 (14)
Location: Bagrami (15) near Kabul
Commencement: March 1968 (16)
Completion: April 1970 (16)
Technical data: Annual production as planned: 200,000 animals and 400,000 eggs (17)
Other details: Mohamed Zahir Shah visited the farm on Dec 8, 1970 (15)

5. Lapis lazuli grinding works

Location: Kabul (18)
Completion: April 1970 (18)

---

(1) NCNA Jun 26, 1969 (2) Kabul Radio Jan 2, 1971 (3) NCNA Apr 2, 1967 (4) NCNA Dec 21, 1968 and Dec 23, 1969 (5) NCNA Nov 1, 1970 (6) NCNA May 23, 1970 (7) NCNA Feb 25, 1968 (8) NCNA Mar 9, 1969 (9) NCNA Feb 25, 1968 (10) NCNA May 23, 1970 (11) NCNA Sep 17, 1972 (12) NCNA Aug 25, 1968 (13) NCNA Mar 9, 1969 (14) NCNA Apr 28, 1967 (15) NCNA Dec 10, 1970 (16) NCNA Jun 1, 1971 (17) BfA/NfA Sep 2, 1966 (18) NCNA Apr 22, 1970

Other details: Chinese experts came to Afghanistan in 1967 to build and equip the grinding works and to train Afghanian workers (1). The grinding works enable Afghanistan to export finished lapis lazuli products (1). Lapis lazuli is minted in Badakhshan province (2).

6. Textile mill
   Location: Bagrami (3), eastern suburb of Kabul (4).
   Commencement: March 1969 (3) or September 1967 (5).
   Completion: Mar 25, 1970 (5)
   Technical data: 20,000 spindles, 600 looms (5)
   Working in two shifts a day, the mill has an annual capacity of 12 million m of cloth and more than 800,000 t of yarn. The mill includes three workshops, for printing and dyeing textiles and for dyeing yarn (6).
   Other details: The Bagrami mill is one of two textile mills to be constructed under the Afghanian Five-Year Plan (7) and will enable Afghanistan to increase her output of cotton cloth by 15 % (6). The mill has so far produced more than 20 million m of printed and dyed cloth coming in 1,000 different shades and designs (8). Mohamed Zahir Shah visited the mill on Dec 8, 1970 (9).
   In May (?) 1972 China gave a new US$ 25m. loan for the extension of the mill which involves the installation of another 240 looms (10).

C. Aid projects under construction

1. Experimental tea plantation
   Protocol: Dec 6, 1967 (11)
   Location: Kunar province (11), in the districts of Kerali and Baghesalar (12)
   Commencement: February 1968 (12)
   Other details: The first Chinese experts arrived in 1966 and 1967. Another protocol on tea planting was signed in December 1969 (12). (We do not know whether this new protocol is related to the old one, or was set up to initiate a new project).

2. Station for the cultivation of silkworms
   Protocol: Sep 25, 1969 (13)
   Commencement: 1967 (14)
   Other details: A Chinese group of experts finished the preliminary work for the development of the station in 1966 (13).

---

(1) BfA/NfA Sep 2, 1966 (2) NCNA Jun 23, 1972 (3) NCNA Dec 24, 1968 (4) KTA 1970 p.393 (5) NCNA Mar 27, 1970 (6) NCNA Mar 29, 1970 (7) NCNA Dec 24, 1968 (8) NCNA Mar 27, 1972 (9) NCNA Dec 13, 1970 (10) FEER Sep 30, 1972 (11) NCNA Dec 14, 1967 (12) NCNA Dec 23, 1969 (13) NCNA Sep 28, 1966 (14) UNDP

3. Hospital

Protocols (1,2)	Exchange of instruments for the construction of a hospital on Jul 25, 1972
Technical data:	Capacity: 200-250 beds (2)
Other details:	The hospital is a gift from China (2)

(1) NCNA Jul 25, 1972 (2) NCNA Nov 21, 1973

General remarks

Those who want to ascertain facts in connection with China's economic aid to Albania face considerable difficulties, since in both countries publications on the subject are scarce, not only as regards the extent of the aid granted (on this there is no information at all and we have to rely on estimates) but also as regards the individual projects. This is particularly true of the time immediately following the beginning of Chinese aid, i.e. the period of Albania's third Five-Year Plan (1961-5). Thus one source implies that China had taken part in Albania's third Five-Year Plan with 25 projects (1), while other details available do not reveal more than seven projects.

The reason for this scarcity of information during the earlier stages of Chinese economic aid to Albania was probably a certain insecurity on both sides, the idea being to wait and see whether this aid, which had to rely solely on sea transport, could be carried into effect at all and if so, how. There is some indication that the caution with which reports were given at that early stage has given way to a tendency to disclose more details since 1966.

It should be noted that we are not in a position to get a full picture of Chinese economic aid to Albania from the sources now open to us. However, since Albania is one of the few recipients of economic aid from China among the Eastern Bloc countries for which data are available at all, it seems to be justified to disclose at least those. In any case they reveal the many-sided engagement of China in this field.

No original sources are available as to the extent of Chinese aid to Albania. The first loan, that of 1961, is said to have amounted to US$ 123m.(1), another one, in 1968, is estimated at US$ 100m. (1) and the last one, in 1970, we estimate to have amounted to US$ 40m.

A. Chinese loans

1961: US$ 123m. (1)

1968: US$ 100m. (estimate)

B. Aid projects completed

1. Asbestos factory (2)
   Location: Vlora
   Completion: Apr 30, 1966
   Technical data: The factory produces asbestos tubes and sheets.

(1) NZZ Dec 8, 1973 (2) NCNA May 1, 1966

2. Caustic soda factory (1)
   Location: Vlora
   Completion: Mar 9, 1968
   Other details: The factory meets the caustic soda demands of Albania's oil, textile, paper, soap, and glass industries. It is one of the key projects in Albania's third Five-Year Plan.

3. Electrification of the rural districts
   The Central Committee of Albania's Workers Party arranged a ceremony to be held on Nov 5, 1970, to celebrate the completion of the rural electrification project. In his speech, Mr.Carcani, member of the Politburo, thanked the PR China for its fraternal help in the development of this project, and said that China had "sent the necessary equipment and material to Albania as soon as possible"(2). This remark permits the conclusion that China has continued a project originally started with Russian aid and stopped when Albania left Russian hegemony. It is difficult to estimate the extent of Chinese aid in this project. The following details may possibly give some hints:-

   The first electrification project completed under the Communist regime was the "Lenin" hydroelectric station in 1951. In 1965 the total power output was kWh 335 million, 252 million being generated in hydroelectric stations. During the fourth Five-Year Plan the power output again rose considerably. In 1970 it amounted to 102 times that of 1938. On completion of the "Mao Tse-tung" hydroelectric station and the Korca thermal power station in 1971, the power output will reach kWh 2,000 million, i.e. twice the output of 1970 (3).

4. Paint factory
   Location: Tirana (4)
   Completion: Trial production commenced in November 1969 (5).
   Technical data: The main two workshops produced 20 different paints, among them oil paints, anticorrosive paints, varnishes, enamel, and inks for printing purposes (5).
   Other details: The factory is associated with the Tirana chemical combine (4).

5. Glass factory (6)
   Location: Kavaja
   Completion: Production commenced in November 1970.

6. Bulb factory (7)
   Location: Vlora district
   Completion: Nov 24, 1969
   Other details: This factory is the first of its kind in Albania.

---

(1)NCNA Mar 11, 1968 (2)NCNA Nov 6, 1970 (3)NCNA Nov 4, 1970 (4) NCNA Apr 25, 1970 (5) ATA Apr 21, 1970 (6) NCNA Nov 29, 1970 (7)NCNA Nov 25, 1969

7. Instruments factory (1)
   Location: Korca
   Completion: Nov 25, 1969
   Technical data: The factory produces cutting tools and measuring instruments
   Other details: This factory is the first of its kind in Albania

8. Cable factory (2)
   Location: Shkodra
   Completion: Mar 29, 1966
   Technical data: The factory produces 400 different kinds of cable, 130 of them, using local material.

9. Coal mine (3)
   Location: Valias
   Other details: This coal mine was mechanized with Chinese aid.

10. "Mao Tse-tung" hydro-power station at Vau i Dejes
    Location: On River Drin (4), Shkodra district (5) in North-East Albania (6).
    Commencement: January 1967 (7)
    Completion: October 28, 1971 (8). The ribbon-cutting ceremony took place in the presence of Mehmet Shehu (8).
    Technical data: Height of the dam 65 m
    Width at foundation: 320 m
    Width at top: 9 m (7).
    The station produces kWh 1,000 million annually (6). It has five turbo-generator units with a total capacity of kW 250,000.(8).
    Other details: The coffer dam was closed in July 1969. This project is the greatest in Albania's fourth Five-Year Plan (4). It is Albania's greatest industrial project (9) and the largest hydro-power station in existence (8).

11. Heat and power station I (10)
    Location: Fieri district
    Completion: Nov 23, 1969

12. Heat and power station II (11)
    Location: Korca
    Completion: The station was officially declared open on Dec 7, 1971

13. Fertilizer plant I
    Location: Fieri (12)
    Commencement: Spring 1965 (13)
    Completion: March 1968 (12). Start of trial production in February 1967 (13).
    Technical data: The plant produces nitrates (12).
    Other details: The plant is Albania's first fertilizer plant (12).

---

(1) NCNA Nov 26, 1969 (2) NCNA Apr 30, 1966 (3) ATA Apr 16, 1969 (4)NCNA Jul 22, 1969 (5)NCNA Jan 13, 1967 (6)NCNA Nov 3, 1969 (7)NCNA Feb 4, 1970 (8)NCNA Oct 29,1971 (9)NCNA Jan 13, 1967 (10)NCNA Nov 25, 1969 (11)NCNA Dec 8, 1971 (12)NCNA Mar 10, 1968 (13)NCNA Feb 25, 1967

14. Fertilizer plant II
    Location: Lac (1), Kruja region (2)
    Completion: Mar 24, 1968 (2)
    Technical data: The plant produces phosphate fertilizers (2).

15. Copper refinery (3)
    Location: Rubik
    Completion: Mar 27, 1968

16. Milk-processing factory
    Location: Shkodra (4)
    Completion: Nov 28, 1970 (5)
    Technical data: Production of the first batch of evaporated milk in September 1970 (6).

17. Metallurgical combine
    Protocol: November 1968 (7)
    Location: Elbasan (7)
    Completion: Oct 16, 1971 (8)
    Technical data: On completion the combine will have a manufacturing capacity of 0.8 million tons of iron-nickel ore (7,9).
    Other details: The combine is one of the greatest projects in Albania's fifth Five-Year Plan (1971-1975) (8).

18. Sewing and embroidery factory (10)
    Location: Korca
    Completion: Oct 23, 1969
    Other details: The factory is associated with the "Hammer and Sickle" knitware combine. There is no exact proof that this project has been carried out with Chinese aid. Our assumption that it was is based on the fact that Chinese experts and members of the embassy at Tirana were present when the factory was inaugurated.

19. Laboratory for nuclear irradiation (11)
    Location: Tirana State University
    Completion: Oct 1, 1970
    Other details: The laboratory is a donation from the PR China.

20. Oil paint and lacquer factory (12)
    Location: ?
    Commencement: Spring 1968
    Technical data: On completion this factory will produce 16 different types of paints and varnishes.

21. Paper mill (13)
    Location: Kavaja
    Completion: Mar 29, 1966

---

(1)NCNA Oct 12, 1968 (2)NCNA Mar 26, 1968 (3)NCNA Mar 28, 1968 (4)ATA Jul 4, 1970, and Sep 10, 1970, NCNA Nov 29, 1970 (5)NCNA Nov 29, 1970 (6)ATA Sep 10, 1970 (7) Roter Morgen Nov/Dec 1969 (8)NCNA Oct 18, 1971 (9)ATA Sep 7, 1970 (10)NCNA Oct 24, 1969 (11)NCNA Oct 3, 1970 (12)ATA Apr 2, 1968 (13)NCNA Apr 29, 1966

22. Computer centre (1)
    Location: Tirana State University
    Other details: This centre will help solve complex problems in many departments of the Albanian economy.

23. Plastics factory (2)
    Location: Durres
    Completion: January 1971

24. Plant for crude-oil processing (3)
    Location: Fieri district
    Completion: Nov 23, 1969

25. Broadcasting station I (4)
    Location: ?
    Other details: Two broadcasting stations constructed with Chinese aid were inaugurated on Oct 1,1967.

26. Broadcasting station II (4)
    Location: ?
    Other details: Two broadcasting stations constructed with Chinese aid were inaugurated on Oct 1,1967.

27. Sawmill (5)
    Location: Tirana
    Completion: Jul 10, 1965

28. Concrete factory (6)
    Location: Shkodra
    Other details: In this factory the first concrete pylons were made (for high-voltage towers?). They are chiefly intended for export purposes.

29. Soda ash factory (7)
    Location: Vlora
    Completion: Feb 25, 1967
    Other details: The plant is one of the biggest in Albania's chemical industry.

30. "Mao Tse-tung" textile combine
    Protocol: Under the Sino-Albanian 1961-1965 loan agreement China provided 55 m. Rub. (=US$ 13.75 m.) for buying Chinese textile equipment and other material (8).
    Location: Berat district (9)
    Commencement: March 1966 (10)
    Completion: First phase, comprising spinning and weaving mills, in October 1966 (11). Second phase, comprising workshops for finishing processes, in May 1967 (10).Third phase and completion of the whole project, in November 1969 (12).
    Other details: The buildings for yarn-dyeing and weaving were completed in February 1968 (13). The combine will provide Albania with 22 mill. million metres of textiles of many varieties every year (14).

---

(1)NCNA Nov 3, 1971 (2)NCNA Jan 14, 1971 (3)NCNA Nov 25, 1969 (4)NCNA Oct 3, 1967 (5)NCNA Jul 10, 1965 (6)ATA Apr 20, 1971 (7) NCNA Feb 26, 1967 (8)JMJP Jan 23, 1966 (9)NCNA May 17, 1967, and Nov 23, 1969 (10)NCNA May 17, 1967 (11)NCNA Oct 23, 1966 (12)NCNA Nov 22, 1969 (13) ATA Feb 28, 1968 (14)NCNA Nov 23, 1969

31. Tractor spare-part factory (1)
    Location: Tirana
    Commencement: July 1963
    Completion: June 1966
    Technical data: The factory produces 416 different spare-parts.

32. Cement plant I (2)
    Location: Elbasan
    Completion: October 1968
    Other details: The plant was put into operation six months ahead of schedule.

33. Cement plant II (3)
    Location: Fushe-Kruje
    Commencement: December 1964
    Completion: March 1968

34. Cement-bag factory (4)
    Location: Shkodra
    Completion: April 1965
    Technical data: Annual capacity: 5 million bags

C. Aid projects under construction

1. PVC and caustic plant
   Protocol: November 1968 (5)
   Location: Vlora (4)
   Commencement: Oct 16, 1971 (6)

2. Hydro-power station
   Protocol: November 1968 (5)
   Location: Fierze (5)
   Commencement: November 24, 1971 (7)
   Technical data: On completion the capacity installed will be kWh 0.4 million (8).
   Other details: The power station is one of the three greatest projects in Albania's fifth Five-Year Plan (7).

3. Cement-mixing plant (9)
   Location: Vau i Dejes
   Completion: May 1969
   Other details: This process obviously belongs to the Vau i Dejes hydro-electric station.

4. Deep-oil processing plant and oil combine
   Location: Fieri (10)
   Other details: The plant is one of the three greatest projects in Albania's fifth Five-Year Plan (10).
   Commencement: Nov 27, 1971
   Technical data: After completion, in 1974, the combine will produce 1.5 million tons (11).

5. Plastic articles factory (12)
   Location: Lushnje
   Commencement: Apr 30, 1972
   Other details: The factory is among the important projects in Albania's fifth Five-Year Plan.

---

(1) NCNA Jun 25, 1966 (2) NCNA Oct 12, 1968 (3) NCNA Apr 2, 1968 (4) NCNA Apr 30, 1965 (5) Roter Morgen Nov/Dec 1969 (6) NCNA Oct 18, 1971 (7) NCNA Nov 25, 1971 (8) ATA Sep 7, 1970 (9) NCNA May 22, 1969 (10) NCNA Nov 11, 1971 (11) NZZ Dec 8, 1973 (12) NCNA May 1, 1972

General remarks

The first Chinese offers of economic aid were based on the friendly relations existing between Peking and the Ben Bella regime. This relationship obviously cooled after Ben Bella's fall. The failure of the Afro-Asian Conference scheduled to take place in Algiers in 1965, in which the Chinese had proposed to take an active part, led to the alienation of the two countries. This is the reason why Chinese aid then concentrated on medical aid, neglecting the other fields.

Relations fell to zero during the Cultural Revolution, when Algerian protested to China because of a public outrage by Chinese nationals against a Soviet diplomat in Algiers. Not until the end of the Cultural Revolution, when China opened towards the outside world again did relations improve. The Chinese offer of an economic aid loan of US$ 40m. to Algeria in 1971 seems to have been meant as a full stop to the years of disharmony between 1965 and 1971. The visit of the Algerian President Boumedienne to China in February 1974 indicates a noticeable change for the better in the relationship between the two countries.

A. Chinese loans

1958, November:	US$ 4.9m., donation (1)
1963, Oct 10:	US$ 51m., free of interest, over 20 years (2)
1965, February:	US$ 2m. (the sum estimated for the 13,000 t freighter promised to Algeria)
1967:	US$ 2m. in cash (3)
1971, Jul 27: (4)	Loan of US$ 40m. (5)

(1) HdE II D 92 p.5f. (2) NCNA Oct 11, 1963 (3) CN Jun 15, 1967
(4) NCNA Jul 27, 1971 (5) NR 8/1973

B. Aid projects completed

1. Exhibition and fair building

Protocol:	Jun 20, 1966 (1)
Location:	Sunawbar al-Bahari Palais near Algiers(2)
Foundation-stone laid:	Nov 19, 1968, in the presence of President Boumedienne (3).
Completion:	September 1970 (4)
Technical data:	The floor space covers 36 000 sq.metres (1). The building is divided into a central pavilion containing three big and four small exhibition halls, an industry pavilion, a local pavilion, and on office building (4).
Other details:	A group of Chinese experts had already come to Algeria in 1965, in order to arrange the preliminary work (1). It had originally been intended to commence construction in 1967 (5). As a result of China's disappointment with Algeria's policy regarding the Afro-Asian Conference scheduled for 1965, the Chinese experts were called back (6).

2. Cargo-ship
   As a donation of the Chinese government, a cargo -ship of 13,000 RT was given to Algeria on Feb 24, 1965 (7).

3. Small-scale industrial plants
   Some plants for small-scale industries were established with money from the 1963 loan (8).

4. Ceramic factory

Protocol:	Sep 9, 1966 (9)
Location:	Gelma (10), Annaba Department in Northeast Algeria (11)
Commencement:	1968 (11)
Completion:	Winter 1971 (11). Production started on Jun 20, 1972 (11).
Technical data:	The original schemes aimed at an annual production of 3,000 t of pottery for daily use.
Other details:	A group of Chinese experts searched for clay from the summer of 1966 till early 1967. Their search was successful in the region of Djebel Debagh in East Algeria (12). In February 1969, 26 Algerians went to China to be trained in the Chinese ceramic industry for between 12 and 18 months (10).

5. Medical groups

Protocols:	Dec 8, 1965 (13) and Mar 17, 1970 (14)

---

(1)NCNA Jun 20, 1966 (2)EpAkL 2/69 (3)NCNA Nov 19, 1968 (4)NCNA Sep 17, 1970 (5) el-Moudjahid Jun 25, 1966 (6) CN 169 (7)NCNA Feb 24, 1965 (8)NZZ Jun 26, 1967 (9)NCNA Sep 26, 1966 (10)EpAkL 3/69 (11)NCNA Jun 21, 1972 (12)NCNA Apr 22, 1967 (13)NCNA Dec 8,1965 (14)NCNA Mar 18, 1970

First group: In Algeria since the summer of 1963 (1). (No protocol was published). The group consisted of 23 persons who returned to China in October 1965, except for 5 persons who remained in Algeria to form the nucleus of the second group. Before their departure the first group gave part of their medical outfit to local health centres as a present (1).

Second group: 35 persons (2). Arrival in Algeria in December 1965 (3), departure in September 1968 (4). The group worked in the Mostaganem and Saida districts (5).

Third group: 50 persons. Arrival in August 1968. Scheduled region of employment: West Algeria (6), 500 km from Algiers (7). By July 1969 the group had attended to 29,000 patients and had made more than 3,500 operations (8).

Fourth group: Arrival in September 1970 (9), departure in January 1973 (10).

Fifth group: Arrival in January 1973 (10). In accordance with a new agreement the number of persons in the Chinese medical group will be 160 in the near future (11).

6. Transport planes
In 1964 the PR China presented Algeria with four transport planes (5).

D. Aid projects planned

1. Irrigation project
In the summer of 1967 a group of Chinese experts examined the possibilities for the construction of dams and the sinking of wells in the Aurès Mountains (5). Obviously, this project has never been carried into practice.

2. Technical school
China was to take part in equipping a technical school at Blida (12). There has been no further information on this project and we therefore assume that it has not been carried into effect.

3. Steel-rolling mill
A summary in the Chinese press mentioned Chinese experts being engaged in studying the possibilities of constructing a steel-rolling mill (12). There has, however, been no further information on this project and we therefore assume that it has not been carried into effect.

---

(1) NCNA Oct 18, 1965 (2)NCNA Dec 8, 1965 (3)NCNA Dec 10, 1965 (4)NCNA Sep 22, 1968 (5)EpAkL 2/69 (6)NCNA Aug 23, 1968 (7)NCNA Jul 17, 1969 (8)NCNA Jul 15, 1969 (9)NCNA Sep 29, 1970 (10)NCNA Jan 26, 1973 (11) NZZ Apr 12, 1972 (12) Algiers Radio Apr 26, 1965 (13) NCNA Feb 15, 1967

4. <u>Cement factory</u>
   Part of the 1963 loan was to be used for the construction of a cement factory (1). A group of seven Chinese experts was in the Skikdah region near Constantine in the spring of 1965 (2) to work on this project. It has, however, not been heard of again and we assume therefore that it has not been carried into effect.

5. <u>Hydrogeological survey</u>
   In December 1972 a Chinese subterranean water surveying and well-sinking team was working at a site in Khinshlah Dairah, Aures Wilayah (3).

---

(1) NZZ Jun 26, 1967 (2) Algiers Radio Apr 28, 1965 (3) NCNA Jan 3, 1973

General remarks

Burma, which also borders on China, is one of the Asian countries that already enjoyed the benefits of Chinese economic aid at a very early date. Considering the extent of loans offered, she takes the fourth place among the Asian recipients of economic aid from China.

When the Cultural Revolution broke out in China, the positive relationship between China and Burma suffered a heavy blow. Mao emblems worn by juvenile Overseas Chinese in Burma gave rise to anti-Chinese riots, which in turn caused China to discontinue her economic aid. In contrast to Indonesia, however, diplomatic relations between Burma and China were not interrupted.

We may safely assume that the governments of both countries were overrun by this political development, which was contrary to their long-term political interests. Shortly after the end of the Cultural Revolution the situation improved: Burma sent an ambassador to Peking in November 1970 (between the autumn of 1967 and November 1970, there had only been a chargé d'affaires ad interim) and Peking followed suit in March 1971. Some months later China decided to resume the economic aid she had stopped in 1967.

A. Chinese loans

1958, Jan 11: Kyat 20m. =US$ 4.2m. Interest: 2.5 % (1)

1961, Jan 9: £30 m. =US$ 84m., free of interest, repayable in equal yearly instalments in the form of goods or in currency (2), between 1971 and 1980.

Donation of US$ 4.2 (?) m. (3).

1971, Oct 7: The unused funds of Kyat 270m. (=US$ 55m.) from the 1961 loan will be spent on projects to be determined by Burma and China (4).

(1) HdE II D 21 p.17 (2) JMJP Jan 10, 1961 (3) This sum is an estimate and the same as that mentioned for the 1958 loan, which had been granted to Algeria for the construction of a cotton-spinning mill. The source of this information is Thakin Tin (FEER Feb 15, 1962) (4) Rangoon Radio Oct 7, 1971, and NCNA Oct 8, 1971

B. Aid projects completed

1. Cotton-spinning mill I

Protocols:	Nov 1, 1958 (1) and Dec 13, 1961 (2)
Location:	Merktila (3)
Completion:	Scheduled for 1967 (4). The first trial production commenced in June 1967 (5).
Technical data:	600 looms, 40,000 spindles (6)
Other details:	When the Chinese aid was interrupted in July 1967, the project had been almost completed (7). (As all machines seem to have been installed by that time and the interval between then and the final putting into operation of the mill had probably been intended for the training of the local staff, we count this project among the economic aid projects completed).

2. Cotton-spinning mill II (8)

Contract:	July 17, 1956
Location:	Thamaing
Technical data:	21,362 spindles, 196 automatic looms, and auxiliary equipment

3. Bridge I

Location:	Upper Salween River, Kunlon district (9)
Commencement:	May 1965 (9)
Completion:	December 1965, 3 months ahead of schedule (10)
Technical data:	Length 247.9 m, width 6.75 m. Steel-chain suspension bridge. The bridge carries a motor highway and two sidewalks, and may be used by 24 ten-tonners at a time (11).

4. Bridge II

Location	Near Takaw (12), Shan state, across the River Salween (13)
Technical data:	Steel-lattice bridge construction. Carrying 60 tons
Other details:	When Chinese aid was suspended, the bridge had been almost completed (12). The construction of the bridge will be resumed (14). A Chinese team arrived on Oct 9, 1972, to resume the construction of the Takaw bridge (15).

5. Power station

When Chinese aid was suspended, this power station (location unknown) had been almost completed (2). The capacity installed was to be kWh 100-500 (6).

6. Paper-mill

Location:	Sittang, Karen state (17)

(1) HdE II D 21 p.17 (2)JMJP Dec 12, 1961 (3)NCNA Feb 12, 1967 (4) NCNA Jun 15, 1967 (5)NCNA Jul 31, 1967 (6)NCNA Feb 12, 1967 (7) NCNA Oct 31, 1967 (8) PCh Sep 16, 1956 (9) NCNA May 10, 1965 (10) NCNA Dec 24, 1965 (11)NCNA Dec 24, 1965 (12) NCNA Oct 31, 1967 (13) NCNA Jul 12, 1967 (14) Rangoon Radio Oct 9, 1972 (15)Rangoon Radio Oct 9, 1972 (16) FEER Feb 15, 1962 (17) Rangoon Radio Jun 2, 1966

Commencement: November 1965 (1)
Technical data: Daily production 43 t (2) or 40 t of paper (3). The raw material used is bamboo from the banks of the Sittang R. The water required for the production process is also taken from that river (1).
Other details: This is Birma´s first paper-mill (4). By April 1966 the construction of the buildings had been almost completed (5). When the Chinese aid was suspended, all necessary machines had been installed and a power station, completed (6). (This is probably the power station mentioned under B. 5. above).

7. Sugar-mill I (5)
Location: Bilin Thaton district
Commencement: March 1965
Completion: March 1966
Technical data: The mill covers a floor space of 20,000 sq. metres. It can process 1,000 tons of sugar-cane and produce 100 tons of sugar a day.
Other details: The construction work was done by 200 Chinese experts and 2,000 Burmese workers.

8. Sugar-mill II
Location: Paungde (7), Prome district, Karen state (8).
Technical data: The mill produces 50 tons of sugar a day (8).

9. Needle knitting mill
In January 1958, China provided Burma with a loan of Kyats 2 m. (=(US$ 0.4 m.) for building a needle knitting mill (9).

C. Economic aid projects not completed

1. Tire factory
Location: Danyingon (10)
Technical data: Capacity:90,000 pairs of tires (11) a year (?)
Other details: When the Chinese aid was suspended (July 1967), the design had been completed, Chinese experts and the first machines had arrived. The remaining machines were ready for shipment (10).

D. Aid projects planned

1. Irrigation and dike project (11)
Location: Yamethin district

2. Diesel engine and water-pump factory (11)
Technical data: Annual production of 800 Diesel engines and 1,500 water-pumps.

3. Poultry-raising and animal husbandry-improving project (11)

(1) Rangoon Radio Jun 2, 1966 (2) NCNA Apr 14, 1966 (3) NCNA Jun 16, 1966 (4) NCNA Feb 12, 1967 (5) NCNA Apr 17, 1966 (6) NCNA Oct 31, 1967 (7) EpAkL 2/69 (8) FEER Sep 19, 1963 (9) TKP Jan 9, 1958 (10) NCNA Aug 29, 1967 (11) FEER Feb 15, 1962

4. Leather and shoe factory (1)
Location: Shan state

5. Hydro-electric survey
After Chinese economic aid had been resumed in October 1971, a Chinese hydro-electric surveying team arrived in Burma on Jul 17, 1972 (2), and left in June 1973 (3).

6. Cement plant
A Chinese team arrived in Rangoon on Oct 30, 1972 to survey the ground for this cement plant (4).

7. Thermo-electric power plant
A Chinese team arrived in Rangoon on Nov 20, 1972, to survey the ground for this thermo-electric power plant (5)

8. Textile plant
A Chinese surveying team worked in Burma in February 1973 to survey the site for a textile plant (6).

9. Rubberball manufacturing factory
A Chinese surveying team worked in Burma in February 1973 (6).

10. Tinned fruit and fruit-juice factory (7)
Location: Rangoon

11. Fruit plantations (7)

12. Two sluices (7)

13. Improvement of silkworm cultivation (7)

14. Plywood factory I
Location: Moulmein (8)
Technical data: Annual capacity: 200 cubic metres (7)

15. Plywood factory II (7)
Location: Rangoon
Technical data: Annual capacity:200 cubic metres (7)

16. Extension of the DEMAG built steelworks (7)
Location: Ywama
Technical data: Expansion of the annual capacity to 20,000 t of steel

17. Road (7)
Location: Wa state
Technical data: Length: 415 kilometres

18. Improvement of tea cultivation (7)

19. Cement factory
A Chinese cement plant survey team arrived in Burma on Oct 30, 1972 (9).

20. Bridge III
A Chinese bridge construction survey team worked in Burma and left the country on Oct 30, 1972 (9)

21. Four hydro-electric stations (10)
Location: Kentung, Kunlong, Machambaw (the fourth location is unknown).
Other details: One of the four stations has been almost completed (see B.5. above).

(1)FEER Feb 15,1962 (2)NCNA Jul 17,1972 (3)NCNA Jun 4,1973 (4) NCNA Oct 30,1972 (5)NCNA Nov 21,1972 (6)NCNA Feb 22,1973 (7)FEER Feb 15,1962 (8)NCNA Jan 1,1963 (9)NCNA Oct 30,1972 (10)NCNA Nov 6, 1967

E. Chinese experts

When the Chinese aid was suspended (July 1967), 412 experts were called back to China (1).

(1) NCNA Oct 30, 1972

General remarks

China and Burundi entered into diplomatic relations in December 1963. Hardly more than 12 months after this, Burundi broke them off on rather dubious grounds: the murder of the Burundian Prime Minister Ngendandumwe was linked with Chinese subversive activities, the allegations being based on unqualified evidence given by an interpreter who had defected from the Chinese Embassy in Bujumbara.

The resumption of diplomatic relations by Burundi in 1971 may be seen as an admission of the earlier accusations being untenable.

In pursuance of the pragmatic line of her foreign policy after the Cultural Revolution, China rewarded Burundi for this admission with an economic aid loan offer of US$ 20m. It is assumed that the fact that China was the first Communist country to offer economic aid to Burundi has played some part in this.

A. Chinese loans

1972, Jan 6: China grants a loan of US$ 20m. (1)

(1) NZZ Jan 6, 1973

General remarks

Cambodia may be regarded as the model recipient of Chinese economic aid. The width of aid offered deserves respect and attention and so does the fact that the aid offered was gratuitous. We cannot understand this properly unless we see the tendency of Chinese foreign policy to try to make friends with China's close neighbours. It would be an over-simplification to regard this aid exclusively as a satisfying of the selfish long-term interests of China. Though the political development in Cambodia after Sihanouk's going to exile in China may point in this direction, we believe that China's intention of making friends with her neighbours, even if they are under feudal rule, is sincere and guided by her wish to encourage the establishment of a goodwill "cordon sanitaire".

Even with this model among economic aid recipients China underwent some negative experiences as a result of the inadequate preparation and planning of certain projects. This is an experience China shares with the Western countries and the Soviet Union. The fact that we go into some detail here is not due to malignant intentions but to our desire to show the common mistakes of all donors of economic aid who, during the first decade of development aid, were by no means guiltless of faulty investments and faulty planning.

1. Cholong paper-mill
The initiators of the project had overlooked the fact that the factory was too far away from the course of raw material so that, for example, the bamboo wood,which served as raw material, had to be transported to the factory by trucks. In addition, the training of the Cambodian staff proved inadequate.

2. Dey Eth plywood factory
Again the problem of profitability - which, as we know, is of considerable interest outside Communist countries- was neglected. Because of the failure to investigate the market before establishing the factory, even the Cambodian's government's prohibition of the importation of plywood failed to save the factory. Another deficiency was that the output of the factory far exceeded Cambodia's own needs. China's offer to buy the products that could not be sold in Cambodia implied an admission of faulty planning. Moreover, the quality of the plywood produced proved unsatisfactory. As a model for this Cambodian project, China had taken a factory in Southern China that worked well, without realizing that a glue blended from pig's blood and soya bean oil was unsuitable for use in Cambodia's monsoon climate.

3. Chakrey Ting cement factory
Again the initiators had overlooked the circumstance that the difficulties in procuring the necessary energy (coal from Haiphong) would make work unprofitable.

However despite these mistakes, and in due consideration of the limited possibilities, the Chinese economic aid to Cambodia must be regarded as a model which, taken as a whole, was designed to achieve an optimum of encouragement of that country's infrastructure and basic industries.

It is not yet evident in what form the Cambodian government in exile (in Peking) is making use of Chinese economic aid. We can only presume that the aid is used for the reconstruction of the areas liberated by the Red Khmer.

This part of Chinese aid did not begin until 1970 when Sihanouk's star began to sink, and should therefore be seen in connection with China's political endeavours to increase Sihanouk's prestige in the eyes of the Red Khmer fighting units, who are more inclined towards North Vietnam and the Soviet Union. Whether or not it will be possible to arrest the waning of Sihanouk's influence in this manner remains to be seen.

A. Chinese loans

1956, Jun 21:	Riel (CR) 800m. (=US$ 22.4m., donation (1)
1958, Aug 24:	US$ 5.6m., donation (1)
1960, Dec 19:	CR 400m. (=US$ 11.4m.), donation (1)
1961-1968 (both years inclusive)	US$ 30.8m., donation (2)
1972, Feb 11:	Economic aid given to the Cambodian government in Peking exile (3)
1973, Jan 13:	Economic aid given to the Cambodian government in Peking exile (4), the two aids amounting to an estimated US$ 30 30m.)

B. Aid projects completed

1. Phnom Penh-Sihanoukville railway-line traced out
   In March 1961 Prince Sihanouk inaugurated the new railway-line from Phnom Penh to Sihanoukville in the tracing out of which Chinese technicians had cooperated (5).

2. Airport

Location:	Sien Rap (6), near Angkor Vat (7)
Completion:	Official inauguration on Jun 22, 1968, in the presence of Prince Sihanouk (8). The airport was transferred to the Cambodian authorities on Oct 5, 1968 (7).
Other details:	This airport was intended to become more important than that of Pochentrong (5).

---

(1) HdE IID 21 p.26 (2) NZZ Dec 15, 1968 (3) NCNA Feb 11, 1972 (4) NCNA Jan 13, 1973 (5) NCNA Mar 3, 1961 (6) Phnom Penh Radio May 6, 1961 (7) NCNA Oct 7, 1968 (8) NCNA Jun 29, 1968

3. Buildings (1)
   Location: Svay Rieng
   Other details: In August 1961, Prince Sihanouk inaugurated five buildings two of which had been constructed with Chinese aid.

4. Glass factory I
   Location: Stung Meanchey (2)
   Completion: June 1968. Inauguration in the presence of Prince Sihanouk (3).
   Technical data: Annual capacity: 3,000 tons (4)
   Other details: This factory was built to meet Cambodia's glass requirements (2).

5. Glass factory II
   Location: Cholung Ek, Kandal province, south of Phnom Penh (5) or Dankor (6)
   Commencement: November 1966 (6)
   Completion: Jun 11, 1968. Inauguration in the presence of Prince Sihanouk (5),
   Other details: The factory was named "Chinese People's Friendship Factory" (7).

6. Hospital I (8)
   Location: Siem Reap
   Completion: February 1960
   Other details: Chinese aid to be used for out-patients' department only. Inauguration in the presence of Prince Sihanouk.

7. Hospital II (9)
   Location: Phnom Noreay
   Remarks: The source only mentions the intention to construct a hospital at Phnom Noreay with Chinese aid. We have not been able to find out whether or not it has been completed.

8. Hospital III (10)
   Location: Preakkat Mealea
   Completion: Jan 10, 1969. Inauguration in the presence of Prince Sihanouk.

9. Fertilizer plant (11)
   Location: Kampot
   Remarks: Neither the Chinese side nor the Cambodians have ever mentioned this project.

10. 12 laboratories and one factory
    Protocol: Jun 5, 1966 (12)
    Location: Royal Compong Cham University (12)
    Completion: July 1968 (13).

---

(1) NCNA Aug 18, 1961 (2) Phnom Penh Radio May 6, 1967 (3) NCNA Jan 23, 1969 (4) NZZ Dec 15, 1968 (5) NCNA Jun 14, 1968 (6) Phnom Penh R. Jun 11, 1968 (7) NCNA Jun 13, 1968 (8) NCNA Feb 5, 1960 (9) Phnom Penh R. May 6, 1967 (10) NCNA Jan 12, 1969 (11) NZZ Apr 16, 1968 (12) Jun 5, 1966 (13) NCNA Jul 20, 1968

11. Teachers' training college (1)
    Location: Preah Outey, Takeo College
    Completion: February 1962. Inauguration in the presence of Prince Sihanouk.

12. Medical institute and hospital (2)
    Location: Takeo Kampot, Royal University
    Completion: January 1967

13. Paper-mill
    Location: Chhlong (3) Kratie province (4)
    Completion: February 1961 (4)
    Technical data: Originally an annual capacity of 5,000 tons had been planned (3). Actual production between March and December 1961: 1,605 t (519 t of paper for newspapers, 142 t of writing paper, and 268 tons of pasteboard etc. (4). In 1962 the production of note-paper was 800-900 tons (3). The total production in that year amounted to 1,300 t (3).
    Other details: 754 workers and clerical staff work in the mill (4) in three shifts round the clock (3). The mill worked unprofitably, because it is located too far away from the raw material supply centres. The bamboo to be used has to be transported in trucks (5). In a letter to the Chinese Prime Minister, Prince Sihanouk thanked the Chinese for their promise to help "transform the paper-mill of the peoples of Cambodia and China" (6). A protocol relating to this transformation was signed on May 21, 1969 (7).

14. Tire factory (8)
    Location: Takhman
    Remarks: Neither the Chinese nor the Cambodians have ever mentioned this project.

15. Broadcasting station
    Location: Stung Meanchey near Phnom Penh (9)
    Completion: February 1963 (9)
    Other details: In a message to Chou En-lai Prince Sihanouk thanked China for her aid in intensifying the transmitting power of the national broadcasting station (10). We have not been able to find out whether or not this station is identical with the one at Stung Meanchey.

---

(1) NCNA Mar 1, 1962 (2) NCNA Jan 6, 1967 (3) FEER May 9, 1963 (4) FEER Jul 5, 1962, and NCNA Jun 11, 1961 (5) FEER May 13, 1965 (6) NCNA May 15, 1969 (7) NCNA May 23, 1969 (8) NZZ Apr 16, 1968 (9) Phnom Penh Radio Feb 26, 1963 (10) Phnom Penh R. Jan 4, 1970

16. School I (1)
Location: Stungtrent
Completion: February 1961. Inauguration in the presence of Prince Sihanouk.

17. School II (2)
Location: Preyvang
Completion: March 1961. Inauguration in the presence of Prince Sihanouk.

18. Plywood factory
Location: Dey Eth (3) near Phnom Penh (4)
Completion: Mar 23, 1962 (4)
Technical data: Daily production of 600 triple-glued wooden boards, size 1.2 x 2.4 m (3). The factory has a repair workshop and a power station of its own (3).
Other details: The factory was named "Sihanouk-Chou En-lai factory". In 1962 the capacity of the factory was found to surpass Cambodia's demands for plywood (4) and the price of its product is three times that of the plywood imported from Hong Kong (3). The factory is so far away from the raw material supply centres that the country prefers to import plywood. Possible new uses for the factory have been considered. Its construction had been delayed as a result of transport difficulties caused by an unusually low water level of the Mekong River (4).

19. Sports town (6)
Location: Southeast of Phnom Penh
Commencement: May 1966
Completion: November 1966
Technical data: The town consists of a block of three-storeyed buildings, with 14 rooms on each floor, a gymnasium with seats for 1,000 spectators, telephone boxes, a laundry, an agency for admission tickets, and a conference room.
Other details: The sports town was built for GANEFO (Games of New Emerging Forces).

20. Textile mill I
Location: Kompong Cham (7)
Completion: December 1960 (3)
Technical data: Annual capacity of the spinning mill: 1,619 t of cotton and 1,450 t of yarn; of the weaving mill: 5,188 million m of cloth (4). Daily capacity of the finishing department: 100 bales (4,000 m) of cloth (7). Equipment of the spinning mill: 28 machines and 11,788 spindles; of the weaving mill: 210 automatic looms (7). 613 workers work in the factory in 3 shifts (7).

---

(1)NCNA Feb 17, 1961 (2) JMJP Mar 9, 1961 (3) FEER May 9, 1963
(4) FEER Jul 5, 1962 (5) FEER May 13, 1965 (6) NCNA Nov 6, 1966
(7) FEER Apr 21, 1960

Other details: The factory (without equipment) cost US$ 3 m. All machines are of Chinese origin (1). The project included a subsequent extension of the factory (2).

21. Textile mill II
Location: Battambang (3)
Completion: May 1967 (3). The mill was put into operation on Mar 30, 1968 (4)
Technical data: 92 looms; 10,400 spindles. Annual capacity: 4.3 million m of cloth and 726 t of yarn (5). Attached to the factory are a foundry, a forge, 10 workshops, a power-station with 3 generators of kW 560 each (5).
Other details: The factory was named "Factory of Friendship with the People's Republic of China" (4).
Signing of the deed of transfer to Cambodia: Mar 30, 1968 (4).

22. Cement factory
Location: Chakrey Ting, Kampot province (2)
Completion: September 1964 (7), originally scheduled for mid 1962 (2), later on for the end of 1963 (7).
Technical data: Annual capacity 50,000 tons (7). In 1967(?) the extension of the factory to an annual capacity of 100,000 t was commenced. Another extension to an annual 150,000 t was planned for some later date to meet Cambodia's cement requirements fully (8). (Neither the completion of the first extension nor the commencement of the second phase has ever been mentioned, so we assume that the plans were all that existed).
Other details: Near the factory, new clay deposits were found and connected with the factory by a railway-line (7). The factory was named "Kossamak-Liu Shao-ch'i" (9). Although it enabled Cambodia to reduce her cement imports, it works unprofitably, because the coal required for operation must be imported via Sihanoukville (10). 1,200 Cambodian workers were trained (6).

23. Sugar mill (14)
Location: Kompong Tram (?)
Remarks: Neither the Chinese nor the Cambodians have ever mentioned this project.

24. Prospecting for minerals (2)
The first phase of China's aid to Cambodia included a project of mineral prospecting.

---

(1) FEER Apr 21, 1960 (2) FEER Jul 5, 1962 (3) NCNA May 3, 1967 (4) NCNA Apr 2, 1968 (5) Phnom Penh Radio May 4, 1967 (6)NCNA Sep 9, 1964 (7) FEER May 9, 1963 (8) Phnom Penh R. May 6, 1967 (9) NCNA Oct 15, 1964 (10) FEER May 13, 1965 (11) NZZ Apr 16, 1968

D. Aid projects planned

1. Steel works

Location: Kompong Cham

Technical data: Annual production 40,000 t of cast iron, 15,000 t of steel sheets, 20 000 t of other steel products (1).

Other details: In the spring of 1962, a Chinese group of experts studied the possibilities to construct steel works (2). The project was abandoned, because no coal was available for smelting (3).

2. Tool factory

Location: near Phnom Penh (4)

Technical data: The factory was to produce spraying equipment, spare parts for textile machinery and other products (4).

Other details: In the spring of 1962 a group of Chinese experts was in Cambodia to study the possibilities for constructing a factory of this type (2).

Remarks: The project probably never got beyond the planning stage.

3. Agricultural aid

The agreement on economic and technical aid of December 1960 included a project to develop the cultivation of rice and tea as well as fruit plantations (4).

(1) EpAkL 2/69 p.87 and FEER Jul 5, 1962 (2) FEER Jul 5, 1962
(3) FEER Jul 25, 1963 (4) FEER Jan 12, 1961

A. <u>Chinese loans</u>

1972, Aug 17:	Loan (1) of unknown amount, estimated at US$ 20 m.
1973, Mar 28:	Loan of unknown amount estimated at US$ 10m.

(1) NZZ Sep 9, 1972 (?)

General remarks

The Chinese loan which was offered in September 1964 has probably never been used, because the CAR broke off its diplomatic relations with China in January 1966, shortly after President Dacko of the CAR had been deposed by a military coup under Colonel Bokassa.

A. Chinese loans

1965, Jan 14: US$ 4.1 m. (1)

(1) GT Jan 18, 1965

A. Chinese loans

1973, Sep 20 (1): US$ 11 m. (2)

(1) NCNA Sep 20, 1973 (2) NZZ May 23, 1973

General remarks

The most favourable terms China has ever granted on repayable loans were offered to Chile (repayment after 50 years!). China's intentions were clear: she wanted to gain a foothold on the Latin American continent which had been closed to her until 1970, having until then been a sphere of influence to the Soviet Union and its satellites. China therefore thought it worth her while to make a generous gesture which would compare favourably with the Soviet Union's very sober terms.

We have been unable to find out to what extent the loan offered comes under the heading of "economic aid" and how far it had been actually paid out to Chile before President Allende's fall.

A. Chinese loan

1972, Jun 8 : US$ 65m. (1), repayable after 50 years (2).

(1) NZZ Jun 14, 1972 (2) FAZ Feb 12, 1973

General remarks

After the fall of the first President of Congo (Brazz.), Abbé Fulbert Youlou, in August 1963, the new President, M.Massamba-Débat, opened the country to leftist influences. When China entered into diplomatic relations with Congo (Brazz.) on Feb 22, 1964(1), she entered at the same time into competition with the Soviet Union there. Ever since the Algerian and Cuban military advisers were called back, the Soviet Union has supported the country's armed forces so that China's influence in the country must be regarded as secondary, although the Chinese have succeeded in making the Défense Civile dependent on them to some extent (2).

The fact that China offered Congo (Brazz.) a new loan in 1972, thus leaving the Soviet Union far behind as a donor of economic aid, leads us to conclude that the Soviets' influence has diminished considerably lately.

A. Chinese loans

1964, Jul 1 :	US$ 5m., half of it in cash, free of interest, repayable from 1977 onward (3).
Oct 2 :	NF 100m. (=US$ 20.4m.), free of interest, repayable in equal yearly instalments between 1980 and 1989 (4).
1968, Aug 12:	US$ 1m. (5)
1972, Oct 19:	Chinese loan estimated at US$ 30m. (6).
1973, Jul 30:	Chinese loan estimated at US$ 10m. (7).

B. Aid projects completed

1. Medical groups

First group:	Protocol of Jan 24, 1967 (8) The group presumably arrived in 1967. Departure in April 1969 (9).
Second group:	Arrival on Jul 28, 1969 (10). On Jul 9, 1970, a new protocol on medical groups to be sent from China to Congo was signed (11), probably relating to the second group. The group was intended to consist of 40 doctors and medical assistants (12) expected to stay in the country for two years (13).

2. Intensifying of the transmitting power of Congo Radio

Protocol:	Jan 17, 1966 (14)
Location:	15 km from Brazzaville (14)
Completion:	Apr 8, 1967 (15).

(1) JMJP Apr 23, 1964 (2) NZZ May 28, 1967 (3) HdE II D 21 p.7 (4) JMJP Oct 3, 1964 and EpAkL 2/69 p.67 (5) EpAkL 2/69 p.67 (6) NCNA Oct 20, 1972 (7) NCNA Jul 30, 1973 (8) NCNA Jan 25, 1967 (9) NCNA May 1, 1969 (10) NCNA Aug 7, 1969 (11) NCNA Jul 9, 1970 (12) CN 369 Jul 16, 1970 (13) EpAkL 8/70 p.102(14) Peking Radio Jan 20, 1966 (15) NCNA Apr 11, 1967

Technical data: The transmitting power will be amplified from kW 25 to kW 100 with Chinese aid (1).
Other details: The short-wave station has been named "Voice of the Congolese Revolution" (2).

3. Broadcasting transmitter station
Location: Kinkolo (3)
Other details: When the station was inaugurated, the Chinese chargé d'affaires ad interim, Mr.Li Ch'en-kuang, said that this project was one of many still to come (4).

4. State farm
Protocol: Aug 12, 1968 (5)
Location: Kombé, 17 km southwest of Brazzaville (6)
Commencement: The laying of the foundation-stone took place on Aug 5, 1970 (7).
Completion: The farm was handed over on Oct 9, 1971 (8).
Technical data: The farm will grow cereals, vegetables, oil seeds, and cotton, and will also raise pigs and poultry (6).

5. Textile combine
Protocol: Sep 13, 1965 (9)
Location: Kinsoundi (10) near Brazzaville (11)
Commencement: Nov 26, 1966 (12)
Completion: May 15, 1969 (13). Transfer to the Congolese authorities on Aug 12, 1969 (13).
Technical data: The textile combine has workshops for spinning, weaving, printing, dyeing, and knitting (13).
Other details: The factory supplies essentially the cotton textiles required by Congo (7).The Chinese experts who had helped with the construction of the combine departed on Aug 20, 1969 (14).

6. Dockyard
Protocols: Feb 8, 1968 (15) and Sep 6, 1969 (16)
Location: Pointe Noire (17) near Brazzaville (16) or Mpila (18)
Commencement: Foundation-stone laid on Jul 23, 1970 (19)
Completion: The yard was transferred to the Congolese authorities on Mar 9, 1972 (20).
Technical data: The dockyard will build small wooden boats (15). The annual capacity will be 14 boats (16). Workshops, a sawmill and a foundry are connected with the dockyard. The boats will be for civilian and naval use. The ones for civilian use will include passenger boats carrying 100 persons and freight-boats carrying 250-500 t (18).

---

(1) ATP Jun 15, 1965 (2) NCNA Apr 11, 1967 (3) Brazzaville Radio Mar 20, 1969 (4) CN 307 Apr 10, 1969 (5) NCNA Aug 13, 1968 (6) NCNA Aug 26, 1969 (7) NCNA May 9, 1970 (8) NCNA Oct 10, 1971 (9) NCNA Sep 14, 1965 (10) NCNA Aug 24, 1969 (11) FEER Jun 1, 1967, and NZZ May 28, 1967 (12) NCNA Nov 27, 1966 (13) NCNA Aug 12, 1969 (14) NCNA Sep 24, 1969 (15) NCNA Feb 9, 1968 (16) NCNA Sep 7, 1969 (17) EpAkL 8/70 (18) Brazzaville Radio Nov 6, 1969 (19) NCNA Jul 24, 1970 (20) NCNA Mar 10, 1972

Other details: The President of Congo (Brazz.), Marien Ngouabi, attended the launching ceremony of the first mixed boat built by the shipyard (1) . The President was present when the first passenger and cargo boat was launched on Aug 11, 1973 (2). Name of the shipyard: "Chacona" (2).

C. Aid projects under construction

1. Hospital (3)
   Protocols: Feb 27, 1970 and Jan 27, 1971
   Location: Fort Rousset

2. Hydroelectric station
   Location: Bouenza (4)
   Commencement: September 1972 (5)

D. Aid projects planned

1. Fish-breeding
   China has promised to develop the Congolese fisheries (6). Among the projects scheduled are fish-pickling factories at Mossaka and Pointe Noire (7).

2. Cotton plantation (7)
   Location: Niari valley (8)
   Technical data: The planation will cover an area of 6,000 hectares (8).

3. Paddy fields (6)
   Location: Congo Basin

4. Palm-oil refinery (6)

5. Radio assembling workshop (6)

6. Tea plantations (6)

7. Water-supply project (9)
   Other details: In August 1970 a group of Chinese technicians arrived in Brazzaville to make plans for this project.

8. Sawmill (10)

9. Technical school (11)

10. Hydroelectric station (13)
   Location: Bouenza
   Other details: A Chinese team to build the station arrived in Brazzaville in September 1972.

E. Chinese experts
In 1965 there were about 180 Chinese experts in Congo (Brazz.). (12). In 1968 their number had increased to some hundred (14).

---

(1) NCNA Mar 24, 1973 (2) Aug 11, 1973 (3) NCNA Jan 30, 1971
(4) NCNA Apr 29, 1970 (5) NCNA Sep 13, 1972 (6) NZZ May 28, 1967
(7) ATP Jun 15, 1965 (8) EpAkL 2/69 p.79 (9) NCNA Aug 30, 1970
(10) NCNA Sep 9, 1972 (11) EpAkL 2/69 p.79 (12) DT Apr 27, 1965
(13) NCNA Sep 13, 1972 (14) FEER Oct 3, 1968

B. Aid projects completed

Machine parts factory (1)

Location:	Havana
Completion:	August 1961
Technical data:	The factory has over 90 machines, employs 250 persons, and can provide more than 600 different machine parts for various machines used in the sugar industry and in agricultural production

(1) NCNA Nov 23, 1971

General remarks

China and Dahomey entered into diplomatic relations in November 1964, but these were broken off after slightly more than 12 months. A military coup under General Sogho on New Year´s Day 1966 overthrew President Apithy´s government. 48 hours after this event the Chinese ambassador was informed that, although "this did not impair the friendly relations between our two countries", official relations had come to an end. It was not until December 1972 that the two countries resumed diplomatic relations. At the same time, they signed an agreement on Chinese economic aid under which China granted Dahomey a loan of US$ 46m.- far more than China gave to other small African countries-, thus bringing Dahomey immediately into the tenth place on the list of African recipients of Chinese aid.

There can be no doubt that China´s intention was to gain a strong foothold in this politically unsettled country.

A. Chinese loans

1972, Dec 29: US$ 46m. (1)

(1) NZZ Jan 19, 1973

General remarks

After the establishment of diplomatic relations in October 1970, China and Equatorial Guinea entered into an agreement on economic and technical cooperation in January 1971 under which China granted her partner a loan of US$ 10m. (estimated).

All the indications are that China has thus established a promising basis for her interests in Equatorial Guinea, which became independent in 1968.

A. Chinese loans

1971, Jan 22 (1): Loan estimated at US$ 10m.

B. Aid projects completed

1. Medical groups
   First group: The group presumably arrived in 1971. Departure in November 1973 (2)

C. Aid projects under construction

1. Cotton experimental farm (3)
   Location: Micomisseng county

2. Mongomo - Ncue road (4)
   Location: Rio Muni province
   Other details: President Francisco Macias Nguema inspected the construction site in Bimbiles county on Dec 9, 1972.

(1) NCNA Jan 22, 1971 (2) NCNA Dec 1, 1973 (3) NCNA Dec 10, 1972
(4) NCNA Dec 12, 1972

General remarks

Egypt ranks twelfth among the countries receiving economic aid, but this does not really mean very much. In reality the Chinese offers of aid have never been taken up. Egypt accepted neither the 1964 loan amounting to US$ 80m. nor the offer, made in 1967, of a donation of 150,000 tons of wheat, worth US$ 10m. The refusal was considered politically imperative by the Egyptians, in view of their friendly relations with the Soviet Union, from which Egypt had received economic aid amounting to US$ 1,198m. by 1972 (Egypt ranks second, after India, among the recipients of Soviet economic aid).

After the relations between Cairo and Moscow had become somewhat strained as a result of disagreements in 1972, followed by the departure of the Soviet military advisers, Egypt's attention again turned to China. In September 1972 Peking renewed its 1964 offer of economic aid and this time Egypt gave the green light for the construction of 15 factories.

However, the October 1973 war forced Egypt back into Moscow's arms and it is doubtful that the Chinese aid will materialize now that the Soviets have regained their powerful position in the country. Everything seems to indicate that in 1972 President Sadat used the Chinese trump card to blackmail the Soviets.

A. Chinese loans

1956, Nov 10:	Donation of SF 20m. (1) (= US$ 4.7m
1964, Dec 21:	Loan of US$ 80m. (2)
1967, June :	China offers a donation of 150,000 tons of wheat (3) worth US$ 10m. (4)
1972, September:	Loan of US$ 80.5m. (5) (As Egypt never made use of the 1964 loan, the 1972 loan seems to be a renewal of the offer for the old loan)

D. Aid projects planned

The 1972 loan is to be used for the construction of 15 plants (6).

1. Sand brick factory (7)
   Protocol: Jun 26, 1973

(1) HdE II D 21 p.12 (2) HdE II D21 p.13 (3) dpa Jun 11, 1967 (4) CN Jun 15, 1967 (5) NZZ Oct 4, 1972 (6) FAZ Oct 2, 1972 (7) NCNA Jun 28, 1973

General remarks

When Chou En-lai stayed in Ethiopia in January 1964 on his tour of Africa (which lasted several months), the Emperor Haile Selassie I showed him unlimited respect. The reason why it took the two countries more than six years after this event to establish diplomatic relations was probably that Haile Selassie did not wish at that time to be the only one in Africa to swim against the anti-Chinese tide, thereby provoking ill-feelings on the part of the Soviet Union, which had just started to grant Ethiopia economic aid.

In 1971 China offered Ethiopia a loan of US$ 80m., which brought the country into the 14th place in the list of recipients of economic aid from China. This enables us to conclude that China attributes great importance to Ethiopia. Although the greater part of the aid is to be used for the extension of the civil air system from which China also benefits under an agreement on civil air transport concluded in July 1972, the high amount offered may also be regarded as a provocation of the Soviet Union, whose financial involvement in Ethiopia totals a mere US$ 102m.

A. Chinese loan
1971, Oct 9 : US$ 80m. (1)

D. Aid projects planned

1. Road building (2)
A Chinese road survey team arrived in Addis Ababa on May 25, 1972.

2. Electrification (3)
A provincial town's electrification study team arrived in Addis Ababa on Jul 7, 1972.

3. Hydro-geological investigation (4)
A hydro-geological investigation team arrived in Ethiopia in Jun 1972.

4. Technical investigation (4)
A technical investigation team arrived in Addis Ababa on Aug 8, 1972.

---

(1) ENA Oct 10, 1971 (2) NCNA May 29, 1972 (3) NCNA Jul 13, 1972
(4) NCNA Aug 14, 1972

General remarks

Among the few countries where China has had negative experiences in the field of economic aid is Ghana. After US$ 42m. had been granted by 1964 and a great number of projects had been initiated, a military coup took place in February 1966 while the Ghanaian President Nkrumah was in Peking on an official visit. As a result, diplomatic relations were severed and Chinese economic aid was discontinued.

It was not until six years later that diplomatic relations between the two countries were resumed (February 1972), China's economic aid being resumed in September 1972.

A. Chinese loans

1961, Aug 18: Ghana £ 7m. (=US$19.6m.), free of interest, payable between July 1962 and June 1967, repayable between 1971 and 1981 (1)

1964, Jul 15: £ 8m. (=US$ 22.4m.), free of interest, to be used in the first Ghanaian Seven Year Plan (1963/64 - 1969/70) (2), repayable between November 1974 and December 1983 (3).

B. Aid projects completed

1. Grass plaiting
   In the summer of 1965 a group of Chinese experts left Ghana after having established some grass-plaiting enterprises and training local workers in this handicraft (4).

D. Aid projects not completed

1. Pencil factory (5)
   Location: Kumasi
   Commencement: January 1966
   Other details: By the beginning of 1966 1,000 t of material for the construction of this factory had been shipped to Ghana. China will bear the expenses of construction.

2. Pisciculture centres
   In November 1963 a group of Chinese fresh-water fish-breeding experts arrived in Ghana to help establish pisciculture centres (6).
   Nothing was heard of these centres later on, so it is assumed that the project has not been carried out in practice.

---

(1) JMJP Aug 22, 1961 (2) JMJP Jul 17, 1964 (3) HdE II D 92 p.7 f. (4) NCNA Jul 22, 1965 (5) OP Apr 22, 1966 (6) CT YB 351 p.21

3. Cotton spinning and knitting mill
   Location: Juapong, Volta district (1)
   Commencement: October 1965 (2)
   Other details: By the end of 1965 7,000 t of material for the construction of this mill had been shipped to Ghana. China will bear the expenses of construction (2).

4. State farm
   Location: Volta district (3)
   Other details: A group of Chinese experts arrived in Ghana in July 1965 to establish state farms (4)

D. Aid projects planned

1. Drug factory (5)
2. Porcelain and enamel factory (5)
3. Soap factory (5)
4. Plywood factory (5)
5. Fish-breeding experimental station (5)
6. Irrigation dam project (6)
   Location: Tano river

(1) NCNA Sep 11, 1965 (2) OP Apr 22, 1966 p.242 (3) NCNA Sep 11, 1965 (4) NCNA Jul 22, 1965 (5) EpAkL 2/69 p.78 (6) Accra Radio Nov 29, 1972

General remarks

Having received economic aid loans totalling US$ 100m. from China, Guinea comes 8th in the list of recipients of Chinese economic aid, which demonstrates the importance China attaches to this country. Guinea is one of the African countries where the economic aid balance is in favour of the Soviet Union and the socialist countries of Eastern Europe. It is this rivalry which explains the ambitious Chinese projects in Guinea, including in particular the Chinese offer to build the Kankan-Bamako railway line, an uneconomic project undertaken solely for prestige.

Owing to the skill of President Sekou Touré, the country profits from this rivalry without provoking resentment on either side.

A. Chinese loans

1960, Sep 13:	Rub 100m. (= US$ 25m.) , free of interest, repayable between 1970 and 1979 (1)
1969 Feb 28 (?)	US$ 45m. (2)
1972, Dec 13 (3)	Loan estimated at US$ 30m.

B. Aid projects completed

1. Bamboo processing centre (4)
   - Location: 9 km northeast of Conakry
   - Commencement: February 1968
   - Completion: December 1969
   - Other details: The centre includes a big processing hall.
2. Oil-pressing works
   - Location: Dabola, Upper Guinea (5)
   - Commencement: Dec 7, 1968 (5)
   - Completion: May 17, 1970 (6)
   - Technical data: The mill processes peanuts and palm kernels (5).
   - Other details: This is Guinea´s first oil-pressing mill (5).
3. Cinema building
   - Protocol: Jun 2, 1966 (7)
   - Location: Conakry (8)
   - Completion: Nov 8, 1968, in the presence of President Sekou Touré (8).
   - Other details: The cinema was named "8th November" (8).

---

(1) JMJP Sep 14, 1960 (2). Since 1960 China has granted Guinea several loans but no figures have been given. According to FEER of Nov 11, 1970, China´s loans had reached US$ 70 m. by 1970. The US$ 45 m. loan was presumably granted under the agreement of Feb 28, 1969 (NCNA Feb 28, 1969) (3) NCNA Dec 13, 1972 (4) NCNA Dec 17, 1969 (5) NCNA Dec 10, 1968 (6) NCNA May 20, 1970 (7) NCNA Jun 2, 1966 (8) NCNA Nov 9, 1968

4. High-voltage lines and transmission station
   Location: Central Guinea (1)
   Completion: May 1970 (1)
   Technical data: The project connects the Kinkon hydro-electric station with the towns of Labe, Pita, Dalaba, Mamou, and others (1).
   Other details: The line between Dalaba and Mamou which is 40 km long, crosses mountainous areas the highest elevations of which are more than 1,ooo m high, as e.g. the Kavendou mountains (2).

5. Conference building
   Protocol: February 1965 (3)
   Location: Conakry (?)
   Commencement: January 1966 (3)
   Completion: September 1967, in the presence of President Sekou Touré (3).
   Technical data: The building has a floor space of 22,000sq.m. and seats for 2,000 persons (4). It is equipped with a simultaneous translating system(5).
   Other details: The building was named "2nd October Palais" (3).

6. Agricultural development
   In 1966 Chinese agronomists were engaged in developing paddy fields. The Government of Guinea plans to grow rice on an area totalling 40,785 hectares in 12 regions (6).

7. Medical groups
   Protocols: December 30, 1967 (7), and March 10, 1970 (8).
   First group: Arrival in October 1968. 34 persons (9). In 1969 the group was divided into four teams working in Conakry, Macenta, Siguiri and Gaoual districts. By September 1969 they they had treated 167,000 out-patients (10). The Gaoual team was received by President Sekou Touré (11). Departure: August 1970 (12).
   Second group: Arrival in July 1970 (13).As laid down in the protocol of Mar 10, 1970, the medical group was reinforced by 2 surgeons, 1 anaesthesist, and some dentists who arrived in December 1970 (14). Departure not mentioned, presumably early 1973.
   Third group: Arrival: Apr 23, 1973 (15).

8. Small steelworks
   A small steelworks was under construction in the summer of 1967 (16) (at an unknown location). The type is supposed to be the one known from Chinese People´s Communes.

---

(1) NCNA May 21, 1970 (2) NCNA Jun 1, 1970 (3) NCNA Sep 26, 1967 (4) NCNA Sep 26, 1967 (5) NZZ Aug 18, 1966 (6) NCNA May 5, 1966 (7) NCNA Jan 1, 1968 (8) NCNA Mar 13, 1970 (9) NCNA Jun 10, 1968 (10) NCNA Sep 23, 1969 (11) NCNA Mar 1, 1970 (12) NCNA Aug 31, 1970 (13) NCNA Jul 29, 70(14) NCNA Dec 5, 1970, and NZZ Mar 13, 1970 (15) NCNA Apr 24 and 28, 1973 (16) FEER Jun 1, 1967

9. Tea plantation and factory (1)
   Location: Macenta in Southeast Guinea
   Completion: February 22, 1968, in the presence of President Sekou Touré and Tanzania's President Nyerere, then a guest in Guinea.

10. Hydroelectric station I
   Location: At the Kinkon Falls of River Kokolou (2) in the Fonda Djallon highlands (Central Guinea), where the rivers Niger, Senegal, and Gambia come from. Distance from Conakry: about 400 km (3).
   Commencement: Jul 2, 1964 (4)
   Completion: Jan 1, 1967 (3)
   Technical data: Dam 235 m in length (5), 21 m in height (5) Reservoir capacity: 3 million cubic metres (5), power capacity installed: kW 3,200 (5) or 3,000 (6). The power station supplies the Pita, Labe, and Dalaba regions with electricity (6).
   Other details: 200 Chinese engineers and technicians took part in the construction of the project (7), at the same time training 470 Guinean technicians (8). The Kinkon project is the first hydroelectric station China built in a foreign country (3).

11. Cigarette and match factory
   Location: 24 km northeast of Conakry (9)
   Commencement: March 1963 (9)
   Completion: September 1964 (10)
   Technical data: Annual capacity 24 million packages (containing 20 cigarettes each) and 45 million match-boxes (9). The workshops cover a floor space of 15,000 sq.m (9).
   Other details: This project made Guinea self-sufficient in cigarettes and matches (9) so that imports of foreign products in this field stopped in 1966 (10). The output has increased from year to year (10). In July 1971 the factory began to turn out high-class filter-tipped cigarettes (10). Over 1,800 workers and clerks are employed in the factory (10). Guinea recently opened 8 tobacco-planting centres in Macenta, Pita and Faranah. A tobacco-testing station will be set up (10).

C. Aid projects under construction

1. Hydroelectric station II
   Location: Tinkosso (11), Pita district (12)
   Other details: The first Chinese study group of experts arrived in Conakry in November 1969 (11).

---

(1) NCNA Feb 28, 1968 (2) NCNA Nov 11, 1964 (3) NCNA Feb 14, 1967 (4) NCNA Jul 2, 1964 (5) NCNA Nov 11, 1966 (6) NCNA Feb 14, 1967 (7) CT YB 351 p.22 (8) NCNA Feb 14, 1967 (9) NCNA Aug 25, 1964 (10) Feb 26, 1972 (11) NCNA Nov 26, 1969, Feb 21, 1972 (12) EpAkL 12/69 p.78

2. Brickworks (1)
   Location: Kankan
   Commencement: October 1969

3. Sugar refinery
   Location: Koba (2), in the coastal Boffa administrative region (3)
   Other details: The Prime Minister Beavogui inspected the construction site on Nov 15, 1972 (3). After completion the sugar complex will not only meet the needs of the Guinean people but will also put an end to the country's import of sugar (4).

4. Monument
   Chinese technicians and workers work on the construction site of the "November 22, 1970 Monument" for which President Sekou Touré laid the foundation stone on Nov 22, 1972 (5).

5. Farm tool plant (6)
   Location: Mamou region
   Other details: The plant was under construction when it was visited by Keita Nfamara, Minister of Social Domain, on Jun 19, 1973.

D. Aid projects planned

1. Repair of the Conakry-Kankan railway line
   China agreed to repair the railway line from Conakry to Kankan (7).

2. Repair of Conakry harbour
   China agreed to repair the port installations of Conakry (8).

3. Agricultural development programme
   China agreed to support an extensive agricultural development programme. A new Chinese agronomists' group arrived in May 1973 (9).

4. Cement plant
   An unconfirmed source mentioned a cement plant being under construction in 1967 (10). As neither the Chinese nor the Guinean presses had referred to this subject, it is assumed that the cement plant was only planned at that time, and is identical with the one Conakry Radio spoke of two years later.
   Technical data: Annual capacity 200,000 t (8).

5. Guinea-Mali railway line
   Agreement: May 24, 1968 (11) between PR China, Guinea, and Mali
   Course: Kankan (Guinea) - Bamako (Mali (12)

---

(1)NCNA Nov 5, 1969 (2) NCNA Feb 21, 1972 (3) NCNA Nov 16, 1972 (4) NCNA Nov 6, 1973 (5) NCNA Nov 23, 1972 (6) NCNA Jun 25, 1973 (7) Conakry Radio Oct 31, 1969 (8) Conakry R. Oct 31, 1969 (9) NCNA May 24, 1973 (10) FEER Jun 1, 1967 (11) NCNA May 25, 1968 (12) FEER Oct 3, 1968

Technical data: Length: 360 km of which 210 km in Guinea (1)

Survey: The first group of Chinese surveyors arrived in Guinea in August 1968 (2). The surveying work in Mali was completed in November 1968. The Chinese team engaged in this work then proceeded to Guinea (3)

Other details: Kankan is the final point of the Conakry-Niger railway line (1). Mali´s present connection with the ocean is the Bamako-Dakar railway line (4). The project of the Kankan-Bamako railway line had been studied by France when she still ruled as a colonial power but was rejected as being uneconomical. After the independence of the former French West Africa the new states of Guinea and Mali revived the project and asked the Soviet Union for help. The Soviets sent an expert team which concluded an expertise but were unwilling to finance the project (1).

Remarks: Obviously this project did not get beyond the stage of planning and surveying. The reason is presumably that the relations between the PR China and Mali became very much cooler following the overthrow of Modibo Keita in November 1968. After Senegal´s refusal to let the Dakar-Bamako railway line be used for the Chinese aid project, the Chinese were forced to abandon the original plan to start work at Bamako. The new plans then envisaged the starting point at Kouroussa (at a distance of 60 km from Kankan). However, the Conakry-Kouroussa railway line was in a deplorable state so that repairs were necessary before it could be used for the transport of material. The Federal Republic of Germany had promised a loan of DM 30 m. for these repairs (an agreement had already been ratified!) when China offered a loan on much more favourable conditions. Guinea then renounced the German loan.
The railway line is of no economic importance whatever, as there is no goods exchange between Guinea and Mali nor will there be any in the near future. Obviously the plans for this line were made for political considerations on the part of both Sekou Touré and Modiba Keita. After Keita´s fall the project was, accordingly, never heard of again.

E. Chinese experts

In the summer of 1967 about 3,000 Chinese experts were in Guinea. Most of them were engaged in agricultural projects, mainly paddy fields (5).

---

(1) FEER Aug 15, 1968 (2) NCNA Sep 27, 1968 (3) NCNA Nov 15, 1968
(4) NZZ May 31, 1968 (5) FEER Jun 1, 1967

General remarks

When China offered Guyana an economic aid loan (US$ 52m.) in April 1972, she was the first Communist country to undertake such activity in Guyana. The high amount of the loan is an indication of China´s endeavours to obtain a key position in this small South American country. It was not until 1970 that China managed to enter any of the Latin American countries, where she had regarded the Soviet predominance as particularly provocative.

A. Chinese loan
   1972, Apr 9 : US$ 52m. (1)

D. Aid projects planned

1. Training of bricklayers
   In the summer of 1972 some Chinese experts were assisting in the training of Guyanese bricklayers in the Government´s programme to encourage building with clay bricks (1). The first group of young bricklayers have completed a three-and-a-half months´training course in New Amsterdam. The name of the clay brick factory is "Alness" (2).

2. Rice plantation (1)
   In June 1972 some Chinese experts were expected to arrive and work on the rice expansion programme.

3. Cotton industry (1)
   In June 1972 some Chinese experts were expected to arrive and help establish a cotton industry.

   A Chinese economic and technical study group stayed in Guyana from September to December 1972 (3)

---

(1) JT Jun 30, 1972 (2) NCNA Oct 18, 1973 (3) NCNA Dec 9, 1972

General remarks

There can be no doubt that the most disastrous chapter in the history of Chinese economic aid is Indonesia. Though the first Chinese loan had been offered as early as 1958, not one of the projects was completed. This was no fault of the Chinese but the consequence of the strange ideas of the then President Sukarno who thought that, even in economic aid, prestige projects should rank before industrial plant. The fact that, out of the considerable total of loans offered, China actually paid a mere US$ 26m. (1) seems to indicate inter alia that the Chinese were not satisfied with the practices of Indonesian economic development policy.

It is a strange coincidence that the greatest lump of China's economic aid to Indonesia, viz. US$ 150m., was offered on September 30, 1965, the very date of the Communist riots which eventually resulted in the severance of diplomatic relations with China. China's failure actually to pay Indonesia more than a minor portion - probably a mere 25 % or so - of the loans offered in the years preceding 1965, when close relations existed between the two countries, should be seen in the light of the fact that the Soviet Union and its satellites made no further investment after the anti-Communist coup in October 1965 either. All the rival Communist countries had to write off Indonesia as a recipient of economic aid.

A. Chinese loans

1958, Apr 17:	SF 48m. (=US$ 11.5m.), at an interest of 2.5 %, repayment over a period of 10 years, starting in 1959 (2).
Oct 8:	US$ 13.5m., at an interest of 2.5 % (2).
1961, Oct 11:	SF 129.6m. (=US$ 30m.), at an interest of 2 % (3).
1965, Jan 25:	US$ 50m. , free of interest (4)
Mar 31:	Loan of unknown amount (4)
Sep 30:	US$ 150m. (including that of Mar 31, 1965) (5)

---

(1) CN Jun 15, 1967 (2) HdE II D 21 p.22 (3) Radio Djakarta Oct 20, 1961 (4) HdE D 21 p.23 (5) HdE II D 21 p.23 (referring to a Soviet source!)

C. Aid projects not completed

1. Paper mill (1)

Protocol: April 6, 1965
Location: Tjiandju, West Java
Technical data: Daily capacity: 40 t
Remarks: When the Chinese aid was suspended (October 1965), the construction of the plant had probably just commenced.

2. Textile mill I

Location: Bandjavan (2)
Other details: When the Chinese aid was suspended (October 1965), about 70 % of the project had been completed (3).

3. Textile mill II (4)

Location: Bandung
Technical data: 30,000 spindles
Other details: When the Chinese aid was suspended (October 1965) 70% of the project had been completed (3).

D. Air projects planned

1. Conference building

Protocol: Sep 14, 1965 (5)
Location: Djakarta (?)
Other details: The Chinese expert group left Indonesia two days after the coup of Sep 30, 1965, taking all the blue-prints with it (6).

2. Textile mills

The 1961 loan of US$ 30 m. had been intended for the construction of 6 textile mills (spinning and weaving mills) (7) totalling 1,000 automatic looms and 160,000 spindles (8). In 1963 China and Indonesia discarded the plan to build the weaving mills and instead agreed to build 8 spinning mills in Bandjermasin, Lombok, Madiun, Madjalaja, Makassar, Padang, Tapanuli, and Timur (9). We have not been able to find out whether, or not, the two textile mills of Bandung and Bandjavan (under C.2 and 3 above) form part of the present programme.

---

(1) NCNA Apr 6, 1965 (2) NCNA Oct 25, 1965 (3) Antara Dec 4, 1965 (4) UPI Dec 15, 1965 (5) NCNA Sep 14, 1965 (6) Antara Nov 18, 1965 (7) Djakarta Radio Oct 20, 1961 (8) FEER Jul 16, 1959 (9) HdE II D 21 p.22 f.

General remarks

Although diplomatic relations between China and Iraq have existed since 1958 and several agreements have been concluded, the first agreement on economic and technical cooperation was entered into only in June 1971 (1). Accordingly, Iraq will soon occupy the sixth place among the Near and Middle East countries receiving economic aid from China.

Since Iraq is one of the countries where the Soviets have placed their centre of gravity in the field of economic aid (Iraq coming fifth on the list of recipients after India, Egypt, Afghanistan, and Iran), the economic aid offered by China does not carry much political weight.

A. Chinese loans

1971. Jun 21: Yüan 100m. = Iraq Dinar (ID) 14m. (2)
(=US$ 36m) (3)

D. Aid projects planned

After having signed the Sino-Iraqi agreement on economic and technical cooperation, Mr. Sa´dun Hammadi, the Minister for Oil and Minerals announced that the Chinese loan would be used for the construction of a factory (2) (probably a textile mill).

(1) NCNA Jun 21, 1971 (2) INA Jun 25, 1971 (3) DW Jun 26, 1971, and NYHT Jun 26, 1971

General remarks

The establishment of diplomatic relations between China and Kenya in December 1964 was followed by a development suggesting a rapidly stabilizing friendship. Less than five months later, Kenya's Home Minister, Odinga, brought back from a visit to Peking two Chinese loans totalling US$ 18m. (1). Shortly afterwards, the Kenyan government established a special committee to deal with the problems arising in connection with China's economic aid (2).

However, before the Chinese aid had been carried into effect, relations were gravely disturbed by the fact that arms of Chinese origin were found in the possession of rebels in Kenya (3), and that a Communist review, later suppressed by the government, was alleged to have been published at Chinese instigation (4). As a result, Chinese diplomats and journalists were expelled from the country, protests were made on both sides and the exchange of delegations which had been in full swing was interrupted (no delegations whatever were exchanged between August 1965 and 1970!). Thus before Chinese economic aid had really begun, it became bogged down in an atmosphere of distrust which has not yet been overcome.

China's endeavours to return to friendly relations with Kenya, as with other countries, after the thaw in foreign policy following the Cultural Revolution, were manifested in an appreciable donation made by the Chinese Red Cross to relieve the effects of a drought catastrophe in Kenya. This was the highest donation (Yuan 1m. = US$ 420,000, one fifth to be paid in cash, four fifths in the form of grain and other foodstuffs and medicines) (1) China had ever given to a country outside the Eastern Bloc. When this donation was handed over, it was the first time in years that a Chinese diplomat was again received by Kenyatta. Even this gesture, however, was unable to make President Kenyatta change his mind. Kenya is the only country which, though it entered into diplomatic relations with China prior to the Cultural Revolution, has not yet sent a permanent diplomatic representative to Peking. Together with Laos, Kenya is the only country to which China has not sent an ambassador though diplomatic relations had existed already before the Cultural Revolution. Nothing will illustrate more clearly the freezing of relations.

A. Chinese loans

1964, May 10: US$ 15m., interest-free (5). US$ 3m. donation (budgetary aid) (6).

B. Aid projects completed

1. Bamboo processing

In March 1966 a group of Chinese experts left Kenya after having trained some Kenyans to make bamboo utensils (7).

---

(1) JMJP May 4, 1964 (2) NCNA Sep 8, 1964 (3) EAS May 29, 1965 (4) The Guardian Apr 7, 1965 (5) HdE II D 21 p.7 (6) EpAkL 2/69 p.67 (7) NCNA Mar 25, 1966

General remarks

Among the recipients of Chinese economic aid Laos has a unique position insofar as the aid began in 1962 before diplomatic relations had been established (Sep 7, 1962). The aid was primarily intended for the benefit of the Pathet Lao, and the initiators surely did not have anything else in mind. This may be seen from the circumstance that when the tripartite coalition in Laos (comprising representatives of the Pathet Lao, the neutralists, and the right-wing faction) fell apart in 1963, Sino-Laotian relations remained practically limited to those between China and the Pathet Lao. The result was, inter alia, that the Chinese embassy in Vientiane sank into insignificance, while the "Chinese Economic and Cultural Mission" at Khang Khay (in the area dominated by the Pathet Lao) developed into a centre of Chinese activity, and hence repeatedly fell victim to US bombers. Accordingly, another Chinese promise of economic aid made immediately before the falling apart of the tripartite coalition was never fulfilled because of interior developments in Laos.

On the other hand, observers are sure that the one road-building project cited has not remained the only item of economic aid from China to Laos. There are, however, no reliable sources relating to other road-building projects. Nor have such roads been built in accordance with agreements between the official governments, but almost entirely out of military aid funds given to the Pathet Lao without previous consultation with the Laotian government.

A. Chinese loans

1962, Jan 13:	US$ 4m. , donation (1)
Dec 4:	Long-term loan of unknown amount (2) (estimated at US$ 6m.)

B. Aid projects completed

1. Road building I

Agreement:	Jan 13, 1962 (3)
Course:	Moungha(Yunnan province) - Pacha - Moung Yong - Boun Neua - Phong Saly (4)
Commencement:	Spring 1962 (5)
Completion:	April 1963 (5)
Technical data:	Width: 6.5 m, total of reinforced road space: 296,000 sq.m (6). Length on Laotian territory 86 km, on Chinese territory, 36 km (6).
Other details:	In 1970, the road was probably extended by 80 km on Laotian territory (7).

(1) HdE II D 21 p.27 (2) JMJP Dec 5, 1962 (3) JMJP Jan 14, 1962 (4) Vientiane Radio Apr 22, 1963 (5) NCNA Apr 16, 1963 (6) NCNA Apr 23, 1963 (7) FCW Mar 7, 1971, as cited in New York Times

2. Other roads
General Praphat Charusatien, Director of the National Security Affairs Division of the National Executive Council told reporters at the NEC press centre on November 24, 1972, that a road being built in Laos by China had reached the Mekong river and a bridge was being constructed across the river. He said the road, which runs from the border of the PR China to the right bank of the Mekong river in the Kingdom of Laos had been opened to traffic (1).

D. Aid projects planned

1. Construction of industrial enterprises (2)
2. Technical equipment for factories (2)
3. Phong Saly - Namtha road (2)

Remarks: No information regarding the completion of these three project has been found. It may be assumed that only the road building project has been carried out.

(1) Bangkok Radio Nov 24, 1972 (2) JMJP Dec 5, 1962

A. Chinese loans

1973, February: US$ 12 m. (1)

C. Aid projects under construction (1)

1. Hotel at Nossi-Bé
Malagasy severed her diplomatic relations with the Republic of South Africa, which had started this project, in June 1972. China promised to complete the hotel.

(1)FAZ Feb 5, 1973

General remarks

After the fall of Modibo Keita at the end of 1968, relations between Mali and China became very much cooler. However, when China normalized and reactivated her foreign policy after the Cultural Revolution, she visibly endeavoured to reestablish friendly relations, the principal reason probably being that the Mali government opened its country to Chinese and Soviet economic aid alike. A new offer of an economic aid loan amounting to US$ 20m. in 1970 and another one three years later (estimated at US$ 10m.) reveals China's growing involvement in the face of increasing rivalry with the Soviet Union.

A. Chinese loans

1961, Sep 22:	Malian Franc (MF) 50m. (=US$ 0.2m.), donation (1). MF 4,800m. (=US$ 19.4m.), free of interest (1) payable within 20 years, repayable over a period of 10 years, after the end of payments (2).
1964, Nov 3:	MF 2,000m. (=US$ 7.9m.), donation (1)
1966, Jun 9 (3):	US$ 3m. (4)
1968, May 24:	Agreement on the construction of the Guinea-Mali railway line (5), loan estimated at US$ 5m.
1970, Dec 21:	Agreement on economic and technical cooperation (6). Chinese loan estimated at US$ 20m.
1973, Jun 24:	Agreement on economic and technical cooperation (7). Chinese loan estimated at US$ 10m.

B. Aid projects completed

1. Exhibition pavilion
   On Mar 1, 1968, China made Mali a present of the agricultural pavilion of the Chinese Economic and Trade Exhibition which had taken place at Bamako at the beginning of 1968 (8).

---

(1) HdE II D 21 p.8 (2) OEL 21, 9/65 p.217 (3) NCNA Jun 9, 1966 (4) EpAkL 2/69 p.68 (5) NCNA May 25, 1968 (6) NCNA Dec 21, 1970 (7) NCNA Jun 24, 1973 (8) NCNA Mar 4, 1968

2. Guinea - Mali railway line
   see Guinea under C.1

3. Tannery (1)
   Location: Bamako
   Completion: Sep 21, 1970
   Technical data: Annual processing of 20,000 hides and production of 35,000 pairs of shoes (2).

4. Handicraft workshops
   Chinese experts were engaged in the construction of workshops for the production of bamboo furniture and agricultural implements (3).

5. Jeeps
   These Chinese government presented Mali with 30 jeeps produced in China. Delivery at Bamako on Apr 13, 1968 (4).

6. Cinema building
   Protocol: Sep 1, 1965 (5)
   Location: Bamako (6)
   Commencement: 1965 (6)
   Completion: May 1967 (7)
   Technical data: 2,500 seats (8)
   Other details: The cinema was named "Babemba" (7). Inauguration in the presence of President Keita (7).

7. Medical groups
   Protocol: Dec 14, 1967 (9)
   First group: Arrival at Bamako on Feb 13, 1968. The group consisted of 19 persons (10). First place of work: Markala, a small town in the Ségou district (11). During the first six months the group attended to 30,000 patients and carried out 350 operations (11). Six members of the group work in the remote Macina region (Ségou district) (11). Departure for China in June 1970 (12).
   Second group: Arrival in June 1970 (12).
   Third group: Arrival in August 1972 (13).

8. Motel
   Protocol: Sep 1, 1965 (14)
   Location: Timbuktu (15)
   Completion: November 4, 1967 (15)

9. Paddy fields
   In January 1962 some Chinese experts arrived in Mali to cultivate paddy fields (16). It may be presumed that this project was duly completed.

---

(1) NCNA Sep 21, 1970 (2) EpAkL 11/70 p.320 (3) EG 8/65 (4) NCNA Apr 13, 1968 (5) NCNA Sep 2, 1965 (6) Bamako Radio Jan 18, 1965 (7) NCNA Jun 7, 1967 (8) EpAkL 2/69 p.80 (9) NCNA Dec 15, 1967 (10) NCNA Feb 13, 1968 (11) NCNA Nov 2, 1968 (12) NCNA Jun 6, 1970 (13) NCNA Aug 18, 1972 (14) NCNA Sep 2, 1965 (15) EpAkL 2/69 p.80 (16) CT YB 351

10. Amplification of the broadcasting station's transmitting power
    Protocol: Sep 1, 1965 (1)
    Technical data: Amplification to 200-360 kW (2)
    Other details: Chinese experts engaged in this project were in Bamako in 1965 (3)

11. Match factory
    Location: Bamako (4)
    Commencement: January 1966 (5)
    Completion: February 1967. Inauguration in the presence of President Keita (4).
    Other details: The factory was named "Eclair" (5). It produces all the matches required by Mali (6).

12. Textile combine
    Protocol: Mar 17, 1965 (7)
    Location: Ségou (8), 250 km from Bamako
    Commencement: February 1966 (9)
    Completion: May 21, 1968 (9), in the presence of President Keita (9)
    Technical data: 24,500 spindles and 400 looms (10). The textile combine comprises more than 20 buildings, including a bleaching and dyeing workshop, a drying hall, a central electricity station, a water-supply and drainage system, a repair workshop, an administrative building, and a hospital (11). Number of workers: 3,200 (12) or 1,500 (13). Cost of the mill: US$ 16 m.(12). The Ségou mill is the second largest in the country (13). In 1971 the combine turned out 15 kinds of cotton yarn and blank cloth, and has tried successfully to produce new varieties of textile fabrics, such as gauze, material for mosquito nets, and Khankis (13).
    Other details: A ceremony of laying the corner-stone for the extension of the combine was held on Mar 19, 1973 (14).

13. Transmitting station (15)
    Location: Bamako
    Completion: Sep 21, 1970

14. Cigarette factory
    Location: Djioliba (16)
    Commencement: January 1965 (17)
    Completion: November 1965. Inauguration in the presence of President Keita (17).

---

(1) NCNA Sep 2, 1965 (2) EpAkL 2/69 p.80 (3) Bamako Radio Jan 18, 1965 (4) NCNA Feb 2, 1967 (5) EpAkL 2/69 p.79 (6) NCNA Aug 17, 1966 (7) NCNA Mar 18, 1965 (8) NCNA Dec 14, 1966 (9) NCNA May 22, 1968 (10) Bamako Radio Jan 18, 1965 (11) OEL 21, 9/65 p.217 f. (12) FEER Aug 15, 1968 (13) NCNA Sep 20, 1972 (14) NCNA Mar 20, 1973 (15) NCNA Sep 21, 1970 (16) NCNA Aug 23, 1966 (17) NCNA Nov 3, 1965

Technical data: When the trial production was started in September 1965, four different sorts of cigarettes were produced (1). This cigarette factory is Mali's first one (2).
Other details: President Nyerere of Tanzania visited the factory on Apr 15, 1965 (3).

15. Sugar refinery
Location: Dougabougou, Ségou district (4)
Completion: First phase in April 1964 (5)
Second (and last) phase in February 1967 (4).
Technical data: Daily capacity: 400 t of sugar cane (5), 40 t of sugar (6). This is Mali's first sugar refinery (2). It is under the administration of the Niger Office, Mali's greatest state enterprise (7). Annual capacity scheduled: 4,000 t of sugar (8).
Other details: The inauguration took place in the presence of President Keita (4).

16. Sugar plantation
Location: Near Markala, northeast of Ségou (8), 300 km east of Bamako (9).
Commencement: 1962 (10)
Completion: May 1965 (10)
Technical data: The plantation covers an area of 500 hectares (11). 1,000 ha (sic!) are reported to be irrigated by a pumping station (12).
Other details: President Keita inspected the plantation in May 1965 (10).

17. Tea plantation and processing factory
Location: Balinkoni near Kanieba, Sikasso district (13)
Commencement: (construction) The foundation-stone for the tea factory was laid on Jan 8, 1971 (14).
(plantation): 1962 (13).
Completion: The inauguration took place on Aug 10, 1973 (15).
Technical data: It is intended to plant tea on 400 ha by 1969.
Annual production scheduled: 3,000 t of tea (13).
Other details: The plantation was developed under the guidance of Lin Kuei-t'ang, Director of the Tea Research Institute of the Academy of Agrosciences, Fukien province (13). The plantation is run and owned by the state of Mali (14).

C. Aid projects under construction

1. Grinding mill (16)
Location: Sevare
Completion: In September 1972, the mill was put into trial operation.

(1) NCNA Sep 20, 1965 (2) NCNA Aug 23, 1966 (3) NCNA Apr 15, 1965 (4) NCNA Feb 11, 1970 (5) CT YB 351 (6) Jul 2, 1966 (7) NCNA Jan 29, 1968 (8) NCNA Mar 25, 1965 (9) EG 8/65 (10) NCNA May 19, 1965 (11) NCNA Jul 2, 1966 (12) EG 8/65 (13) PR Jan 18, 1966 (14) NCNA Jan 18, 1971 (15) NCNA Aug 13, 1973 (16) NCNA Sep 13, 1972

2. Guinea-Mali railway-line
   see Guinea, C. Aid projects under construction

D. Aid projects scheduled

1. Hotel
   Protocol: September 1965 (1)
   Location: Bamako (2)
   Other details: At the beginning of 1965 Chinese experts were studying the project (2).

2. Watch factory (3)
   China promised to construct a watch factory in Bamako.

E. Chinese experts

1962: Arrival of the first group of experts (4)
1964: At the beginning of that year the number of agricultural Chinese experts in the country was about 400 (5).
1965: The number was 155 (3)
1967: 1,200-1,500 Chinese experts were in Mali (6).

Most of the experts endeavour to learn the Bambara language but they hardly ever mix with the people. No Chinese is staying longer than two years unless the Malian government asks them to (3).

(1) NCNA Sep 2, 1965 (2) Bamako Radio Jan 18, 1965 (3) AN May 6-12, 1965 (4) PR Jan 18, 1966 (5) CT YB 351 (6) FEER Jun 1, 1967

General remarks

China's economic aid to Malta must be seen primarily from a political point of view. It is easy to imagine the satisfaction Peking felt when called upon to help an underdeveloped European country, the more so since China herself had been subject to treatment as a sort of colony by a number of European countries no more than four decades ago. Now she had an opportunity to demonstrate to the world that, with all its wealth and technical knowledge, Europe could not prevent one of its weakest members from seeking aid in Peking.

A. Chinese loans

1972, Apr 8 (1): US$ 42.6m. (2)

D. Aid projects planned

1. Dock (3)
   Chief among the Chinese development projects is the construction of a new dock to take ships of up to 300,000 tons. 17 Chinese are reported to study the dockyard and many more are expected.
2. Chocolate factory (4)
3. Ornamental glass factory (4)

E. Chinese experts

A general study team of Chinese technicians was received by Mr.Anthony Mamo, Governor-General of Malta.(5)

(1) NCNA Apr 27, 1972 (2) NZZ Apr 29, 1972 (3) DT Oct 23, 1972
(4) Il-Hajja Nov 17, 1973 (5) NCNA Oct 31, 1972

General remarks

In Mauritania China´s economic aid is primarily directed to irrigation projects. There is no other field where greater merit can be acquired in this desert country.Bilateral relations seem to be firmly established; however, this apparent situation is somewhat marred by the fate of the Chinese medical groups. The first medical team came to Mauritania in April 1968, the medical workers being as a rule replaced by others after two or three years. Under a new protocol signed in August 1972, the third medical group arrived in October 1972 but it had left the country already by August 1973. This somewhat abrupt departure suggests that difficulties may have arisen.

A. Chinese loans

1967, Feb 16 (1): US$ 4m. (2)

1971, Apr 1: CFA 650m. (3) =US$ 2.7m. or (more reasonable) CFA 5,650 (=US$ 23.5m.) (4).

B. Aid projects completed

1. House of Youth (5)
   Location: Nouakchott
   Completion: Transfer on Nov 27, 1970 (the tenth anniversary of Independence)
   Other details: The house is a Chinese gift.

2. Home of Culture
   Location: Nouakchott (6)
   Completion: President Moktar Ould Daddah presided over the inaugural ceremony on Apr 8, 1972 (6).

3. Hospital (7)
   Location: Kiffa (capital of the third region)
   Completion: February 1970
   Technical data: The hospital is equipped with modern Chinese instruments.
   Other details: In this hospital the Chinese medical group trained several Mauritanians for medical work. The inauguration took place in the presence of the President of Mauritania.

4. Educational material (8)
   In February 1968 China presented Mauritania with equipment and material for chemistry and physics lessons in secondare schools.

5. Medical groups
   Protocols: Nov 8, 1967 (9) and Aug 21, 1972 (10).
   First group: Arrival on Apr 11, 1968 (11). The group worked at Kiffa Selibaby (12), Aioum (capital of the Second Region (13), Lassaba and Guidimaka (14), and consisted of 24 persons (14). Departure: June 1970 (15).

---

(1) NCNA Feb 16, 1967 (2) FEER Apr 18, 1968 (3) MAPA Apr 19, 1971 (4) Bfa/NfA Jun 21, 1971 (5) NCNA Nov 28, 1970 (6) NCNA Apr 11, 1972 (7) NCNA Feb 20, 1970 (8) EpAkL 2/69 p.80 and NCNA Feb 22, 1968 (9) NCNA Nov 10, 1967 (10) NCNA Aug 21, 1972 (11) NCNA Apr 12, 1968 (12) FEER Apr 18, 1968 (13) NCNA Feb 9, 1970 (14) EpAkL 2/69 p.80 (15) NCNA Jun 23, 1970

Second group:	Arrival June 1970 (1) Departure October 1972 (2)
Third group:	Arrival October 1972 (2) Departure August 1973 (3)

6. Water supply project

Protocol:	Sep 29, 1971 (4)
Location:	Idini Nouakchott (4), 60 km southeast of Nouakchott
Commencement:	1971 (4)
Completion:	The completion of the first stage was marked by a ceremony held at Idini on Dec 3, 1973, in the presence of President Moktar Ould Daddah (4).
Technical data:	The system supplies the capital with 6,000 cubic metres of water daily (4). On completion of the final stage, it will supply Nouakchott with 20,000 tons of desalted water per diem (5).
Other details:	The water comes from 18 wells at Idini. The first pipes along the line Idini-Nouakchott was laid in July 1972 (4). In the first years after independence water had to be fetched in wagons from the Senegal river, more than 2,000 km away. The desalination plant in Nouakchott and the three water pumps in Idini completed in recent years cannot meet the demand for water from the fast-growing population of Nouakchott (4).

C. Aid projects under construction

1. Wells

Protocol:	Nov 27, 1969 (6)
Locations:	Kiffa, Kankossa, Boumdeit districts and elsewhere (6).
Technical data:	The number of wells to be sunk with Chinese aid is 50 (6).
Other details:	In April 1970 the Mauritanian President inspected the drilling at Kankossa (7).

2. Experimental farm

Location:	M'pourie Plain on the Lower Senegal R. (8), 7 km from Rosso town (9).
Commencement:	Spring 1968. The first rice-growing experiments started in 1967 (10).
Technical data:	The project began with the construction of a dam of 13 km length, protecting 6,000 ha of land from being flooded while irrigating the soil during the dry season (11). The dike protects 300 ha of arable land, and will open still more land for cultivation(12).

---

(1) NCNA Jun 27, 1970 (2) NCNA Oct 25, 1972 (3) NCNA Aug 8, 1973 (4) NCNA Dec 3, 1973 (5) NCNA Jul 27, 1972 (6) NCNA Nov 29, 1969 (7) NCNA Apr 25, 1970 (8) NCNA May 27, 1968 (9) NCNA Dec 24, 1968 (10) NCNA May 27, 1968 (11) NCNA Dec 24, 1968 (12) EpAkL 2/69 p. 80

The areas where paddy rice can be grown and animals raised cover 4,000 ha (1).

Other details: The first Chinese group of experts arrived at Rosso in August 1966 (2). The first rice harvest was carried out in November 1970 (3). In eight rural collectives composed of six villages the first rice harvest began in November 1973. The area cultivated with help from the M'pourie state farm is 58 ha (4).

D. Aid projects planned

1. Harbour for ocean-going ships (5)
Location: near Nouakchott (5)
Other details: China has offered aid amounting to CFA 5,650m. (=US$ 23.5m.).

(1) EpAkL 2/69 p.80 (2) NCNA Dec 24, 1968 (3) NCNA Nov 3, 1970
(4) NCNA Nov 24, 1973 (5) BfA/NfA Jun 21, 1971

A. Chinese loans

1972, Aug 9 : US$ 32 m. (1)

(1) NZZ Sep 9, 1972

General remarks

The People's Republic of Mongolia is one of China's three socialist neighbours, to which it used to feel a special obligation because both were in the same camp. The first bilateral economic aid agreement was entered into as early as 1955, and carried out from about 1957 onwards.

What economic aid China actually granted to Mongolia cannot be clearly ascertained. (The principles guiding the release of information on economic aid between socialist countries seem inexplicable to foreign observers.) Still we have been able to trace 40 projects, a total which suggests a wide range of economic aid. Nothing, however, has been disclosed on the number of projects carried out. Thus, for example, the sources open to us reported ten bridges built with Chinese aid, though the number of bridges actually built was more than 190.

It was the People's Republic of Mongolia which gave Peking its first bitter experience in the field of economic aid. When the Mongolians took Russia's side in the Sino-Soviet conflict, Peking discontinued its economic aid to Mongolia. Of the Chinese technicians and workers, of whom between 6,000 and 12,000 were working in Mongolia at various times since the beginning of Chinese economic aid, the last group left the country on July 8, 1964. China, the betrayed one-time friend, then announced that the Chinese workers had created immense wealth for the Mongolian people. They stated that Chinese constructors, together with Mongolian workers, had built houses with a total floor-space of 2.7 million square metres. They had built innumerable miles of railway track, more than 190 bridges and more than 200 kilometres of roads, and laid more than 9,000 kilometres of electric cables. Chinese agricultural workers had raised tens of thousands of tons of vegetables ..... (1). This implies that the Chinese forces had been withdrawn as a result of "force majeure", Peking feeling no guilt whatever in connection with this regrettable development.

Critical observers cannot overlook the exemplary goodwill and generosity which characterized China's aid to Mongolia. Surely this was the result of China's recognition, enforced by the Soviets in 1950, of Mongolia's independence which Peking had tolerated (or had to tolerate?) and to which it then felt bound. We may safely assume that it no longer feels bound by this earlier obligation.

---

(1) JMJP Jul 9, 1964

B. Aid projects completed

1. Bridge I (1)
   Location: Ulan Bator, crossing the Dungol river
   Completion: scheduled for the end of 1958 (2)

2. Bridge II (3)
   Inauguration: Oct 10, 1958 (2)

3. Road I (3)
   Inauguration: Oct 10, 1958 (2)

4. Road II (3)
   Inauguration: Oct 10, 1958 (2)

5. Road III
   Inauguration: October 10, 1958 (2)

6. Vegetable-growing farm (4)
   Transfer: November 1958

7. Residential quarters (4)
   Location: Ulan Bator
   Completion: November 1958
   Technical data: 4-storeyed house

8. School (4)
   Location: Ulan Bator
   Transfer: November 1958

9. Sports stadion (sports hall)
   Location: Ulan Bator
   Transfer: November 1958
   Technical data: 15,000 seats for spectators (5)

10. Power station I
    Location: Suke Bataar (6)
    Completion: Dec 23, 1958 (6)
    Technical data: Capacity kW 6,000 (5)

11. Sanatorium (7)
    Location: Ulan Bator
    Transfer: November 1959
    Technical data: 100 beds
    Other details: The sanatorium is a Chinese donation.

12. Bridge III (8)
    Location: in the suburbs of Ulan Bator
    Transfer: October 28, 1959
    Technical data: Total length of bridges II - V: 460 m

13. Bridge IV (8)
    Location: Bulegan province
    Transfer: Oct 28, 1959
    Technical data: Total length of bridges III - V: 460 m

14. Bridge V (8)
    Location: Ara Changai province
    Transfer: Oct 28, 1959
    Technical data: Total length of bridges III - V: 460 m

---

(1) NCNA Aug 7, 1958 (2) Projects 1-5 are probably in Ulan Bator (3) JMJP Oct 13, 1958 (4) NCNA Nov 12, 1958 (5) Montsame Radio Sep 26, 1962 (6) JMJP Dec 24, 1958 (7) JMJP Nov 5, 1959 (8) JMJP Oct 29, 1969

15. Wool-spinning mill
    - Location: Ulan Bator (1)
    - Commencement: 1958 (1)
    - Completion: Jan 15, 1960
    - Technical data: Annual capacity: 1.2 million m of cloth (1), 0.8 million m of woollen cloth, and 0.2 million blankets (2).
    - Other details: The mill is a Chinese donation. It was constructed by Chinese technicians according to Russian designs. The machines are Chinese and British. The capacity of the mill suffices to supply the country with woollen goods (4).

16. 11 roads (3)
    - Location: Ulan Bator
    - Transfer: Oct 27, 1960
    - Technical data: Total surface 495,000 sq.metres
    - Remarks: The width is presumed to be 7 m, the total length of the eleven roads will be 70 km.

17. Bridge VI (3)
    - Location: Ulan Bator
    - Transfer: Oct 27, 1960

18. Bridge VII (3)
    - Location: Ulan Bator
    - Transfer: Oct 27, 1960

19. Bridge VIII (3)
    - Location: Ulan Bator
    - Transfer: Oct 27, 1960

20. Bridge IX (3)
    - Location: Ulan Bator
    - Transfer: Oct 27, 1960

21. 23 canals (3)
    - Location: Ulan Bator
    - Transfer: Oct 27, 1960

22. Irrigation system (3)
    - Location: Ulan Bator
    - Technical data: Length 9.4 km

23. Residential quarters (4)
    - Location: Ulan Bator
    - Completion: May 9, 1961
    - Technical data: Floor space 50,000 sq. m. A floor space of 50,000 sq.m corresponds to 500 apartments of 100 sq.m each, or to 835 apartments of 60 sq.m each.

24. Store (5)
    - Location: Ulan Bator
    - Transfer: Jun 26, 1961
    - Technical data: Height 40 m

25. Hotel (5)
    - Location: Ulan Bator
    - Transfer: Jun 26, 1961

---

(1) JMJP Jan 19, 1960 (2) FEER Yearbook 1961 (3) JMJP Oct 31, 1960
(4) JMJP May 11, 1961 (5) JMJP Jun 28, 1961

26. Hotel II (1)
    Location: Ulan Bator
    Transfer: Jun 26, 1961

27. Power station II
    Location: Tolgotin (suburb of Ulan Bator (2)
    Transfer: Dec 27, 1961 (3)
    Technical data: Capacity kW 12,000 (3). Floor space 24,442 sq.m (3)
    Other details: About 2,000 Chinese technicians and workers took part in the construction of the station (3). In 1962 the station was extended (4).

28. Power station III
    Location: Aimak Dornod (4)

29. Poultry farm (4,5)
    Location: Central Aimak

30. Alcohol factory (4)
    Location: Ulan Bator
    Technical data: Annual production 1 million litres of alcohol.

31. Wood-processing factory (6)

32. Factory of wooden prefabricated houses (7)

33. Glass factory (7)
    Technical data: The factory produces articles for daily use.

34. Brick factory (7)
    Technical data: Annual capacity 25 million bricks (6).

35. Guest-house (7)
    Location: Ulan Bator
    Completion: Inauguration on Oct 5, 1962
    Technical data: 3 buildings having a total floor space of 4,200 sq.m.

36. Apartment houses for workers
    Location: Ulan Bator (8)
    Completion: First phase: Dec 25, 1964, covering a floor-space of 88,871 sq.m. This includes 30 houses, 7 special buildings for infant nurseries, kindergartens, canteens, shops, etc. (9).
    Technical data: Floor space 220,000 sq.m (8).
    Other details: Among the apartment houses there is one of 11 floors, now the highest building in Ulan Bator (9).
    Remarks: A floor space of 220,000 m corresponds to 3,700 apartments of 60 sq.m each.

37. Potato-processing factory (8)

38. Road IV
    Route: from Ulan Bator to Nalaiha (coal-mines) (8)
    Completion: Sep 27, 1965 (10)
    Technical data: Length 23 km (10)

---

(1) JMJP Jun 28, 1961 (2) Montsame Radio Sep 26, 1962 (3) JMJP Dec 28, 1961 (4) FEER Aug 16, 1962 (5) JMJP Oct 6, 1962 (6)Montsame Radio Sep 26, 1962 (7) JMJP Oct 5, 1962 (8) JMJP Oct 6, 1962 (9) NCNA Dec 25, 1964 (10) NCNA Sep 28, 1965

39. Poultry farm II (1) (identical with poultry farm I?)
    Location: Ulan Bator
    Transfer: Nov 22, 1964

40. Bridge X (Budong Bridge) (2)
    Location: Selenga province
    Technical data: Length 228 m, width 8.9 m

---

(1) NCNA Nov 22, 1964 (2) NCNA Nov 5, 1965

General remarks

Among China's border states and heighbours, Nepal is almost the only one to have enjoyed relatively undisturbed relations with Peking since the establishment of diplomatic relations in August 1955, apart from minor tensions during the Cultural Revolution. Both parties are no doubt equally interested in the maintenance of such friendly relations. Nepal has exercised great skill in freeing herself to some extent from India's dominating influence by opening up toward China - without, however, spoiling her relationship with India. Moreover, Nepal even profited from the Sino-Indian dispute and promptly arrived at a border agreement with China who did not even try to bargain, in order to demonstrate her readiness to reward a friendly attitude.

The economic aid reflects these friendly relations and has been particularly favourable to Nepal, more than half of the Chinese offers (totalling US$ 98.7m.) being in the form of donations.

One of the characteristics of China's aid to Nepal is that it includes huge quantities of consumer goods, such as bicycles, clothing, household goods, etc., which are sold by governmental trading agencies in Nepal. The proceeds are used to finance part of the Chinese projects.

At the request of the Nepalese government, China discontinued work on two planned projects which had, however, not gone beyond the planning stage, viz. the Ithari-Dhalkewar road, 170 km. long, and an irrigation system near Kamala.

As both projects are close to the Indian frontier, India seems to have successfully protested against the presence of Chinese in these parts. This interlude also illustrates Nepal's skill on the one hand and China's on the other.

Nepal's fear that China might use its presence in connection with the economic aid projects to increase Communist influence has proved unjustified.

A. Chinese loans

1956, Oct 7:	Indian Rupees (IR) 60m. (1) (=US$ 12.7m.), one third in the form of financial aid to be paid in two instalments in 1957 and 1958, two thirds in the form of goods. Donation (1).
1960, Mar 21:	IR 100m. (=US$ 21.2m.), donation (2).
1961, Oct 15:	£ 3.5m. (=US$ 9.8m.), donation (3).
1966, Dec 21:	Nepalese Rupees (NR) 150m. (=US$ 20m.), free of interest, payable between December 1966 and December 1977 (4).
1971	The Chinese recently increased their annual aid contributions to US$ 6.5m. (5).
1972, Nov 18: (6)	estimated at US$ 35m.

(1) NCNA Oct 7, 1956; NCNA Feb 5, 1958, HdE II D 21 p.28 (2) EpAkL 2/69 p.74 (3) JMJP Oct 16, 1961,and HdE II D 21 p.28 (4) NCNA Dec 22, 1966 and HdE II D 21 p.28 (5) FEER Apr 1, 1972 (6) NCNA Nov 18, 1972

B. Aid projects completed

1. Warehouse I
   Location: Kathmandu (1)
   Commencement: October 1965 (1)
   Completion: September 1967 (2)
   Technical data: Floor space 7,000 sq.m (1)

2. Warehouse II (3)
   Location: Birgunj
   Commencement: 1965
   Completion: March 1967
   Technical data: Floor space 7,000 sq.m

3. Leather and shoe factory
   Location: Bansbari (4) near Kathmandu (5)
   Commencement: May 1964 (6)
   Completion: June 1965 (7)
   Technical data: Annual capacity: 21,000 pieces of leather, 30,000 pairs of shoes (8)
   In 1972 the factory produced 31,000 pieces of leather and 66,000 pairs of shoes. The hides used for leather-making are from Nepal. 90 % of the sole leather are produced for export. The number of persons working in the management and production lines of the factory is 400. One working shift lasts 7 hours and 30 minutes (9). The factory produced more than 26,000 pairs of shoes in the fiscal year of 1968/69 and more than 63,000 pairs in fiscal 1971/72, the output growing by 2.4 times in four years. The output of leather was over 99,800 kg in fiscal 1968/69 and reached more than 167,200 kilograms in fiscal 1971/72, an increase of 70 %. The total output value of the factory amounted to NR 2.66 m in fiscal 1971/72 which was 60 % more than the 1.64 m. NR in fiscal 1968/69. By making use of scrap leather the factory has now begun to produce glue, sheath, belts, and other commodities, thus slashing production costs and increasing the variety of products. Nepal had no leather and shoe-making industry before 1965 (10).
   Other details: The tannery attached to the factory started trial production in April 1965 (11). At the beginning of 1967 the factory had to be closed down, due to the shortage of leather. There have been considerations to give the factory to a private owner (5). At the fifth anniversary of the inauguration a ceremony was held on Jun 2, 1970, in the presence of Navaraj Subedi, Minister of Industry and Commerce (12).
   Cost of construction: NR 7 m.(5).

(1) NCNA Feb 19, 1966 (2) NCNA Sep 27, 1967 (3) NCNA Mar 25, 1967 (4) NCNA Jun 4, 1970 (5) FEER Mar 23, 1967 (6) NCNA May 13, 1964 (7) NCNA Jun 2, 1965 (8) NCNA Mar 30, 1964 (9) Information given to the author when he visited the factory in Feb 1973 (10) NCNA May 17, 1973 (11) FEER Apr 22, 1965 (12) NCNA Jun 4, 1970

4. Town-hall (1)
   Location: Kathmandu
   Completion: Inauguration on Nov 11, 1970

5. Kathmandu - Kodari road (2) (Aranika Road) (3)
   Agreement: Oct 15, 1961
   Course: Four fifth of the road pass along the banks of the rivers Chakchola, Indravati, Sunkesi, and Bhote Kosi, in heights of between 600 m and 1200 m. The final section which is 26 km long, leads to the frontier pass via difficult rocky territory (4).
   Commencement: June 1963 (5)
   Completion: The road was provisionally opened for traffic of up to 3 t (7) in December 1964 (8).
   Technical data: Length 114 km (9). The five large bridges permit the transport of loads of 30 m/t per axle (10). The longest bridge (176 m) is the Dolalghat bridge, 57 km north of Kathmandu, at the confluence of Rivers Idravati and Sunkosi. The width of this bridge which is made of reinforced concrete is 8 m (11). Length of the "Bridge of Friendship" at the frontier village of Bhaise where it crosses the river: 45 m (10). The road builders started work simultaneously in 5 different places (4). The first 88 km are paved with asphalt, the last 26 km from Barahbise to Kodari, with broken stones. Of the 37 bridges, 11 are in the last 26k-section (12).
   Other details: 12,000 Nepalese workers took part in the road-building work. The number of Chinese technicians working on the first sections was between 50 and 90 (4). 500 Chinese workers worked on the 15 km section from Kodari to the south (8). The use of the road without a special permit by the Nepalese government was, in 1967, restricted to a distance of 40 km from Kathmandu (13). During the construction of the road the doctors accompanying the group of Chinese experts gave medical aid to more than 100,000 Nepalese nationals (14). In June 1970 a Chinese road maintenance group left the country (15). On Mar 9, 1971 a protocol was signed under which China agreed to repair all sections of the road that had been destroyed by floods and landslides (16).

---

(1) NCNA Jun 12, 1970 (2)NCNA Oct 16, 1961 (3) NCNA Mar 7, 1971 (4) FEER Feb 20, 1964 (5) NCNA May 26, 1967 (6) NCNA May 28,1967 (7) NCNA Dec 29, 1964 (8) FEER Jan 16, 1965 (9) NCNA Apr 29, 1964 (10) FEER Jun 29, 1967 (11) NCNA Jun 7, 1966 (12) Information obtained by the author when he visited the road in Feb 1973 (13) New Delhi Radio May 25, 1967 (14) NCNA May 28, 1967 (15) NCNA Jun 4, 1970 (16) NCNA Mar 7, 1971

6. Brick and tile factory

Location: Lalitpur (1), at a distance of 5 km from Kathmandu

Commencement: October 1965 (1)

Completion: Inauguration on Mar 12, 1969, in the presence of King Mahendra (2).

Technical data: Annual capacity 20 million bricks and 0.5 million tiles (3)
The factory produced nearly 30 million red bricks in the fiscal year of 1971/72 while the output of red tiles doubled, as compared with the previous year (4). Since the factory went into operation, it has increased its output year after year (5). The factory needs 3,000 t of coal p.a. which is imported from India (6). The staff includes 6 officers, 21 assistants and 23 clerks working in the administration and 5 officers, 37 assistants and 450 labourers working in production (6). China has agreed to expand the factory (7). On Mar 14, 1972 letters were exchanged between China and Nepal regarding the said expansion (8) the object of which is to double production (6).

7. Hydroelectric station

Protocols: May 25, 1964 (9) and May 25, 1967 (10).

Location: at the Sunkosi river in northeastern Nepal (10,11), at the Kathmandu-Kodari road (12), 80 km from Kathmandu (13)

Commencement: End of 1968 (10). Surveying had commenced in June 1967 (13).

Completion: Nov 24, 1972 (14)

Technical data: Capacity 10,000 kW (11). In December 1973 Nepal had an installed power of 55,000 kW of which hydroelectric power production accounts for more than 33,000 kW (15).

Other details: In September 1968 60 Chinese technicians arrived in Kathmandu to direct the construction work (16).

8. Overhead transmission line I

Course: from Sunkosi to Kathmandu (16)

Commencement: End of 1968 (10).

9. Kathmandu-Bhaktapur highway

Protocol: Sep 27, 1968 (17)

Course: from Kathmandu to a place west of Bhaktapur whence it follows the Kathmandu-Kodari road (17)

Commencement: Surveying commenced in October 1968 (18)

Completion: 1970 (19)

---

(1) NCNA Feb 18, 1966 (2) NCNA Mar 13, 1969 (3) EpAkL 2/69 (4) NCNA Sep 26, 1972 (5) NCNA Nov 24, 1972 (6) told to the author when he visited the factory in Feb 1973 (7) NZZ Dec 1, 1972 (8) NCNA Mar 15, 1972 (9) NCNA May 28, 1964 (10) NCNA Jun 9, 1969 (11) NCNA May 28, 1967 (12) NZZ Jun 14, 1970 (13) NCNA Jun 17, 1967 (14) NCNA Nov 27, 1972 (15) NCNA Dec 10, 1973 (16) NCNA Sep 19, 1968 (17) NCNA Sep 29, 1968 (18) NCNA Oct 30, 1968 (19) NCNA Sep 16,1970

Technical data: Length 16 km. Bagmati bridge: length 87 m, width 20 m, roadway 14 m, 2 sidewalks of 3 m each. Period of construction: April-August 1970 (1)

C. Aid projects under construction

1. Kathmandu-Pokhara (Prithvi) highway

Protocol: August 1965 (2)

Course: The road starts at Naubise, located 20 km from Kathmandu at the road to the Indian frontier. It follows the left bank of the Trisuli river, in a westerly direction, to Tribeni Ghat. Thence it proceeds in a northwesterly direction, following the right bank of Marsyandi Khora river to Chyanglitar where it turns westward to Khairani and then again northwest, following the left bank of the Seti river to the Pokhara valley (3).

Commencement: November 1965 (4)

Technical data: Length 176 km (5). The 125 m suspension bridge is built to cross the Trisuli river (6) at Munglingtar (7). It was inaugurated in the presence of Prime Minister Bistra on Apr 2, 1972 (7). The number of bridges in the course of the 176 km road totals 41, the longest being (a) the one across the Trisuli river at Munglingtar and (b) the one across the Madi river at Damauli which is 370 m long and 7.5 m wide (9), 350 m long(10), at a distance of about 156 km from Kathmandu(14).

Other details: The Chinese technicians engaged in this project had previously constructed the Kathmandu-Kodari road (8). By July 1969 the first 74 km of the road were ready to be used with jeeps (11). China will render assistance in constructing a bitumen infiltration pavement for the highway (12)

2. Trolley-bus project (13)

Protocol: Mar 14, 1972

Highway used: Kathmandu-Bhaktapur

Other details: A Chinese team was engaged in surveying the project between May 2 and Sep 9, 1972 (3)

Commencement: Dec 29, 1973 (14)

D. Aid projects planned

1. Overhead transmission line II (15)

Protocol: Dec 24, 1970

Course: from Sunkosi to Chantara and Barahbise

---

(1) Told to the author by a Nepalese official in Feb 1973 (2) NCNA Nov 7, 1968 (3) NCNA Sep 10, 1972 (4) NCNA May 7, 1966 (5) May 28, 1967 (6) NCNA Feb 25, 1972 (7) NCNA Apr 4, 1972 (8) FEER Jun 29, 1967 (9) Information obtained by the author when he visited the road in Feb 1973 (10) NCNA May 5, 1973 (11) NZZ Oct 18,1969 (12) NCNA Jul 17, 1971 (13) NCNA Mar 15, 1972 (14)NCNA Dec 30, 1973 (15) NCNA Dec 24, 1970

2. Survey on mineral deposits (1)
At the request of the Nepalese government the Chinese government will send two survey teams to conduct surveys on iron, phosphorite, coal, and petroleum deposits in Nepal.

3. Cotton planting
China will dispatch a cotton planting survey team for surveys on, and experimental growth of, cotton (2). This is the first project with which the Chinese have gained access to Nepal's Terai region near the Indian frontier (3),

4. Textile mill (4)
A seven-member Chinese expert team arrived in Kathmandu on Jul 17, 1973, for a detailed study. The site for the factory and its production capacity will be determined on the basis of this study (5). The factory will have a capacity for 10 million m of fabrics a year, enough to meet 50 % of Nepal's total requirement for textile fabrics. The mill is expected to go into production two years after the commencement of construction (6).

5. Pokhara - westward road
A Chinese team arrived in Kathmandu on May 22, 1973, to start work on a survey for a road connecting Pokhara with the far western region (7).

(1) NCNA Oct 28, 1971 (2) NCNA Jul 17, 1971 (3) FEER Jan 15, 1972 (4) NZZ Dec 1, 1972 (5) Kathmandu Radio Jul 17, 1973 (6) Kathmandu Radio Aug 4, 1973 (7) Kathmandu Radio May 22, 1973

A. Chinese loans

1972, Nov 3 : Under the aid agreement Nigeria was given a loan of US$ 3 m (1)

D. Aid projects planned

1. Agricultural development
A Chinese agricultural study team arrived on Feb 11, 1973 (2).

(1) NZZ Jan 6, 1973 (2) NCNA Feb 13, 1973

General remarks

Having been granted loans amounting to US$ 445m., Pakistan occupies the first place on the list of recipients of Chinese economic aid. China did not start offering aid to Pakistan until after India and Pakistan had gone to war over the Rann of Kutch. In this dispute China resented India's refusal to come to a reasonable border agreement and decisively took Pakistan's side.

The correctness of China's political assessment also became evident when, some weeks before the outbreak of the armed conflict, which resulted in the breaking away of East Pakistan, she offered Pakistan's government aid for no less than ten projects for the development of East Pakistan, as an implicit reproach to the government that it had neglected that part of the country and in the hope that it would help ward off the impending danger. However, it was too late. Some months later East Pakistan became the new state of Bangladesh.

The struggle for liberation in Bangladesh had been characterized by all the classic tactics which should, in theory, have gained China's ideological support.

Well-meaning China watchers were surprised to see that ideological principles were sacrificed to power politics, in which the Pakistan card was to trump the Indian card. If there is a region where China's ideology has lost its credibility, it is Bangladesh.

A. Chinese loans

1965, Jun 15 (1): US$ 60m. (2), one half in currency, the other in the form of goods delivered (3), free of interest (1), term: 20 (?) years), repayable in goods, after a period of grace of 10 years (4).

The greater part of the loan, originally meant for 5 years, was exhausted as early as 1967 (5). Half of the loan was used in the fiscal years 1965/66 and 1966/67 for the importation of steel, coal, cement, aluminium conductors, galvanic sheets, steel for construction, and electric installations. The remainder was used for the Taxila heavy machinery complex (6). A sum of US$ 36m. was used for imports from China, 15 m. for the Taxila heavy machinery factory, 9m. for two technical institutes (one in West Pakistan and one in East Pakistan) (7).

1967, December: US$ 40m., free of interest, term: 20 years, repayable after a grace period of 10 years (5).

---

(1) NCNA Jun 23, 1967 (2) Karachi Radio Jun 15, 1965 (3) Karachi Radio Dec 24, 1967 (4) OEL 21, 9/65 p.217 f. (5) Karachi Radio Dec 28, 1967 (6) FEER Jan 11, 1968 (7) FEER Feb 15, 1968

1968, Dec 26: Yuan 100m. = Pakistan Rupees (PR) 200m.(1) (=US$ 42m.) (2), interest-free (1), term: 20 years, repayable after a grace period of 10 years (1).

1970, Nov 14 (3): Yuan 500m. (=US$ 210m.), free of interest, repayable after a grace period of 10 years (4).

1971, January (?): Yuan 7.1m. (=US$ 3m.), free of interest (5).

May: Extension of the November 1970 loan from US$ 210m. to 300.7m. (6).

1972, June: China writes off two project-cum-commodity loans of about US$ 110m. (probably the ones of 1965 and 1968) and defers the repayment of the US$ 210m. loan of 1970 for 20 years (7).

B. Aid projects completed

1. Technical Institute I (8)
   - Location: West Pakistan
   - Other details: US$ 9m. of the 1965 loan were used to construct two technical institutes, one of them in West Pakistan.

2. Technical Institute II (8)
   - Location: East Pakistan
   - Other details: US$ 9m. of the 1965 loan were used to construct two technical institutes, one of them in East Pakistan.

3. Halleh Kush-Khunjerab Pass road (9)
   - Course: from Gilgit in a northeasterly direction, following the silk road to Kashgar, then branching off to the east (10) - Halleh Kush (10)-Khunjerab Pass (4,900 metres above sea level) where the frontier between China and Pakistan is (10).
   - Commencement: 1966 (10)
   - Completion: The opening ceremony took place in Baltit (Hunza) (11) on Feb 16, 1971 (12).
   - Technical data: Most sections of the road are double-tracked. The road may be used in all weather. Length: 280 km. (11). To be used by trucks up to 5 tons (13).
   - Other details: The length of the road as constructed by Chinese workers and technicians on Pakistan territory is not known but it is presumed to be at least 100 kilometres. The number of Chinese, most of them soldiers of the PLA Engineering Corps (10), who have helped in the construction of the road, is believed to have been between 12,000 and

---

(1) Karachi Radio Dec 26, 1968 (2) EpAkL 2/69 p.76 (3) NCNA Nov 14, 1970 (4) Karachi Radio Nov 14, 1970 (5) Karachi Radio Jan 8, 1971 (6) NZZ May 18, 1971 (7) FEER Jul 8, 1972 (8) FEER Feb 15, 1968 (9) NCNA Feb 14, 1971 (10) NZZ Mar 7, 1971 (11) NCNA Feb 18, 1971 (12) Karachi Radio Feb 16, 1971 (13) FCW Mar 7, 1971

15,000. The Pakistan-built section of the road was done by officers and soldiers of the "Frontier Works Organization", most of them members of the Pakistan Engineering Corps (1).The road ia intended to replace the century-old caravan route which, after having been closed for 20 years, was reopened in August 1969, when a Chinese caravan, including 50 camels, went to Pakistan via the Mintaka Pass (north of the Khunjerab Pass (2).

4. Heavy machinery factory

Protocol: Jun 23, 1966 (3)
Location: Taxila, 30 km northeast of Rawalpindi (4)
Commencement: 1968 (?)
Completion: Nov 25, 1971 (5)
Technical data: The factory produces equipment for cement factories and sugar mills, low pressure boilers, road-making machinery, cranes, railway material etc. (6). The complex consists of a cast-iron foundry, a steel foundry, and a mechanical forge. The cast iron foundry has a hot-air coupling furnace having a melting capacity of 5 tons/h, the steel foundry, two electric blast furnaces with a capacity of 10-12 tons each. Annual capacity: 3,000 tons of cast steel and 22,000 steel ingots (7). Annual capacity of the whole complex: machinery having a total weight of 14,500 tons. In the training workshop, 200 skilled workers will be trained annually (8). The complex will produce heavy machinery worth PR 60m. (9) (= US$ 12.5m.) a year.

Road rollers were on top of the production list, followed by equipment for cement factories, sugar mills, boilers, cranes, railway equipment, road-making machines and steel constructions to be used in ships (10). The full programm is scheduled to start with 1975 and is then expected to reach an annual capacity of 14,500 tons of equipment worth PR 61.2m. (11). In December 1970, 95 machines had been installed in five workshops (12).

Other details: This is Pakistan's first heavy machinery factory (13). In 1969, 300 Pakistanis were trained in the factory's training centre. A group of leading technicians were given special training in China (14). Trial production started in December 1970 (12).

---

(1) Karachi Radio Feb 12, 1971 (2) FCW Mar 7, 1971 (3) NCNA Jun 23, 1966 (4) NCNA Aug 3, 1968 (5) NCNA Nov 26, 1971, and Pakistan Radio Nov 22, 1971 (6) NCNA Jun 23, 1967 (7) NZZ Feb 17, 1968 (8) NCNA Jun 28, 1968 (9) Karachi Radio Apr 8, 1970 (10) Karachi Radio Apr 8, 1970 (11)Karachi R. May 2, 1970 (12) Karachi R. Dec 25, 1970 (13) NCNA Aug 3, 1968 (14) Karachi R. Oct 26, 1969

The annual capacity of the foundry is 50,000 (60,000) tons of melted steel (1). The final equipment for the complex was sent from China to Taxila in the spring of 1971 (2). On completion, 2,600 workers will work in the complex (3).

Total cost of the complex: PR 300m. (4) (= US$ 63m.) or PR 120m. (5) (=US$ 25m.), or PR 170m. (6) (=US$ 36m.).

A revised plan of the West Pakistan Corporation for Industrial Development stated the total cost to be PR 176m. (=US$ 37m.) Original estimate: PR 143.5m. (7) (=US$ 30m.). Another source states the total cost as being PR 210m. (8) (=US$ 44m.).

It is estimated that, when the plant goes into full production in 1975, its annual turnover will be worth approximately PR 100m. (9).

The first sugar-making plant in Pakistan, which has a capacity of 1,500 tons of cane daily was manufactured by the Taxila heavy mechanical complex in a matter of six months (10).

5. Ordnance factory (11)
   - Location: Gazipur, East Pakistan, 25 miles north of Dacca
   - Completion: Formal inauguration by President Yahya Khan in April 1970

6. Paper-mill
   - Location: Chittagong (12)
   - Commencement: 1966 (13)
   - Completion: 1969 (13)
   - Technical data: The raw material used is bamboo (14). The mill produces paper in lengths of 10 yards and widths of 30 ft. (14). Annual capacity: 45,000 tons of cellulose processed to yield 15,000 tons of paper (13).

D. Aid projects planned

1. Refractory project
   - Protocol: April 9, 1970 (15) and Dec 2, 1971(17)
   - Location: West Pakistan (16)
   - Technical data: Annual (more likely: monthly) capacity: 30,000 bricks 20,000 of them high-quality ones, and 10,000 magnesite bricks (15).

---

(1) Karachi Radio Apr 9, 1970 (2) Karachi R. Feb 18, 1971 (3) HB May 21, 1970 (4) New Delhi Radio Dec 12, 1967 (5) Karachi R. Jul 10, 1969, Apr 8, 1970, Dec 25, 1970 (6) NZZ Nov 27, 1971 and Karachi R. Mar 24, 1972 (7) Karachi R. Jul 9, 1970 (8) Karachi R. Aug 6, 1970 (9) Pakistan R. Nov 22, 1971 (10) NCNA Dec 23, 1973 (11) Pakistan Radio Nov 22, 1971 (12) FEER Apr 14, 1966 (13) NCNA May 1, 1971 (14) BfA/NfA Feb 7, 1966 (15) Karachi R. Apr 9, 1970 (16) Pakistan R. Mar 18, 1971 (17 NCNA Dec 2, 1971

2. Fertilizer plant I (1)
   Protocol: Apr 9, 1970
   Location: East Pakistan
   Technical data: Daily capacity: 150 tons of synthetic ammonia to be processed to urea (1). Annual production: about 100,000 tons of fertilizer (2).

3. Fertilizer plant II
   Location: North West Frontier Province (3) near Peshawar (4)
   Technical data: The plant will have an annual capacity of 70,000 tons of urea. Estimated costs: 170m. rupees (5).
   Other details: A Chinese expert team arrived in April 1973 in Peshawar to examine the feasibilities of establishing the factory (4).

4. Sugar mill I
   Protocols: Apr 9, 1970 (1) and April 28, 1971 (6)
   Location: West Pakistan (1), probably Hyderabad (7)
   Other details: The equipment for the mill is to be produced in Taxila (1) (see B.4 above). In December 1970 a group of Chinese experts came to West Pakistan in order to find a suitable location for this factory (8).

5. Sugar mill II
   Protocol: Apr 28, 1971 (9)
   Location: Larkana (9)
   Technical data: Daily capacity: 1,500 tons of sugar-cane. 3,000 workers are to work in this mill (9). Annual production: 15,000-18,000 tons of sugar (10).
   Other details: The mill is expected to cost PR 50m. (10) =US$ 11m.), or 65m.rupees (11). A six-member team of Chinese civil engineers arrived on Mar 16, 1973 (11).

6. Newsprint mill (10)
   Location: Lower Sind
   Other details: The project will cost PR 150m. (=US$ 32m.)

7. Iron ore project
   Location: Baluchistan (12), Kashmor in Sind (13)
   Technical data: The Pakistan Government plans to set up a pig-iron works in Baluchistan with Chinese aid. It will have a production capacity for about 100,000 tons of pig-iron a year and will cost 270m. rupees, including a foreign exchange component of about 210m. rupees. It will utilize high-grade iron ore from the (?Chawi) district of Baluchistan (14). A preliminary report on the Chilghazi iron ore deposit had been sent

---

(1) Karachi Radio Apr 9, 1970 (2) BfA/NfA May 5, 1970 (3) BfA/NfA Oct 5, 1972, Karachi R. Mar 31, 1971 (4) Karachi R. Apr 21, 1973 (5) Karachi R. Jun 14, 1973 (6) NCNA May 1, 1971 (7) Karachi R. Feb 20, 1971 (8) Karachi R. Dec 26, 1970, and Jan 6, 1971 (9) Pakistan R. Apr 28, 1971 (10) Karachi R. May 10, 1972 (11) Karachi R. Mar 16, 1973 (12) Karachi R. Jun 23 and Dec 30, 1973(13) Karachi R. Apr 6, 1973 (14) Karachi R. Nov 18, 1972

to the Chinese, who are preparing a feasibility study for a pig-iron works (1). The annual production capacity will be 150,000-200,000 tons. Building will start in two years, after a site has been selected (2). The plant will be based on the iron ore deposits of Chilgazi in Baluchistan and will initially produce 100 tons of pig-iron a day. Later it will be expanded to 300 tons a day (3).

Other details: A team of six Chinese experts arrived in Karachi in May 1972 to conduct survey of the West Pakistan Industrial Development Corporation-sponsored iron ore project to be set up in Sibi, based on the recently discovered high-grade iron ore in Baluchistan (4).

8. Two steel mills (5)
Two medium-sized steel mills using indigenous iron ore are to be set up with Chinese help. Sites for the mills are being selected near the source of iron ore, which is available in considerable quantity.

9. Transmission line (6)
Location: between Tarbela and Wah
Technical data: Length: 58 km
Other details: The 200kW double-circuit line will connect Tarbela with the national grid. The project is expected to cost 70m. rupees. Half of the costs will be met by the Chinese Government in foreign exchange under the agreement on economic and technical cooperation of November 1970 (7).

10. Thermal power station (8)
Location: Quetta, Baluchistan

11. Textile mill I (9)
Location: Tarbela
Technical data: The mill will have 25,000 spindles and produce about 14 million pounds of yarn.
Other details: The mill is estimated to cost 34m. rupees.

12. Textile mill II (10)
Location: Mirpur in Azad Kashmir
Technical data: The mill will have 25,000 spindles and is estimated to cost 45m. rupees.

13. Aid projects in East Pakistan
In mid-October 1971 China had agreed to help Pakistan in setting up small fertilizer factories run on gas in different parts of East Pakistan and inserting 5,000 tube wells

---

(1) Karachi Radio Jun 23, and Dec 30, 1973 (2) Karachi R. Dec 30, 1973 (3) Karachi R. Apr 6, 1973 (4) Karachi R. May 28, 1972 (5) Karachi R. Nov 17, 1972 (6) Karachi R. Nov 18, 1972 (7) Karachi R. May 22, 1973 (8) Karachi R. Nov 29, 1972 (9) Karachi R. May 21, 1973 (10) Karachi R. Nov 24, 1973

in the northern districts of the province. At that time a list of ten development projects had been forwarded to the Chinese government to seek its help in the implementation thereof. The projects were: a new Dacca-Chittagong railway line, railway signalling, telephone and telegraph lines for the railway, the Jaipurhat limestone and cement project, the Tista project, the Rupsa bridge, a Khulna-Mongla railway line, a textile project, a Brahmaputra bridge, the Ranipukurhat rock project, and a power supply system for the irrigation projects of the East Pakistan Agricultural Development Corporation.

Chinese experts were to come to East Pakistan in November 1971 (1). None of the project has been commenced.

(1) Karachi Radio Oct 14, 1971

General remarks

Peru was the first Latin American country to receive an economic aid loan from China. The offer was made as early as three weeks after diplomatic relations had been established. This showed China´s satisfaction at having at last found an opportunity in Latin America to practice economic aid on exceptionally good terms. By offering Peru a loan of US$ 42m., China immediately surpassed the Soviet Union which had granted a mere US$ 28m., but in this connection we must not overlook the fact that the loans offered to Peru by the European Eastern bloc countries totalled US$ 153m. and that the COMECON countries are sure to have harmonized their respective offers.

A. Chinese loans
1971, Nov 28: Soles 1,841m. (1) (=US$ 42m.)

(1) Radio del Pacifico, Lima, Nov 29, 1971

General remarks

The relations between Peking and Bucharest, which have been excellent for a long time, experienced a further improvement when Romania decided to accept economic aid from China. This was another step in the direction of Romania's policy of withdrawing, as far as possible, from Soviet hegemony. The flood catastrophe in May 1970 was probably used as an opportunity to force the Soviets to approve economic aid from China, Romania having thus become the first Warsaw Pact country to accept, or be allowed to accept, such aid from China.

The US$ 245. loan is among the highest loans granted by China, second only to the one granted to Tanzania for the construction of the Tan-Zam railway line (if we exclude the combined economic and military aid loans granted to North Korea and North Vietnam in 1960). This classification reveals the political significance of the loan to Romania, for even a country like Albania received a similar amount in three instalments between 1961 and 1970. The Chinese intention,of course, is to strengthen Romania's independent attitude towards Moscow, by means of generous financial aid, in the same way as Albania was encouraged to oppose Moscow by the offer of financial security from Peking.

Nothing has yet been disclosed regarding the use of the Chinese loan, and in this we must rely entirely on guesses. In August 1970 a Romanian group for the study of irrigation systems travelled through China, followed by machine engineers in October 1970 and February 1971, the latter being mainly experts on "complete machinery equipments". China despatched her Minister of Agriculture and Forestry and her Minister for the Metallurgical Industry to Romania in 1972. These activities suggest that the Chinese aid is probably concentrated on projects of flood protection, complete industrial plants and the metallurgical industry, as well as agriculture and forestry.

A. Chinese loans

1970, Nov 25:	Long-term loan, free of interest, provided for the delivery of industrial equipment (1). Sum granted: US$245m. (2) or US$ 300m. (3)
1971, Oct 28:	Long-term loan, free of interest (4)

(1) NCNA Nov 25, 1970 (2)FAZ Nov 2, 1971 (3) Hong Kong Radio Nov 20, 1971 (4) NCNA Oct 29, 1971

General remarks

The Chinese loan of US$ 20m. in 1972 was the first loan offered to Ruanda by a Communist country. It was, moreover, a comparatively high one in relation to the very small size of the country, and is thus of some political consequence.

A. Chinese loans

1972, May 13: US$ 20m., free of interest, repayable over a period of 15 years in the form of goods delivered (1)

D. Aid projects planned

1. Road link between Ruanda and Tanzania (2)
2. Cement works (2)

(1) NZZ Sep 9, 1972 (2) DN Nov 13, 1972

General remarks

As the only previous aid to Senegal from a Communist country had been a US$ 7m. loan from the Soviet Union, we feel justified in assuming that the Chinese economic aid loan of November 1973 was rather high (something in the order of US$ 20m.), because the Chinese generally try to surpass all other donors of economic aid,and in particular the Soviet Union.

A. Chinese loans

1973, Nov 23: Agreement on economic and technical cooperation (1). Chinese loan estimated at US$ 20m.

D. Aid projects planned

Since March 1973 a Chinese agrotechnical group has been working in Senegal. Its leader, Ning Tzu-ming, was received by the Minister of Rural Development, Adrien Senghor, on April 18, 1973 (2).

(1) NCNA Nov 23, 1973 (2) NCNA Apr 18, 1973

A. Chinese loans

1971, Jul 29: The loan granted under the agreement of July 1971 is estimated at US$ 20m.

B. Aid projects completed

1. Medical group

First group: Arrival Apr 6, 1973 (1). Part of the group in August 1973 worked in the Rotifunk hospital in Moyamba district, southern province (2).

C. Aid projects under construction

1. Stadium

Protocol: Aug 3, 1973 (3)

Other details: An eleven-member stadium study group from China was in Sierra Leone from February until May 1973 (4).

2. Rice technique extension station (5)

Location: Mange Bure, in the northern province

Technical data: The station includes a three-cropping rice experimental plot and a sugar-cane experimental plot.

D. Aid projects planned

1. Bridge I (6)

Location: Mange

2. Bridge II (6)

Location: Kambia

(1) NCNA Apr 13, 1973 (2) NCNA Aug 28, 1973 (3) NCNA Aug 4, 1973 (4) NCNA Feb 17, 1971, Mar 1 and May 11, 1973 (5) NCNA Jan 6, 1973 (6) NCNA Dec 3, 1973

General remarks

Since the establishment of diplomatic relations (Dec 17, 1960), China and Somalia have been on good terms with each other, a situation that did not even change when President Shermake was assassinated in October 1969. In spring 1971 Somalia accepted a Chinese offer to build a cigarette and match factory which, being the first Chinese industrial project, may be taken as an indication of the lasting friendly relations between the two countries.

A. Chinese loans

1963, Aug 9: US$ 20m., free of interest (1) for 10 years (2), repayable over a period of 17 years (3). Donation of US$ 3m.

1971, Jun 7: Loan of US$ 110m. (4).

B. Aid projects completed

1. Rice and tobacco experimental station

Protocol	Aug 19, 1967 (5)
Location:	Jowkar, 100 km from Mogadishu (6) on the Shebeli river (7).
Commencement:	June 1966 (7)
Completion:	End of 1969 (8). Delivery on Apr 5, 1970 (8).
Other details:	Hao Hsiang-chien led the Chinese expert group (9). Samples of the first "Somali Cigarettes" produced were handed over to the Supreme Revolutionary Council on Dec 22, 1969 (10). Early in 1970 China agreed to enlarge the experimental station (11). The President of the Supreme Revolutionary Council, Mohamed Siad Barre, visited the station on Jul 24, 1970 (12).

2. Medical groups

First group:	Arrival: July 1965 (13) Departure: November 1967 (14)
Second group:	Arrival: November 1967 (14) The group worked in Mogadishu, Beletwen and Galcaio (15). Departure: January 1970 (16).
Third group:	Arrival: December 1969 (17)
Fourth group:	Arrival not mentioned, presumably in 1971 Departure: Jul 18, 1973 (18)
Fifth group:	Arrival: July 1973 (18)

(1) FEER, according to Reuter, Sep 19, 1963 (2) EpAkL 2/69 p.68 (3) CT YB 351 (4) NR 8/1973 (5) EpAkL 2/69 p.69 (6) NCNA Apr 12, 1968, and Jun 29, 1968 (7) NCNA Apr 12, 1968 (8) NCNA Apr 5, 1970 (9) NCNA Aug 6, 1970 (10) NCNA Dec 22, 1969 (11) Mogadishu Radio Jun 24, 1970 (12) NCNA Jul 26, 1970 (13) NCNA Jan 26, 1966,and Nov 23, 1967 (14) NCNA Nov 23, 1967 (15) NCNA Jan 20, 1970 (16) NCNA Jan 9, 1970 (17) NCNA Dec 26, 1969 (18) NCNA Jul 19, 1973

Remarks: The Chinese press mentions the dismissal of the first group in January 1970 (1), but the group which departed in November 1967 was also marked as "first group" (2). This contradiction may be explained as follows: The group referred to as the "first" one in our study was a small group consisting of few persons only, who were sent to Somalia to convince the government of the value of medical aid. As it was small, the official Chinese counting started with the delegation of the first group of "normal size" (30-40 persons), which arrived in Somalia in November 1967 (2).

3. Theatre

Protocol: Dec 16, 1965 (3)
Location: Mogadishu (3)
Commencement: November 1966 (4)
Completion: November 1967. Inauguration in the presence of President Shermake (5)
Technical data: 1,200 seats. All the equipment was sent from China. The theatre can be used as a cinema and conference room, too (5). Floor-space: 4,100 square metres. Height: 24 metres (6).
Other details: This project was the first one constructed under the Chinese aid programme for Somalia (7).

C. Aid projects under construction

1. Well-sinking I

Protocols: Mar 18, 1969 (8) and Feb 3, 1971 (9)
Location: Hargeisa (8)
Other details: A group of Chinese technicians started construction work in August 1969 (10). At Ged Gedleh near Hargeisa six wells were sunk to supply the two places with 4,000 cubic metres of water per day (9).

2. Road

Course: Beletwen - Bender Cassim (Bosao) - Hargeisa (11)
Technical data: Distance from Beletwen to Hargeisa: 1,400 km. Distance from Garowe to Hargeisa: 600 km (11).
Other details: Chinese experts surveyed the Garowe-Burao section early in 1971 (12).

D. Aid projects planned

1. Well-sinking II (13)

Protocol: Mar 18, 1969
Location: Beletwen

---

(1) NCNA Jan 9 and 20, 1970 (2) NCNA Nov 23, 1967 (3) NCNA Dec 16, 1965 (4) NCNA Nov 14, 1966 (5) NCNA Nov 27, 1967 (6) EpAkL 2/69 p.81 (7) Mogadishu Radio Apr 29, 1969 (8) NCNA Mar 18, 1969 (9) Mogadishu R. Mar 3, 1971 (10) NCNA Aug 4, 1969 (11) Mogadishu R. Dec 22, 1970 (12) Mogadishu R. Jan 7, 1971 (13) NCNA Mar 18, 1969

2. Well-sinking III (1)
   Protocol: Mar 18, 1969
   Location: Baidaba

3. Well-sinking IV (1)
   Protocol: Mar 18, 1969
   Location: Galkaayu

4. Meat (?) factory I (2)
   Location: Juba region
   Other details: At the end of 1970 a group of Chinese experts visited the lower Juba region in order to find a site for the factory.

5. Meat (?) factory II (2)
   Location: Mogadishu (?)
   Other details: A factory of the type planned in the Juba region will probably be constructed in Mogadishu.

6. Research institute I
   Under a protocol signed in 1970, China gave a loan for the construction and equipment of two research institutes (3).

7. Research institute II
   Under a protocol signed in 1970, China gave a loan for the construction and equipment of two research institutes (3).

8. Cigarette and match factory (4)
   Protocol: Mar 6, 1971
   Location: Mogadishu
   Technical data: Annual capacity: 33,000 boxes of 10,000 cigarettes each and 12,000 boxes containing 1,000 match-boxes each.
   Other details: The production will meet the country´s demand and yield a certain surplus. Owing to the factory´s production, the country will save Somalia Shillings 12m. which used to be spent on the import of cigarettes and matches.

9. Water conservancy project
   A Chinese survey team for water conservancy arrived in Mogadishu on Mar 31, 1973 (5).

(1) NCNA Mar 18, 1968 (2) Mogadishu Radio Dec 22, 1970 (3) EpAkL 8/70 (4) Mogadishu R. Mar 6, 1971 (5) NCNA Apr 9, 1973

General remarks

Both South Yemen (People´s Republic since 1970) and Yemen form a point of intersection of Chinese and Soviet interests. This country´s strategic position is an invitation to super-power involvement. In supporting the Dhofar guerillas materially and by propaganda, the Chinese have succeeded in gaining a favourable position. They have supported South Yemen´s ambitious plans to dominate the south coast of the Arabian Peninsula. The project of a road connecting the First and Sixth Regions must be seen before this background.

China´s high stake in this country - a loan of US$ 72.8m., including the 1972 loan estimated at US$ 20m., which is more than four times higher than the aid offered by the Soviet Union - shows that China has succeeded in gaining a strong foothold in a region which was one of the key positions of the old British Empire.

A. Chinese loans

1968, Sep 24 (1): Denare 4m. =US$ 9.6m. (2)

1970, Aug 7: Denare 18m. = Yuan 100m. (3) =US$ 43.2m. (4), free of interest, for 20 years starting with 1971 (3)

1972, Jul 12: Loan under the agreement on economic and technical cooperation (5), estimated at US$ 20m.

B. Aid projects completed

1. Medical groups
   Protocol: Dec 4, 1969 (6)
   First group: Arrival: February 1970 (7)
   Location: Mahzen hospital, Third Gouvernat (8)
   Other details: The group consisted of 26 persons. In February 1970 the group got 20 tons of medicines from China (9). For its work in 1971, the group received 617 boxes of medicines at the end of 1970 (10), 517 boxes on Jan 21, 1971 (10), and 600 boxes in June 1971 (11).
   Departure: Jun 30, 1972 (12)
   2nd group: Arrival: Jun 4, 1972 (13)

2. Hospital equipment
   On Feb 26, 1970, the "People´s Hospital" was inaugurated in Aden. The medical equipment and medicines came from China. The medical group working in the country helped to establish the hospital (14).

(1) Aden Radio Sep 26, 1968 (2) Aden R. Dec 9, 1970 (3) OR 5/70 (4) FT Aug 18, 1970 (5) NCNA Jul 12, 1972 (6) NCNA Dec 6, 1969 (7) NCNA Feb 5, 1970 (8) NCNA Apr 29, 1970 (9) Aden R. Feb 3, 1970 (10) Aden R. Jan 21, 1971 (11) ANA Jun 6, 1971 (12) NCNA Jun 28 and 30, 1972 (13) NCNA Jun 10, 1972 (14) NCNA Feb 26, 1970

C. Aid projects under construction

1. Road between First and Sixth Provinces

Course:	Am Ain (First Province) - al Mahfed (Third Province) (1) - Mukalla town (Sixth Province) (2)
Technical data:	Length 480 km (3) or 420 km (4). First section: 145 km (3) (Am Ain - al Mahfed)(5), second section: 335 km (3). The road will be covered with asphalt (6).
Commencement:	The surveying work began in February 1970 (7). Road-work on the first section began in January 1971 (5).
Completion:	Scheduled for 1976 (4)
Other details:	The first section is financed by the 1968 loan, the second, by that of 1970 (3). In the first section bridges will be built at Zingibar (8) and Abyan (9).

2. Wells

Location:	Along the Am Ain - Mukalla road (see C.1, Road!).- In the first section 14 wells will be sunk (10). The number of wells totals 30 (8) or 40 (10).
Other details:	The 14 wells of the first section were financed out of the 1968 loan, the remainder out of the 1970 loan (10).

3. Salt production

Protocol:	Jul 7, 1971 (11)
Other details:	At the end of 1970, a group of Chinese experts started the project for salt production (12). The project includes the reconstruction of the Khormaksar salt works (11).

4. Textile mill

Protocol:	Jul 7, 1971 (13)
Location:	Aden (14)
Other details:	The project is one of the main items of South Yemen's Three-Year Plan for economic development. Upon completion, the mill, which will use home-grown cotton as raw material, will primarily meet the needs of South Yemen for cotton cloth (15).

(1) RA (DMS) Aug 1, 1970 (2) OR 3/4- /70 (3) Aden R. Dec 9, 1970 (4) ANA Apr 8, 1971 (5) RA (DMS) Jan 28, 1971 (6) OR 3/4 -/70 (7) RA (DMS) Oct 14, 1970 (8) RA (DMS) Aug 1, 1970 (9) RA(DMS) Aug 15, 1970 (10) RA(DMS)Dec 9, 1970, and Aden Radio Dec 12, 1970 (11) NCNA Jul 8, 1971 (12) Aden R. Dec 16, 1970 (13) NCNA Jul 8, 1971 (14) NCNA Oct 11, 1973 (15) NCNA Jun 4, 1973

D. Aid projects planned

1. Agricultural machinery and equipment
   Part of the 1970 loan will be used to supply agricultural machines and equipment (1).
   In April 1971 a group of Chinese experts arrived in South Yemen to study this project (2).

2. Wharf for fishing-boats
   A wharf for fishing-boats will be built from the 1970 loan (1).

---

(1) RA (DMS) Aug 15, 1970 (2) NCNA Apr 24, 1971

General remarks

Sri Lanka is an example of the dependence of economic aid on political conditions. All the important economic aid projects were discontinued when the Leftist Bandaranaike government lost the elections. It was only when Mrs. Bandaranaike was reelected Prime Minister in 1970 that the projects initiated five years earlier were resumed.

Since that time relations between the two countries have been very close. This is shown, on the one hand, by the loans China has granted to Sri Lanka since 1970 and which have brought that country to the sixth place among the recipients of Chinese economic aid. On the other hand, it is shown by the readiness of both countries to play down the political significance of the rebellion of young Leftists in the spring of 1971 which caused Sri Lanka to sever her diplomatic relations with North Korea. The visit to Peking in 1972 of Mrs. Bandaranaike, who was even received by Mao Tse-tung, may be regarded as an expression of the mutual desire to put an end to a short interlude of distrust.

A. Chinese loans

1957, Sep 19:	Ceylonese Rupees (CRp) 75m. = US$ 15.8m., in instalments of CRp 15m. between 1958 and 1962, donation (1). In 1962 extended until 1967 (2).
1958, Sep 17:	CRp 50m. = US$ 10.5m. at an interest of 2.5 % (3), converted into an interest-free loan on Mar 15, 1964 (4).
1962, Oct 3:	CRp 50m. = US$ 10.5m., donation (4)
1964, Oct 21:	CRp 20m. = US$ 4.2m., free of interest, covering the period from 1965 till 1967, repayable in 10 annual instalments commencing in 1967 (5).
1970, Sep 12:	Yuan 22.155m. = US$ 9.3m. (6)
1971, May 27:	CRp 150m. (7) = US$ 31.5m., payable in two instalments in 1971, repayable over a period of 12 years (7), after a 3 year period of grace.
Oct 10:	Interest-free loan in the form of 100,000 metric tons of rice (8), estimated value: US$ 13m.
1972, Jun 29:	Interest-free loan of CRp 307 (=US$ 33.26m.) of which CRp 260m. are to be paid in hard currency and 47m., for a textile mill and flood control projects (9).
Sep 16:	Loan on providing a cargo-ship (10), estimated at US$ 2m.

(1) HdE II D 21 p.19 (2) NfA No.129, Jun 6, 1962 (3) VVRCh 1 p.66 (4) HdE II D 21 p.20 (5) NCNA Oct 26, 1964, and FEER Oct 15, 1964 (6) EpAkL 9/70 p.181 (7) Colombo Radio May 27, 1971 (8) NCNA Oct 8, 1971 (9) FEER Jul 15, 1972 (10) NCNA Sep 16, 1972

B. Aid projects completed

1. Rolling stock

Protocols: Under the 1957 agreement, CRp 25m. (out of a total of 75m., as granted in 1957) were to be used for several items of rolling stock (1) supplied, viz.
202 goods carriages,
14 tank carriages
8 passenger coaches (1).
Under some supplementary arrangements, the quotas were increased to
202 goods carriages
653 tank carriages
70 passenger coaches (2).
Under the protocol of Jul 13, 1965, China undertook to supply another 162 railway carriages to be paid with part of the CRp 20m. loan of 1964 (3). These 162 carriages are worth CRp 6.3m. (excluding freightage) (4).

First delivery: By October 1962,
202 goods carriages
13 tank carriages
8 passenger coaches (5)
had arrived in Sri Lanka.

Second delivery: In 1964, 235 passenger coaches and goods carriages worth CRp 12m. (6) or CRp 17.75m. (7) were delivered.

Third delivery: 1965/66: 116 passenger coaches and goods carriages worth CRp 4.85m. (7).

Other details: The carriages of the third batch were intended for use on the reopened Puttalam line so as to improve transport facilities to the second cement plant in this district (8).

2. Small textile mills

50 small textile mills, each of them equipped with 48 looms, are under construction in Sri Lanka with Chinese aid (9). The cost of one mill is CRp 0.5m. (10), hence the costs of all 50 mills total CRp 25m. This sum is taken out of the Chinese 50m. CRp donation of 1962. By March 1968, 25 mills had been completed (9). Afterwards the completion of the following mills was announced:

1968, March: Kegalle district, Sabaragamuve province. Inauguration in the presence of the Prime Minister Mr. Senanayake (9).

August: Eheliyagoda (10)

December: Rambukkana, 100 km. northeast of Colombo. Inauguration in the presence of the Prime Minister, Mr.Senanayake (11).

(1) FEER Jan 4, 1962 (2) FEER Sep 27, 1962 (3) NCNA Jul 13, 1965 (4) FEER Aug 12, 1965 (5) FEER Oct 11, 1962 (6) NCNA Jul 7, 1964 (7) Colombo Radio Jun 21, 1965 (8) Colombo R. May 2, 1965 (9) NCNA Mar 27, 1968 (10) NCNA Aug 4, 1968 (11) NCNA Dec 19, 1968, and Colombo R. Dec 19, 1968

3. <u>Conference hall</u>

Protocol:	February 1964 (1)
Location:	Colombo (2)
Foundation-stone laid:	March 1964, in the presence of the Prime Minister, Mrs. Bandaranaike (1).
Commencement:	November 24, 1970, in the presence of Mrs. Bandaranaike (3).
Completion:	May 7, 1973, in the presence of Mrs. Bandaranaike and, as Chinese guest, Hsu Hsiang-chien, Vice-Chairman of the CCP Military Council (4).
Technical data:	The original design of 1964 was for an 8-storeyed building with a congress hall seating 1,500 persons and equipped with a simultaneous translation system for English, French, Russian, Chinese, Spanish, Singhalese, and other languages. The whole block, erected on a surface of 11ha, also contains rooms for sessions, exhibitions, for banquets, and other purposes, the total floor-space being 32,000 square metres (5). On the perimeter of the magnificent structure are 40 white marble columns, 24 metres high, each topped with a golden capital beneath deep eaves. Peach-coloured marble walls and four white sculptured marble pillars flank the front entrance, in Sri Lanka national style. In front of the entrance gate is a 10m high fountain. In the large entrance hall is a bust of the late Prime Minister Solomon Bandaranaike (4). The Chinese government has donated an additional US$ 1.25m. for maintenance and repair of the hall (6).
Cost:	CRp 35m. (7) (= US$ 3.8m.)
Other details:	A group of 6 Chinese experts arrived in Colombo on Aug 12,1970 (8). It consisted of architects and technicians who were to complete the preparatory work for the project within six weeks (9). The conference hall is a Chinese gift (10). More than 400 Chinese workers and technicians went to work on the conference hall. The work was completed ahead of schedule (11). This project had been accepted by the first Bandaranaike government in 1964 but was interrupted when the new Senanayake government thought it too colossal (10). Work on the project therefore did not begin until Mrs.Bandaranaike had returned to power. There is no information as to whether or not the project was constructed according to the design from 1964.

(1) Colombo Radio Apr 30, 1965 (2) NCNA Aug 13, 1970 (3) NCNA Nov 25, 1970 (4) NCNA May 18, 1973 (5) FEER Jan 14, 1965 (6) Colombo R. Nov 20, 1973 (7) Colombo R. May 27, 1971 (8) NCNA Aug 13, 1970 (9) CDN Aug 15, 1970 (10) NZZ Jan 25, 1967, and Colombo R. May 18, 1973 (11) Colombo R. May 18, 1973

C. Aid projects under construction

1. Textile mill

Protocols: June 1959 (1), November 1964 (2), and June 29, 1972 (3)
Location: Pugoda (4)
Technical data: The mill will comprise workshops for spinning, weaving, printing, and dyeing (5).
Other details: A Chinese team of textile engineers arrived in Sri Lanka on Jul 8, 1971, to discuss and arrange the preparations for the construction of the mill.

2. Geological prospecting

In the spring of 1971, a group of Chinese geologists arrived in Sri Lanka to engage in prospecting work at the Ceylonese government´s orders (6).

D. Aid projects planned

1. Textile mill

Protocol: Feb 8, 1970 (7)
Location: Minneriya (7), between Colombo and Kandy (8).
Technical data: 600 power looms, 25,000 spindles (7).
Other details: China will supply the machinery and the building material, and is responsible for designing and constructing the project (7).

2. Flood control

Part of the June 1972 loan will be used to devise a scheme for controlling the annual floods of the Mahaweli, Gin, and Kalu Ganyas rivers (9). In February 1973 the Chinese experts who are to undertake a feasibility study extended their stay by six months (10). The project also calls for the development of irrigation facilities and the building of reservoirs (11).

---

(1) FEER Jan 14, 1965 (2) NfA No.141, Jun 21, 1965 (3) NCNA Jun 29, 1972 (4) EpAkL 2/69 p.84 (5) NCNA Jun 29, 1972 (6) NCNA Apr 8, 1971 (7) NCNA Feb 9, 1970 (8) EpAkL 3/70 (9) FEER Jul 15, 1972 (10) Colombo R. Feb 25, 1973 (11) Colombo R. Oct 14, 1973

General remarks

The Soviet position in the Sudan was weakened after the vain coup d'état in July 1971, and this offered China a welcome opportunity to strengthen her contacts with this country. This is the reason why the first economic aid loan in 1971 was promptly followed by an even higher loan in 1972, which Vice-President Khalid Hassan Abbas brought home from his visit to China. It is easy to understand that to make a new friend at the expense of the Soviet Union is worth some money to Peking. It has therefore not been surprising to see China forthwith initiating a number of ambitious projects in the Sudan, among them the road from Medani to Gedaref.

Though China first granted economic aid to the Sudan in 1970 (diplomatic relations being established as early as 1959), she surpassed the Soviet Union's aid in this country in 1971.

A. Chinese loans

1970, Aug 12 (1): £ 14.5m. (2) = US$ 35m. (3)

1971, Dec 20: US$ 40m. (4)

B. Aid projects completed

1. Medical group
   - Protocol: Dec 14, 1970 (5)
   - First group: Arrival: April 1971 (6) The group worked in Buluk Hospital at Omdurman (7).

C. Aid projects under construction

1. Road I
   - Course: Medani-Gedaref (8)
   - Technical data: The road is 250 km (8) (231 km(9)) long and 7 metres wide (9). It will be the longest asphalt road in the country, exceeding in length the Khartoum-Medani road (180 km) which was constructed with American aid during the rule of M.J. Abboud (9).
   - Other details: The first batch of Chinese and technical staff arrived in March 1972. The road is particularly important because it traverses the agricultural regions of Central and East Sudan (8). It will cost about £ 8m.(9). The road cuts through the Blue Nile valley, with a bridge at Wad Medani (10). This concrete bridge is half a kilometre long and 22 metres wide. By mid December 1972, both banks of the river had been surveyed and cleared of forests and trees. The major

(1) NCNA Aug 12, 1970 (2) Omdurman Radio Jul 26, 1970 (3) NZZ Jul 11, 1970 (4) NR 8/1973 (5) NCNA Dec 15, 1970 (6) NCNA Apr 6, 1971 (7) NCNA May 9, 1971 (8) Omdurman R. Jun 10, 1971 (9)ChR 12/73 (10) NCNA Sep 5, 1973

part of the work of earth removal and excavation on both banks and in the middle of the river had been completed and concrete laid. 200 Sudanese workers, carpenters, masons, and blacksmiths had been engaged. Equipment weighing 200,000 tons of steel were supplied by China. From Port Sudan on the Red Sea, 800,000 tons of equipment were transported to Medani in more than 200 railway carriages to the eastern bank of the river at the bridge site. (1)

2. Road II (2)
   Course: Nyala - Kas - Zalingei
   Technical data: The road is 200 km long.
   Other details: The road will connect Nyala with the Jabal Marrah district.

3. Conference building (3)
   Location: Khartoum (?)
   Other details: In June 1971 a group of Chinese experts stayed in Sudan engaged in design work. The building is expected to cost £ 1.5m.(1).

4. Cotton centre (4)
   Location: Wad Medani

5. Paddy fields (5)
   Location: In the outskirts of Wad Medani (capital of the Blue Nile Province).

6. Other projects (4)
   Since the end of 1971, Chinese technicians have been working on 10 different projects.

7. Experimental rice-growing station (6)
   Location: Gezira area
   Technical data: The experiment in growing rice on a plot of 1.5 feddaus began in 1972.
   Other details: The Sudan Gezira Board has decided to start large-scale production of rice under the Gezira scheme in 1974.

D. Aid projects planned

1. Hotel
   In 1965 China promised to build a hotel worth 2m. £ (7)

2. Industrial projects
   In December 1970 three groups of Chinese experts arrived in Khartoum to work on several projects to be carried out with Chinese aid (8). Among their tasks is geological surveying and prospecting work (9).

3. Textile factory
   Location: Hasahisa (10)
   Technical data: After completion the factory is expected to produce 16 million metres of cloth annually (1).

---

(1) ChR 12/1973 (2) Omdurman Radio Mar 14, 1971 (3) NCNA Jun 22, 1971 (4) NCNA Feb 29, 1972 (5) NCNA Sep 29, 1972 (6) NCNA Dec 2, 1973 (7) NZZ Jun 22, 1967 (8) NCNA Dec 30, 1970 (9) SANA Nov 7, 1970 (10) Omdurman R. Apr 28, 1973

Cost: £ 4m. (1), £ 3m.(2)

Other details: In June 1973 Chinese experts started studies and other preparatory work in connection with the factory project (3).

4. Prospecting of chrome deposits (4)
According to the Sudanese News Agency, 100 Chinese experts were shortly expected, in November 1973, to engage on a project of prospecting for chrome deposits.

5. Exploitation of aquatic products (2)
Location: Numa Lake in the northern part of Sudan
Technical data: The project will include the establishment of a deep-freezing system in Old Halfa, Atbara and Halfa (2), a factory at Wadi Halfa, workshops for the maintenance of boats and fishing nets, and cold-storage depots for salting fish(5).

6. Farm for rice production II (2)
Location: Owel in Bahr al-Ghazal in southern Sudan.

(1) Omdurman Radio Apr 28, 1973 (2) ChR 12/1973 (3) Omdurman R. Jun 17, 1973 (4) Omdurman R. Nov 20, 1973 (5) Omdurman R. Jan 25, 1973

General remarks

The first economic aid loan offered by China in 1963 was not used by Syria until 6 years later. Syria´s reluctance to make use of this loan was due to consideration of the Soviet Union, who had for years been the chief donor of economic and military aid. It was only when the Soviet Union refused, at short notice, to supply Syria with more arms in 1967 after the Six Days´War that the relationship between Moscow and Damascus became somewhat cooler so that China could put her foot in. Within the short period of two years, China built a cotton-spinning mill in Syria which obviously proved good enough to let the Syrians ask China for two more mills.

Though the Soviet Union (US$ 317m.) and Moscow´s East European satellites (US$ 287m.) supplied Syria with considerable economic aid, China,having offered US$ 99m., has attained a very respectable position and Syria now ranks tenth in the list of recipients of Chinese economic aid.

A. Chinese loans

1963, Feb 21(1):	US$ 16.4m. (2), free of interest (1). Repayment between 1976 and 1985 in equal yearly rates (2).
1971, June:	SF 64m. (3), US$ 36m. (4)
1972, May 24:	US$ 47m. (5)

B. Aid projects completed

1. Cotton-spinning mill I

Protocol:	Apr 13, 1967 (6)
Location:	Suburb of Hama in Central Syria (6)
Commencement:	February 1969 (7)
Completion:	March 1971 (8)
Technical data:	Annual capacity: 6,000 (9) or 4,500 tons of textiles (10). 31.000 spindles, later to be enlarged to 50,000 spindles (11).
Other details:	Cost of the project: US$ 4m. (12), Syria £ 18m. (13).

D. Aid projects planned

1. Cotton-spinning mill II

Protocols:	Dec 14, 1971 (14) and May 24, 1972 (15)
Location:	Idlib (13)
Other details:	Upon a request by the Syrian government, China promised to built a second cotton-spinning mill, the cost of which will be SF 64m. (16) (=US$ 20m.).

(1) JMJP Feb 22, 1963 (2) BfA/NfA (k) Mar 3, 1966 (3) SANA Jun 6, 1971 (4) NY HT Jun 26, 1971 and DW Jun 26, 1971 (5) Ch.a. 7/1972 (6) NCNA Apr 16, 1967 (7) NCNA Mar 6, 1971 (8) Damascus Radio Mar 4, 1971 (9) SANA Oct 20, 1968 (10) CT YB 444, 9/67 (11) NfA Jun 23, 1971 (12) CCA 12/67 (13) NfA Jul 11, 197 (14) NCNA Dec 14, 1971 (15) NCNA May 24, 1972 (16) SANA Jun 6, 1971

2. Cotton-spinning mill III (1)
   Location: Deir ez-Zor
   Other details: With the 1972 loan two cotton-spinning mills are to be built. A Chinese textile study group arrived in Syria on May 30, 1973 (2).

3. Indoor stadium
   Location: Damascus(1)
   Other details: An eleven-member group of experts left Peking for Syria to inspect the site of the stadium which is to be built with Chinese aid (3)

(1) NfA Jul 11, 1972 (2) NCNA Jun 6, 1973 (3) NCNA Nov 9, 1972

General remarks

China's greatest economic aid project is the Tan-Zam railway line. Involving US$ 405m. (270m. to Tanzania and 135m. to Zambia), it exceeds all other projects. From the Chinese point of view, it is an example of unselfish aid, of which the propaganda effect will, however, be far-reaching. Peking will do its best to make this project a complete success. This is true of the time-table and of the economic consequences for the two receiving countries. However, difficulties are liable to arise out of certain terms of the loan agreement, under which Tanzania is bound to import Chinese consumer goods in order to pay for the local expenses, which amount to 52 % of the total cost. This led to a curtailment of Tanzania's development plans for 1971/2 as a result of a shortage of foreign currency. As early as 1971 President Nyerere was criticized by his opponents from left to right, who found fault especially with the narrow choice of the Chinese consumer goods and the fact that they did not meet with approval by the Tanzanians. It is up to Peking to take care of these facts. China's considerable displeasure with the mistakes made in Tanzania's planned economy might also easily harm the good prospects of the Tan-Zam railway.

A. Chinese loans

This includes the loans given to Zanzibar until that country and Tanganyika united to form Tanzania (April 25, 1964).

1964, Feb 21:	£ 0.175m. (1) = US$ 0.5m. (2), at an interest of 2.5 % (3).
Jun 8:	£ 5m. (3) = US$ 14m. (2), free of interest (3). The loan is to serve Zanzibar's development (4). £ 1m. (3) =US$ 3m. (5), donation, given to Zanzibar (3).
Jun 26 (6):	£ 10m. (3) = US$ 28m., free of interest (3), half of the loan to be given in free currency (3).
1966, Mar 22:	£ 30,000 = US$ 85,000. Donation for the development of Dares Salam University (3).
Jun 8 (7):	East Africa Shilling 40m.(3) = £2m.(8) = US$ 5.6m. (2), free of interest (3). EA shillings 20m. (3) =£ 1m. (8) = US$ 2.8m.(2).
Jul 7:	US$ 3.5m. (estimated value of the two freighters of 10,000 register tons each (9).
1970, Jul 12 (10):	US$ 270m. (two thirds (11) of the 405m. loan jointly given to Tanzania and Zambia) (12), free of interest (12), repayment over a period of 30 years (12), starting in 1983 (13) or 1976 (14).

(1) NZZ Feb 24, 1964 (2) EpAkL 2/69 p.69 (3) HdE II D21 p.10 (4) FT Jun 9, 1964 (5) NT Jun 1, 1965 (6) JMJP Jun 17, 1964 (7) NCNA Jun 8, 1966 (8) FEER Jun 23, 1966 (9) NCNA Jul 7, 1966 (10) JMJP Jul 13, 1970 (11) estimate (12) Dares Salam Radio Jul 12, 1970 (13) NZZ Nov 8, 1970 (14) NZZ Aug 22, 1970

B. Aid projects completed

1. Pharmaceutical laboratory, equipment for (1)
   Location: Zanzibar, "Lenin Hospital"
   Completion: 1968
   Other details: China supplied the equipment for the production of medicines and injections.

2. Five (2) irrigation projects on Zanzibar and Pemba islands
   Locations:
   1. Makundishi (2) on Zanzibar. Inauguration Oct 10, 1969 (2)
   2. Chaani on Zanzibar. Inauguration Jun 27, 1969 (3).
   3. Machui on Pemba. Inauguration: Oct 11, 1969 (2)
   4. Donge Mbiji, north of Zanzibar city. Inauguration: Jun 25, 1969 (4).
   5. unknown

3. College building
   Location: Dares Salam University (5).
   Completion: Mar 19, 1968 (5)
   Technical data: The complex includes a bookshop, a bank, and a post-office (5).
   Peking University donated a large quantity of scientific instruments and illustrative material (5).
   Other details: The project is a Chinese donation promised by Chou En-lai during his state visit in 1965 (5).
   Cost of the project: £ 30,000 (1).

4. Printing office I
   Location: Saateni on Zanzibar (6)
   Completion: Inauguration in the presence of First Vice President Karume on Oct 6, 1967 (7).
   Technical data: The printing shop is equipped with modern machinery capable of printing coloured pictures, maps, and booklets (7).

5. Printing office II (6)
   Location: Dares Salam
   Completion: January 1967
   Technical data: The printing press is capable of printing 20,000 newspapers daily.
   Other details: The printing office is a Chinese donation.

6. Vaccine factory
   Location: Mabibo near Dares Salam (8)
   Commencement: End of 1969 (8)
   Completion: Apr 23, 1971 (9)
   Technical data: The factory produces vaccines against smallpox and tuberculosis. Annual production: Smallpox vaccines for 1.4 million persons, for tuberculosis, for 12-14,000 persons (8).
   Other details: There are plans to enlarge the factory (8).

(1) NCNA Aug 24, 1968 (2) NCNA Oct 13, 1969 (3) EpAkL 6/69 and NCNA Jun 28, 1969 (4) NCNA Jun 25, 1969 (5) NCNA Mar 20, 1968 (6) EpAkL 2/69 p.81 (7) NCNA Oct 7, 1967 (8) NT Apr 24, 1971 (9) NCNA Apr 28, 1971

7. <u>Hospital</u>

Location:	Mkoani, South Pemba (1)
Commencement:	The laying of the foundation-stone took place in the presence of President Nyerere on Jul 12, 1969 (2).
Completion:	Jul 15, 1970.
Other details:	The medical equipment and furniture are Chinese donations (3). Name of the hospital: "Abdallah Mzee" Hospital (3).

8. <u>Agricultural tools factory I</u>

Protocol:	Jan 5, 1965 (4)
Location:	Ubungo (5), in the suburbs of Dares Salam (6).
Commencement:	The laying of the foundation-stone took place in the presence of Second Vice-President Kawawa on Feb 10, 1968 (6).
Completion:	March 1970 (7). Official inauguration by Kawawa on Jun 5, 1970 (8).
Technical data:	The factory produces agricultural tools conforming to conditions prevailing in Tanzania (6), as e.g. ploughs, hoes, etc. (7). The number of workers in the factory is 140 (9). Annual production: 300,000 hoes and 3,000 ploughs (10).
Other details:	This factory helps to save imports worth East African Shillings 10m. (11) (=US$ 1.4 m.). The construction of the factory costs EA Shillings 5.4m. (11) (=US$ 0.6m.). In the first year of operation the factory had a deficit of East African Shillings 584,000 because its capacity was not fully utilized (12).

9. <u>Agricultural tools factory II</u>

Location:	Mbweni (13)
Completion:	Autumn 1968 (14)

10. <u>Leather and shoe factory</u>

Location:	Maruhubi, in the northern suburb of Zanzibar city (15), or at Mtoni on Zanzibar (15).
Commencement:	April 1967 (15).
Completion:	Inauguration on Feb 15, 1968 (16).
Technical data:	Floor-space 10,400 sq.m(on ground) (15). Annual capacity: 12,000 pieces of leather, 20,000 pairs of shoes and sandals (15).
Other details:	The factory is one of the largest on Zanzibar (15). The Chinese experts who helped to construct the factory arrived in the country in November 1966 (16).

---

(1) NCNA Jul 12, and Dec 15, 1969 (2) NCNA Jul 12, 1969 (3) NCNA Jul 16, 1970 (4) NCNA Jun 6, 1970 (5) Dares Salam Radio Jun 5, 1970 1970 (6) NCNA Feb 11, 1968 (7) NCNA Jun 4, 1970 (8) Dares Salam R. Jun 7, 1970 (9) NCNA Jun 6, 1970 (10) NT Apr 15, 1971 (11) Dares Salam R. Jun 2, 1970 (12)NT Apr 15, 1971 (13) NCNA Nov 7, 1970 (14) Peking Radio Oct 27, 1968 (15) NCNA Mar 13, 1968 (16) NCNA Feb 16, 1968

11. Medical groups I
    Location: Zanzibar
    First group: Arrival 1966 (?), 1967 (?) (1), (2)
    The group trained 19 persons as medical staff in the "Lenin Hospital" (1).
    Departure: May 1969 (3).
    Second group: Arrival: April 1969 (2)
    Part of the group worked on Pemba island (4).
    Third group: Arrival: December 1970 (5)

12. Medical groups II
    Location: Tanzania
    First group: Arrival: Jan 20, 1968 (6)
    Departure: October 1970 (7)
    In summer 1969 two teams of this group worked in the Musoma, Tarime, and Mara districts (8). In spring 1969 the group worked in 8 hospitals of 3 regions: Mara (northwestern Tanzania), Dodoma (Central Highlands), and Mtawara (central district, bordering on Mozambique) (9).
    On Jul 11, 1970, President Nyerere visited the group in Mpwapwa district, Dodoma region. In cooperation with the inhabitants, the Chinese medical personnel established a health centre in Mkoko village (50km from Mpwapwa town). During the last two years, the Chinese started 130 actions in which they treated 35,000 patients in the surrounding districts (10).
    On Aug 8, 1970, Second Vice-President Kawawa inaugurated a surgical station in the district hospital of Nachingwea in Mtawara district, which had been established by the Chinese medical group (11).
    Second group: Arrival: October 1970 (12). Late in 1970, the group was working in Musoma, Mara district (13). Part of the group departed in June 1971 (14). Another part departed in October 1972 (15).

13. Medical groups III (?)
    Since 1968 two Chinese medical groups were possibly working in continental Tanzania. According to Chinese sources, the first group arrived in January 1968 (16), and was followed by another one in April 1968 (17). The latter may, however, have been the second team of the first group. The assumption that there were two different groups was verified by NCNA (Aug 2, 1969) in a report stating that two medical groups were working in Musoma, Tarime, and Mara districts (18). Parts of the group returned to China in June 1971 (19).

(1) NCNA Feb 18, 1968 (2) NCNA Apr 9, 1969 (3) NCNA May 11, 1969 (4) NCNA Jun 14, 1970 (5) NCNA Dec 9, 1970 (6) NCNA Jan 24, 1968 (7) NCNA Oct 6, 1970 (8) NCNA Sep 2, 1968 (9) NCNA Mar 17, 1969 (10) NCNA Jul 11, 1970 (11) NCNA Aug 9, 1970 (12) NCNA Oct 6, 1970 (13) NCNA Dec 12, 1970 (14) NCNA June 22 and 27, 1971 (15) NCNA Oct 18, 1972 (16) NCNA Jan 24, 1968 (17) NCNA Mar 17, 1969 (18) NCNA Aug 2, 1969 (19) NCNA Jun 22, 1971

14. Party building (1)
Location: Zanzibar
Other details: The building of the Afro Shirazi Party headquarters was set up with Chinese aid.

15. Police-school, extension of
Location: Moshi (2)
Commencement: The laying of the foundation-stone took place on Jan 29, 1967 (3)
Other details: The project is a donation of the People's Republic of China (4). In 1969, Chinese instructors taught at this school (5).

16. Prospecting work (6)
In November 1967 a Chinese expert group came to Tanzania to engage in the prospecting of iron and coal deposits. Within four months it discovered four coal deposits.

17. Pumping station (7)
Location: Donge, on Zanzibar
Remarks: This project became known, when Fang Yi, Director of the Commission for Foreign Economic Relations, visited Tanzania in October 1970 (8).

18. Rice and tobacco farm (9)
Location: Kilombero, on Zanzibar
Commencement: November 1966
Other details: China was to supply this state farm with 42 tractors and agricultural machines.

19. Repair-shop for tractors and agricultural tools
Location: Mbweni, 3 km south of Zanzibar city (10).
Completion: August 1968 (11)
Other details: A group of Chinese technicians trained local workers for this repair-shop in summer 1968 (11). In August 1970, the group was replaced by another one (12).

20. Shoe factory (13)
Location: Mgulani National Service Camp on the outskirts of Dares Salam.
Technical data: The factory is small.

21. Broadcasting station, extension of
Protocol: May 11, 1965 (14)
Commencement: The foundation-stone was laid on Dec 28, 1965 (15).
Completion: Inauguration on Dec 7, 1967 (16).
Technical data: One 100 kW short-wave transmitter and one 150 kW medium-wave transmitter were installed (14).
Other details: All the equipment is of Chinese origin (17).

(1) NCNA Nov 7, 1970 (2) NZZ Aug 11, 1968 (3) NCNA Jan 30, 1967 (4) NCNA Jan 30, 1967 (5) NZZ Aug 3, 1969 (6) NCNA Mar 5, 1968 (7) NCNA Nov 8, 1970 (8) NCNA Oct 28, 1970 (9) EpAkL 2/69 p.82 (10) NCNA Aug 31, 1968 (11) NCNA Aug 31, 1968 (12) NCNA Aug 12, 1970 (13) NCNA Mar 14, 1972 (14) NCNA May 11, 1965 (15) NCNA Dec 28, 1965 (16) NCNA Dec 7, 1967 (17) NCNA Aug 27, 1966

22. Two freighters
When the Joint Chinese-Tanzanian Shipping Company was founded in 1966, China gave Tanzania two freighters, of 10,000 tons each, for a present (1).

23. State farm I

Location:	Ruwu, 80 km west of Dares Salam (2).
Technical data:	Cultivated crops: paddy rice, cotton, grain, vegetables (2). The farm includes a poultry farm and a small rice-mill (3) and has 18 tractors, trucks, and harvesting machines (4). Cultivated area: ha 1,750 (5) or ha 2,800 (6), including ha. 800 for paddy rice (6). On the site of the farm is a dam at Kibunda, the construction of which started in summer 1968 (7).

24. State farm II

Location:	Upenja (8), in Central Zanzibar (9).
Commencement:	The first Chinese expert group arrived in 1965 (10).
Completion:	Scheduled for 1968 (9). The delivery took place on Jan 11, 1969, in the presence of First Vice-President Karume (8).
Technical data:	Area covered: ha 520 (8). Cultivated crops: Rice, tropical fruit, vegetables (8), tobacco, and sugar-cane (9). The farm includes a poultry farm (8), a store, and lodgings for the workers (9). The paddy field is irrigated by 13 deep wells, sunk between January and October 1966 (11).

25. Stadium I

Location:	Zanzibar, near the government's seat (12).
Commencement:	The foundation-stone was laid on Mar 26, 1968, in the presence of President Nyerere and First Vice-President Karume (12).
Completion:	Jan 12, 1970 (13)
Technical data:	Area covered: sq.metres 90,000 (14), number of seats: 10,000 (15). The stadium has an electricity supply and a broadcasting system of its own, and also includes a three-storey hotel for the sportsmen (12).
Other details:	The stadium has been named "Peace Stadium" (16).

26. Road (17)

Course:	Maziwangombe-Wete (on Zanzibar)
Completion:	1964

(1) FEER Jul 14, 1966 (2) NCNA May 5, 1967 (3) NCNA May 24, 1968 (4) TT Jan 6, 1965 (5)NCNA May 5, 1967 (6) NCNA May 24, 1968 (7) EpAkL 2/69 p.82 (8) NCNA Jan 11, 1969 (9) NCNA Mar 5, 1968 (10) NCNA Jan 9, 1969 (11) NCNA Nov 10, 1966 (12) NCNA Mar 26, 1968 (13) NCNA Jan 12, 1970 (14) NCNA Mar 5, 1968 (15) NCNA Jan 11, 1969 (16) NCNA Nov 8, 1970 (17) EpAkL 2/69 p.82

27. Textile mill
    Location: Ubungo, suburb of Dares Salam (1)
    Commencement: July 1966 (2)
    Completion: Feb 6, 1968 (3) (scheduled for July 1968) (4). The inauguration took place on Jul 6, 1968, in the presence of President Nyerere (1).
    Technical data: 978 looms, 40,000 spindles (1). Annual production: 20 million square metres of Khangas Vitenge (printed material for African dresses) and kg 900,000 cotton yarn (5). The textile combine consists of more than 20 buildings (5) among them workshops for spinning, weaving, dyeing, and cloth printing (6). More than 2,000 workers work in the mill, 400 of them in the cloth printing and dyeing workshops (5). The mill processes about 5 per cent. of Tanzania's cotton crop (6).
    Other details: Name of the mill "Friendship" (7) (originally the intention had been to name it "Mao Tse-tung Mill")(8). By the beginning of 1968, 1,000 workers and technicians had been trained (9). The mill cost £ 2.5m. (8) or 3.32m. (10). It is one of the largest textile mills in East Africa (11). Since it was put into operation, the mill has worked with a heavy deficit (12).

28. Cloth sewing factory of the National Service (13)
    Location: Ruvu, 50 km from Dares Salam
    Completion: Dec 10, 1972, in the presence of Prime Minister Kawawa

29. Wood furniture manufacturing factory (13)
    Location: Nachingwei Camp of the National Service in the Lindi region of southern Tanzania
    Completion: Dec 8, 1972, in the presence of Prime Minister Kawawa.

C. Aid projects under construction

1. Tanzania-Zambia railway
   Agreements: Sep 5, 1967, between China, Tanzania, and Zambia (14)
   (One) China undertakes to finance and construct the railway-line
   (Two) China offers an interest-free loan covering the costs
   (Three) The preparations will begin in the first three months of 1968 (15)

---

(1) NCNA Jul 6, 1968 (2) NCNA Jul 29, 1966 (3) NCNA Feb 6, 1968 (4) NCNA Mar 5, 1968 (5) NCNA Jul 18, 1968 (6) FEER Jul 18, 1968 (7) NCNA Feb 6, and Jul 18, 1968 (8) TT Jan 6, 1965 (9) NCNA Mar 5, 1968 (10) FEER Jul 18, 1968 (11) NCNA Jul 29, 1966 (12) NZZ Apr 1, 1970 (13) NCNA Dec 11, 1972 (14) NCNA Sep 5, 1967 (15) FEER Sep 14, 1967

Apr 8, 1968
Protocol on terms of loan
Protocol on the despatch of Chinese technicians and their working conditions
Protocol on surveying and design work (1)

Apr 27, 1968
Loan agreement
Protocol on technical principles (2)

Nov 14, 1969
Supplementary protocol (no details
Protocol on preparatory work preceding the construction
Protocol on additional technical proposals (3)

Jul 7, 1970
Protocol relating to the sums involved and the terms of repayment
Protocol on a "Report on planning and design"
Protocol on details of the negotations (4)

Line: Starting-point as originally planned: Kidatu (5), terminal of a branch-line from the Dares Salam - Kigoma railway line (at Lake Tanganyika). According to a protocol of Nov 14, 1969, the starting-point was transferred to Dares Salam (3). From there, the line goes in a southwesterly direction, crossing the plain of the Kilomboreo valley and later the Mkumbaku mountain ranges with their ravines, to the mountain-enclosed highlands in Southern Tanzania up to the Mbeya Pass at the Zambian border, whence the line crosses the Chambeshi river and the Zambian hills until it reaches the copper belt (6). Terminal: Mposhi (7). The most difficult section is between Mlimba and Makumbaku in Tanzania (8).

Commencement: Official start on Tanzanian territory (in Dares Salam) on Oct 25, 1970(9), on Zambian territory (in Mposhi) on Oct 28, 1970 (10), both in the presence of the Presidents of Tanzania and Zambia, Nyerere and Kaunda, respectively (11).

Completion: Scheduled for 1975 (12)

---

(1) NCNA Apr 9, 1968 (2) NCNA Apr 27, 1968 (3) NCNA Nov 17, 1969
(4) NCNA Jul 12, 1970 (5) NCNA Oct 20, 1968 (6) PR Nov 18, 1969
(7) NZZ Nov 8, 1970 (8) NCNA Oct 26, 1970 (9) NCNA Oct 25, 1970
(10) NCNA Oct 29, 1970 (11) PR Nov 10, 1970 (12) NZZ Mar 17, 1971

Preparatory work: The first group of Chinese surveyors and designers, totalling 154 persons, arrived in Tanzania at the beginning of 1968 (1), and was followed by another 200 technicians in April 1968 (1). The first technical group on Zambian territory arrived in Lusaka on Sep 21, 1968 (2), and was followed by a second group in October 1968 (3). Further groups of engineers and technicians arrived in March 1969 (4), July 1969(5), August 1969(250 persons)(6), September 1969 (100 persons)(7). In November 1969 (8) a group of 290 (7) came to Tanzania, and two more groups, in January 1970 (9) (10). The surveys on Zambian territory were completed in February 1970 (11) and the Chinese experts then returned to China (12).

Technical data: The length of the line from Dares Salam to Kapiri Mposhi is 1859 km (13), or more than 1900 km (14),(15).
Length on Tanzanian territory: 708 km (16).
The line will be single-tracked (17). Annual capacity: 1.75 million tons of goods in each direction (17) (18).
The sub-base has a carrying capacity of 45 kg/m, as against a mere 30 kg/m of the old East African railway, thus permitting a maximum speed of 100 km/h, as against 60 km/h (18).
Gauge: 1.064 m, which corresponds to that used in Zambia, while the gauge of the East African railway is only 1,00 m (18).

Other details: The Presidents of Tanzania and Zambia are said to have agreed that the number of Chinese technicians and workers admitted to their countries should be limited to a total of 25,000 (18).
The headquarters of the Chinese experts in Zambia is in Mkushi (19).
The first load of 1,800 tons of rails and other equipment arrived in Dares Salam in September 1969 (20).
In autumn 1969, it was not known whether or not China would also supply the engines and wagons (20). The rolling stock was to be ordered from China(21).

---

(1) NZZ Apr 30, 1968 (2) NCNA Sep 22, 1968 (3) NCNA Oct 30, 1968 (4) NCNA Mar 28, 1969 (5) NCNA Jul 26, 1969 (6) NCNA Aug 17, 1969 (7) Lusaka Radio Sep 30, 1969 (8) NCNA Nov 7, 1969 (9) NCNA Jan 1, 1970 (10) NCNA Jan 13, 1970 (11) NCNA Feb 25, 1970 (12) NCNA Apr 24, 1970 (13) NZZ Nov 8, 1970 (14) PR Nov 18, 1969 (15) NCNA Jul 10, 1969 (16) NCNA Sep 29, 1968, and PR Nov 12, 1968 (17) FEER Nov 7, 1970 (18) NZZ Nov 8, 1970 (19) NCNA Jun 15, 1969 (20) Lusaka Radio Sep 30, 1969 (21) Lusaka R. Oct 22, 1969

One of the railway officials declared that it was planned to instal modern security devices to protect the railway against sabotage (1).
In March 1969 a Chinese group of surveyors had a clash with a group of US technicians building a road from Tanzania to the Zambian copper belt, near Mbeya. The Chinese demanded that the Americans should stop their work while the Chinese were surveying the ground, but the Americans refused to do so. After 5 hours of quarrelling the police had to settle the dispute (2).
In summer 1970 a prefabricated concrete factory, a machine repair shop and a saw mill were erected at Mangula near Kidatu (3). The station at Dares Salam was completed within 26 days (4). In autumn 1970, a repair shop for engines and wagons, a depot for material, and a reception centre were started (4). By October 1970, 110 bridges had been built and the railway dams, prepared over wide sections of the line (5). In November 1970 the production of about 2,000 sleepers daily was begun (5).

Chinese loans: The loans offered by China for the construction of the railway line have been indicated as follows:

£ 100m. (5)
Kwacha 170m. (6)
Kwacha 256m. approximately (7)
Kwacha 19,836billion (8)
US$ 300m.(9)
Tanzania Shillings 2.866 billion (10)= £ 169m.
Tanzania Shillings 2.866 billion = SF 1.5 billion (5)
US$ 400m.(11)
£ 167m. (12)

Terms of loan: Repayment is assumed to begin after a five years' period of grace, and to go on for 25 years. The local costs are to be covered by the proceeds from the sale of Chinese goods (7). The loan will be free of interest and repayable over 30 years (10). The local costs are calculated at 52 % of the loan, and will be covered by the importation of Chinese commodities under a commodity loan agreement between China and the governments of Tanzania and Zambia (5).

(1) Lusaka Radio Oct 22, 1969 (2) Ta Mar 21, 1970 (3) NCNA Aug 28, 1970 (4) NCNA Oct 25, 1970 (5) NZZ Nov 8, 1970 (6) Lusaka R. Sep 30, 1969 (7) Lusaka R. Oct 22, 1969 (8) Lusaka R. Nov 3, 1969 (9) Ta Mar 21, 1970 (10) Dares Salam Radio Jul 12, 1970 (11) FEER Nov 7, 1970 (12) WHChM Oct 18, 1970

Estimated time of construction:	8 years (1) 5 years (2)
Chinese staff:	The number of Chinese staff working on the railway was estimated at between 7,000 and 10,000 at the beginning of 1971. They are working in cooperation with about 5,000 local workers (3).
History:	The history of the construction of this railway line is long. It began in 1964, when Zambia attained independence. The country then considered it incompatible with its national interests on the long run to transport its copper exports via Rhodesia and the Portuguese colony of Mozambique to the port of Beira, the only port at that time attainable by rail. Zambia´s annual copper production amounts to 700,000 tons and its yield is more than half of the total export revenue of the country. After the declaration of Independence, Zambia sought new ways of rendering her copper exports independent of possible interference from racist or colonial states. As early as 1967, the amount of copper conveyed to Beira via Rhodesia had sunk to a mere 200,000 tons. Another 200,000 tons have since been transported to Dares Salam by road over a distance of almost 2,000 km. 180,000 tons go to the Atlantic port of Lobito in Angola, via the Congo, by rail. 50,000 tons are transported by "Zambia Aircargoes" to Dares Salam, another 50,000 t go to Malawi by road and thence to Beira by rail. It cost a lot of money to open up and maintain all those new ways of transportation. After the World Bank had made an analysis and declared the construction of a railway between Tanzania and Zambia to be unprofitable, a Canado-French consortium arrived at the opposite result. However, neither Tanzania nor Zambia succeeded in arousing Western interest in this project and President Kaunda of Zambia never concealed his disappointment over this. Eventually the two states accepted an offer which the Chinese Prime Minister, Chou En-lai, submitted to the Tanzanian President, Nyerere, in summer 1965.

2. <u>Housing project</u> (4)

Location:	Michenzani
Remarks:	The existence of this project came to be known when Fang Yi, Chairman of the Commission for Economic Relations with Foreign Countries, visited it in October 1970.

---

(1) NZZ Nov 8, 1970 (2) Lusaka Radio Nov 3, 1969 (3) NZZ Mar 17, 1971 (4) NCNA Nov 7, 1970

3. Housing project II (1)
Location: Kilimani
Remarks: The existence of this project came to be known when Fang Yi, Chairman of the Commission for Economic Relations with Foreign Countries, visited in October 1970.

4. Saw-mill (2)
Protocol: Jul 31, 1970
Location: Zanzibar
Other details: A Chinese technical group engaged in planning this project was received by the First Deputy President Karume a short time before its departure.

5. Brick-works
Location: Koani (3) or Mkoani on Pemba (4)
Commencement: Second half of 1970 (3)

6. Pharmaceutical plant (5)
Location: Dares Salam
Commencement: Nov 2, 1973
Costs: Shillings 3m.
Other details: The Chinese medical team working in Tanzania and Chinese technical personnel are helping with the construction of this plant.

D. Aid projects planned

1. State farm III (6)
Protocol: May 8, 1970
Location: Mbarali

2. Extension of the stadium (7)
Protocol: Jun 24, 1969
Location: Dares Salam

3. Cigarette factory and technical instruction centre for the planting of tobacco
Location: Zanzibar (8)
Other details: A group of Chinese experts, who had studied the feasibility of the construction of this factory and instruction centre, returned to China in April 1970 (8).

4. Sugar refinery and sugar-cane plantation (8)
Location: Zanzibar
Other details: A group of Chinese experts, who had studied the feasibility of the construction of the refinery and the development of the plantation, departed in April 1970.

5. Technical school for workers and peasants (8)
Location: Zanzibar
Other details: A group of Chinese experts, who had studied the feasibility of the construction of this school, departed in April 1970.

---

(1) NCNA Nov 7, 1970 (2) NCNA Aug 4, 1970 (3) Zanzibar Radio Jun 1, 1970 (4) EpAkL 7/10 (5) NCNA Nov 4, 1973 (6) NCNA May 10 and 11, 1970 (7) NCNA Jun 24, 1969 (8) NCNA Apr 25, 1970

E. Chinese experts

1968:	On Zanzibar there were between 300 and 500 Chinese experts, who partly worked on agricultural projects and partly, as military instructors (1). On the continent there were between 700 and 800 experts, 300 among them engaged in planning the Tanzania-Zambia railway line (1).
1970:	4,700 Chinese technicians and workers were engaged in constructing the railway line (2).
1971:	As told by President Nyerere at the beginning of the year, the number of Chinese engaged in the construction of the railway line was 7,000 (3), or between 7,000 and 10,000 (4).
1973:	The number of Chinese working on the railway was 16,000 (5).

---

(1) NZZ Aug 11, 1968 (2) NZZ Nov 8, 1970 (3) DT Feb 4, 1971 (4) NZZ Mar 17, 1971 (5)FAZ Feb 21, 1973

General remarks

When diplomatic relations were established in September 1972, China granted an appreciable economic aid loan of US$ 45m. This was the first time Togo accepted a loan from a socialist country and the loan has helped to give China a strong position in Togo.

A. Chinese loans

1972, Sep 27: Loan of US$ 45m. (1)

(1) NR Jun 15, 1973, p.4

General remarks

Sino-Tunisian relations have by no means always been very friendly. Having been established in 1964, diplomatic relations between the two countries were interrupted in 1967 when the Cultural Revolution was in full swing. The Chinese closed their embassy after the President Bourguiba had shown - in the Chinese view - an unfriendly attitude by rather pointedly questioning China's claim to Taiwan. The embassy was not reopened until October 1971.

Since then relations have been satisfactory. In 1972 China offered Tunisia an economic aid loan of US$ 36m., thereby surpassing the Soviet Union who had by then granted Tunisia US$ 34m. In addition, Tunisia finally opened an embassy in Peking in December 1973, having long been one of the few countries with a Chinese embassy in their own country, without itself maintaining an embassy in China.

A. Chinese loans
1972, Aug 27: Loan of US$ 36m. (1)

B. Aid projects completed

1. Medical group
First group: Arrival Jul 1, 1973 (2)

(1) NR Jun 15, 1973, p.4 (2) NCNA Jul 2, 1973

General remarks

The economic aid loan offered by China in 1965 was obviously not used by Uganda until 1971, at a time when the rulers had manoeuvred their country into an isolated position in international politics, as a result of a dubious domestic policy.

A. Chinese loans

1965, Apr 21: US$ 12m., without interest (1), half of it to be repaid in hard currency (2).
US$ 3m. as a donation (1)

C. Aid projects under construction

1. Rice scheme (3)
   Location: Kibimba in Busoga district, eastern Uganda
   Commencement: Nov 17, 1973

2. Dam (3)
   On November 17, 1973, President Amin visited a dam under construction with Chinese aid.

3. Spillway (3)
   On November 17, 1973, President Amin visited a spillway under construction with Chinese aid.

4. Brick factory (3)
   On November 17, 1973, President Amin visited a brick factory under construction with Chinese aid.

(1) Kampala Radio May 3, 1965, and EpAkL 2/69 p.70 (2) NZZ Sep·9, 1972 (3) NCNA Nov 22, 1973

A. Chinese loans

1973, Sep 8:	Agreement on economic and technical co-operation (1). Chinese loan estimated at US$ 10m.

(1) NCNA Sep 15, 1973

General remarks

Yemen is one of the strategic points where Chinese and Soviet interests intersect. While China was on pretty good terms with the Royalist Government of Yemen, relations became less satisfactory after the coup d´état. The reason seems to be that China refused to evacuate her diplomatic mission from Sana (1), thus arousing the suspicion of opportunistic behaviour. As a result, the Yemeni Prime Minister Hasan al-Amry cancelled his announced visit to China - obviously under Soviet pressure, the Soviet Union being at that time the main supplier of arms to Yemen.

The fact that the Sana - Sada road,which was commenced in September 1967,is still not completed is an indication of the fact that the relations between Peking and Sana have become somewhat cooler. It was the political pragmatism adopted by the People´s Republic of China after the Cultural Revolution which gave relations a turn for the better, as may be seen from the loan offered to Yemen in 1972 (US$ 22m.).

Following is a table comparing Chinese and Soviet aid with each other (2) (3)

People´s Republic of China	mill. US$	Soviet Union	mill. US$
1.Hodeida-Sana road	15	1. Wadi Sardud agricultural project	18
2. Sana - Sada road	28	2. Hodeida-Taiz road	34
3. Textile mill	2.5	3. Cement factory	10
4. 1972 loan	22.1	4. Hodeida harbour	15
		5. Fish-processing plant	7
	67.6		84

A. Chinese loans

1958, Jan 12 (4): US$ 16m. (5), free of interest (6)

1959, Jan 23 (7): US$ 0.142m., free of interest (6)

1962, Nov 24: US$ 4.8m. (5)

1964, Jun 9: (8) US$ 28.2m., free of interest (6)

1972, Jul 21: US$ 22.1m., free of interest, payable over 20 years (3).

---

(1) AW Dec 18, 1967 (2) FML (3) upi Aug 7, 1972 (4) NCNA Jan 13, 1958 (5) HdE II D 21 p.25 (6) EpAkL 2/69 p.73 (7) NCNA Jan 24, 1959 (8) NCNA Jun 9, 1964

B. Aid projects completed

1. Wells

In September 1965 Chinese experts started to sink wells 10 km north of Sana (1).

In June 1968 a well sunk with Chinese aid was inaugurated at al-Maamara (20 km from Sana). This well is113.84 m deep and the only artesian well in that region. It supplies the water necessary for the building of the Sana-Sada road (2). Vice-Premier Abdel Salam Sabrah received a Chinese team at Khmr (90 km north of Sana) on Jan 30, 1969, which was then engaged in sinking deep-water wells (3).

Chinese experts were busy sinking wells in the Sana - Hoth section of the Sana - Sada road for almost two years. They also sunk three wells in Sana (4).

2. Donation of teaching material

The Chinese Ministry of Education gave Yemen 283 crates filled with teaching material (5).

3. Medical groups

First group:	Arrival in July 1966 (6) Departure in May 1969 (7)
Second group:	Arrival in March 1968 (6) In summer 1968 the group worked in the hospital of Ibb (8). In spring 1969 the group established an X-ray station in Taiz and trained Yemeni medical personnel (9). Departure in April 1970 (10).
Third group:	Arrival in April 1970 (10) Departure in May 1971 (11)
Fourth group:	Arrival in May 1971 (11) Departure in June 1972 (12)
Fifth group:	Arrival in June 1972 (12)

4. Technical school

Protocol:	Jul 14, 1969 (13)
Commencement:	The foundation-stone was laid on Jul 21, 1969 (14).
Completion:	The inauguration was on Sep 26, 1970 (15).
Other details:	The school is a gift from China (13). A well will be sunk to provide it with water (16).

5. Road I

Protocols:	Jan 12, 1958 (17) and Jan 23, 1959 (18)
Course:	Hodeida - Baital - Manacha - Sana (19)
Commencement:	December 1958 (20)

---

(1) NCNA Sep 12, 1965 (2) NCNA Jun 5, 1968 (3) NCNA Jan 31, 1969 (4) NCNA Aug 11, 1969 (5) NCNA Mar 3, 1968 (6) NCNA Mar 15, 1958 (7) NCNA May 15, 1969 (8) NCNA Jul 24, 1968 (9) NCNA May 27, 1969 (10) NCNA Apr 11, 1970 (11) NCNA Jul 23, 1969 (12) NCNA Jun 28, 1972 (13) NCNA Jul 16, 1969 (14) NCNA Jul 23, 1969 (15) NCNA Sep 27, 1970 (16) EpAkL 1/70 (17) NCNA Jan 13, 1958 (18) NCNA Jan 24, 1959 (19) FT 2/61 (20) NCNA Dec 26, 1958

Completion: December 1961 (1)
Technical data: Length 231 km (2).
55 bridges and 489 drainage canals (3).
The length daily covered with asphalt-surfacing was 1 km. (4).
Other details: Cost of the road US$ 15m. (8). Chinese engineers and technicians as well as 10,000 Yemeni workers were engaged in the construction of the road (4). During the construction 857 Yemeni workers received vocational training (5). The Chinese experts left the country in March 1962 (6). Ten of them and one interpreter remained for repairs (7).

6. Textile mill
Protocols: Jan 23, 1959, and Mar 23, 1965 (9).
Location: Sana (10)
Commencement: The foundation-stone was laid on Sep 27, 1964 (10).
Completion: March 1967 (11), delivery Sep 25, 1967 (11).
Technical data: Annual production: 7 million metres of cotton cloth (11). The mill works up one third of Yemen's cotton production which is between 3,000 tons and 4,000 tons annually (11). Since the putting into operation of the mill, 30 varieties of cloth were produced, including gabardine and dyed poplin (11). 1,000 Yemeni workers and 20 Chinese experts worked in the mill in 1970 (8). Upon the Yemeni Government's request, Chinese experts were still working in the mill in 1971 (12). In January 1967 printed cloth was produced for the first time (13).
The cotton-spinning shop of the mill was put into operation on Apr 13, 1972 (14).
The mill carries out all the processes, commencing with the raw material and including the printing and dyeing of cotton cloth. It is the largest single modern enterprise in the country and has 360 looms and 10,000 spindles. The mill caters for a substantial proportion of Yemen's demand in respect to plain white cloth, various kinds of calico cotton prints, poplin, khaki dyed, and venetian cloth. The mill employs more than 1,500 workers and staff. Over 1,300 of them are already skilled spinners, weavers, printers, or dyers. 70 others are technicians and managing personnel. The mill has been producing on a 3-shift system since the beginning of 1970, which has replaced the one-shift system of the mill's early operation. There are now 300 women workers in the mill (15).

(1) NCNA Dec 31, 1961 (2) PR Jan 5, 1961 (3) NCNA Nov 12, 1961 (4) JMJP Oct 20, 1960 (5) PR Jan 5, 1962 (6) JMJP Mar 8, 1962 (7) NCNA Mar 18, 1962 (8) FML (9) NCNA Jan 23, 1959, and Mar 23, 1965 (10) NCNA Sep 27, 1964 (11) NCNA Sep 25, 1967 (12) NCNA Feb 20, 1971 (13) NCNA Jan 30, 1967 (14) NCNA Apr 14, 1972 (15) NCNA Jul 18, 1972

Other details: Parts of the textile mill were destroyed and several Chinese hurt on Jul 25, 1968, when royalist forces bombarded it (1). Costs of the mill: 2.5m. US$ (2).

C. Aid projects under construction

1. Road II

Line: Sana - Sada (3)
Commencement: September 1967 (3)
Technical data: Length 300 km (4).
Other details: Most of the road goes up to heights of more than 2,000 m above sea-level (5). Eight wells were sunk along the Sana-Huth section (122.4 km) (6). Costs of the project: US$ 28m. (2). The Sana-Hamir section was opened to traffic on Feb 16, 1972 (7), the Sana-Huth section (128 km) on Sep 25, 1972 (8). In October 1966 the Yemeni government asked the Chinese government to speed up the construction of the road (9).

D. Aid projects planned

1. Agricultural development

On Dec 30, 1971, a Chinese agricultural investigation group arrived in Yemen (7)(10).

2. Hospital

Protocol: Mar 16, 1972 (11)
Location: Taiz (11)
Other details: A Chinese hospital investigation group stayed in Yemen from September 1971 (10) to March 1972 (10) (12).

E. Chinese experts

In 1967 the number of Chinese in Yemen totalled 3,300 (9).

---

(1) NCNA Jul 31, 1968 (2) FML (3) NCNA Sep 26, 1967 (4) EpAkL 2/69 p.85 (5) NCNA Dec 13, 1969 (6) EpAkL 1/70 (7) NCNA Feb 17, 1972 (8) NCNA Sep 26, 1972 (9) CTYB 440 9/67 (10) NCNA Jan 10, 1972 (11)NCNA Mar 21, 1972 (12) NCNA Sep 16, 1971

General remarks

President Mobuto said in September 1966: "My Government does not at present want a rapprochement with the People´s Republic of China because of all the damaging deeds committed by those people. Our wounds are too fresh for us to be able to forget what they have done to us. The People´s Republic of China played an important part in the insurrection movement in many parts of our country in 1964". This was Mobutu´s comment on a declaration by Mao Tse-tung on November 28, 1964.

China´s relations with what later came to be Zaire were strained, above all, by her support of the separatist Lumumba who had pronounced the Republic of Congo (Stanleyville). With that state China had entered into diplomatic relations on February 20, 1961, a couple of days after Lumumba had been killed. Those relations did not last for more than some months and were fictitious, because the Republic of Congo (Stanleyville) never became a reality.

The exceptionally high loan of US$ 115m., which China offered Zaire in January 1973, and which brought Zaire right into the seventh place on the list of recipients of Chinese economic aid, must therefore be interpreted as a means to buy back some political goodwill. Its importance is exceptional, as it is the first economic aid loan ever granted to Zaire by a Communist country.

A. Chinese loans

1973, Jan 14: Agreement on economic and technical cooperation (1). Chinese loan of US$ 115m.(2).

(1) NCNA Jan 14, 1973 (2) NZZ Feb 1, 1973

General remarks

Relations between China and Zambia developed rather slowly. Though the two countries had entered into diplomatic relations as early as 1964 and China had immediately set up an embassy at Lusaka, more than four years passed before Zambia sent her first ambassador to Peking (January 1969). It was not until June 1967, when President Kaunda paid his first visit to Peking, that relations became really friendly. On that occasion China probably submitted a practical offer for the construction of the railway line from Zambia to Tanzania, which resulted in an agreement three months later.

Though the railway line is expected to solve an essential economic problem for the non-maritime African countries and Zambia ought to be grateful for this Chinese offer, minor differences keep coming up: thus Zambia has found fault with the medical standards of the Chinese medical groups which, they say, do not meet the high standards valid in Zambia. Another criticism was that, early in 1971, the medium and short-wave radio transmitting station, the completion of which had been promised for 1970, had still not been provided with the intended technical equipment (1) - by the way of a donation from China.

However, there was not much of such carping, unfounded criticism and there cannot be any doubt that the relations between the two countries are on the whole friendly. This was once more shown by the visit of President Kaunda to China in February 1974, when he was granted another loan of US$ 19m. (2).

A. Chinese loans

1967, May 26:	US$ 7m. (3)
Jun 23:	US$ 16.8m., free of interest (3)
1970, Jul 12 (4):	US$ 135m., one third (5) of the Chinese loan to Tanzania and Zambia which totalled US$ 405m. (6) (see Tanzania, A. Chinese loans).
1973, May:	US$ 10m. (7)

B. Aid projects completed

1. Road project I

Protocols:	Feb 2, 1969 (8) and Jan 30, 1970 (9)
Commencement:	Surveying started in October 1969 (10) (11) The actual construction started in July 1970 (11)
Completion:	September 1972 (12). Opened to traffic on May 26, 1973 (13).
Course:	Lusaka - crossing the Katue river - Mankoya - ending 25 km behind Mankoya (10).

(1) Lusaka Radio Sep 9, 1970, and FEER Nov 7, 1970 (2) NCNA Feb 26, 1974 (3) EpAkL 2/69 p.68 (4) JMJP Jul 13, 1970 (5) estimate (6) Dares Salam Radio Jul 12, 1970 (7) NZZ May 30, 1973 (8) NCNA Feb 15, 1969 (9) NCNA Jan 31, 1970 (10) Lusaka Radio and NCNA Nov 4, 1970 (11) NCNA Nov 4, 1970 (12) NCNA Nov 16, 1972 (13)NCNA May 27, 1973

Technical data: Length 630 km (1) or 400 km (2) or 600 km (3) or 388 km (4). Asphalt road (5).
The largest bridge crosses the Kafue river (6). It is 282 metres long and was completed in May 1972 (7).

Other details: The cost of the road will be Kwacha 12m. out of the loan of Jun 23, 1967 (2).

2. Medium- and short-wave radio transmitting station

Protocols: Dec 31, 1969 (8) and Mar 23, 1970 (9)

Location: Shorthorn, 17 km from Lusaka, at the old Mumbwa road (10).

Commencement: May 20, 1970 (11)

Completion: Apr 25, 1973 (11). The transfer took place on May 28, 1973 (12).

Technical data: The transmitters installed are: two 50 kW short-wave transmitters and one 200 kW medium-wave transmitter (Chinese donation) (10).

Other details: China pays for the shipment of the equipment to Dares Salam (13). Although the completion had been scheduled for the end of 1970, the three transmitters were not delivered until January 1971 (14).

C. Aid projects under construction

1. Tanzania-Zambia railway
see Tanzania, C. Aid projects under construction

2. Road projects II

Protocol: Jan 30, 1970 (15)

Line: Lusaka - Kaoma (Western Province) (16)

Commencement: July 1970 (16)

Technical data: Length 380 km (16)

Remarks: This road is presumably identical with the Lusaka-Mankoya road or forms part thereof. There was a somewhat misleading report in Lusaka Radio saying that the first section of the road from Mongu to Kaoma was to be constructed by the British Burton Construction Company and to be completed in September 1971, while the section between Lusaka and Kaoma, more than twice the length of the British section, was to be built by the People's Republic of China and was to be completed in autumn 1972 (17).

(1) Lusaka Radio Oct 1, 1969, and NCNA Nov 4, 1970 (2) CN No.307 Apr 10, 1969 (3) Lusaka R. Apr 8, 1971 (4) NCNA Nov 16, 1972 (5) EpAkL 8/70 (6) Lusaka R. Jan 24, 1969 (7) NCNA Jul 24, 1972 (8) NCNA Jan 5, 1970 (9) NCNA Mar 26, 1970 (10) Lusaka R. Dec 31, 1969 (11) NCNA May 29, 1973 (12) NCNA May 30, 1973 (13) EpAkL 3/70 (14) Lusaka R. Jan 16, 1971 (15) NCNA Jan 31, 1971 (16) NCNA Nov 4, 1970 (17) Lusaka R. Apr 8, 1971

THE CHINESE AID PROJECTS ACCORDING TO BRANCHES

The agreements forming the basis of Chinese economic aid having been specified in Part I, and the various projects in Part II, Part III sums up the projects specified in Part II according to branches. The principal object of this part is to show how the centres of gravity in Chinese economic aid are distributed.

Table 11 contains a list of all projects, of which 200 had been completed, 61 were under construction and 90 were still in the stage of planning at the end of 1973. The majority (namely 36 %) of the 351 projects are light industrial, the most important branch aided. The 127 projects in this field are distributed over 55 different sectors - an indication of the wide range covered by Chinese economic aid. While there is no light industrial sector in which China does not seem willing to give active support, she has been reluctant to offer aid in the field of heavy industry, where the Taxila project is as yet the only one she has undertaken. This clearly shows China's limitations technically speaking.

The author would like here to insert a short note on this subject. While there is no field in technology and science in which China has not reached the top by world standards, she still lacks, in many fields, the broad basis of technicians that would enable her to join the ranks of the industrial nations of the world. The efforts she has made, and is making, in this direction are immense and deserve our highest respect, but they cannot possibly lead to full success within a year or two. We may safely assume, however, that China will be the first of the less developed countries to reach the status of an industrial nation. Her leaders'method of organizing mass campaigns with the aim of making the population take an active interest in the technological development of the country has certainly resulted in a widespread and deep involvement, so that the principles of modern management are entering into the consciousness of the masses to an ever-increasing extent. The much-ridiculed campaign of "front-garden furnaces" was also a positive contribution, not to be underestimated. Unless development is interrupted, this policy is sure to make China one of the leading industrial nations in the world within the space of a decade. Her political claim, as manifest in the economic aid offered, is a sort of anticipation of what China will be justified to claim after ten years.

Another centre of gravity in Chinese economic aid, as revealed by the table, is transport. Here China has done much in all fields, particularly road building, so that the infrastructure in all recipient countries has profited appreciably. This will also be true when China's most ambitious economic aid project, the Tan-Zam railway, is complete. In that project China is setting new standards in the world's economic aid schemes, with regard to both its comparatively low costs and the short time of construction.

All the other projects can only illustrate the great variety of China's ability and potential for making economic aid of real benefit to the recipients.

Table 11

THE CHINESE AID PROJECTS

according to branches and stages

		completed	under construction 1)	planned
Heavy industry		1		
Mining		2		1
Oil Industry		1	1	
Light industry		63	9	28
Textile mills		13	9	5
Broadcasting stations		9		
Buildings		31	4	6
Power stations	hydroelectric	7		5
	thermoelectric	2		2
Electrification		3		4
Transport	Roads	12	8	4
	Railway-lines	1	1	2
	Bridges	11	2	2
	Miscellaneous	2	1	1
Medical aid	Medical groups	4	10	
	Hospitals	7	3	
	Pharmaceutical plants	3		
Agriculture		16	9	13
Irrigation and water supply		10	4	6
Other projects		6		11
	Total:	200	61	90

1) including ten projects, which had not been completed when economic aid was discontinued in Burma, Ghana, and Indonesia

HEAVY INDUSTRY

Heavy machine factory

Country	Location	Time of construction
Pakistan	Taxila	1968-1971

MINING

Mechanization of mine

Country	Location	Time of construction
Albania	Valias	-1969 (?)

Metallurgical combine

Country	Location	Time of construction
Albania	Elbasan	-1971

Iron ore project

Country	Location	Time of construction
Pakistan	Baluchistan	planned

OIL INDUSTRY

Plant for crude-oil processing

Country	Location	Time of construction
Albania	Fieri district	-1969

Deep-oil processing plant and oil combine

Country	Location	Time of construction
Albania	Fieri	1971-

LIGHT INDUSTRY

Agricultural tools factory

Country	Location	Time of construction
Tanzania	Ubungo	1968-1970
	Mbweni	-1968

Alcohol factory

Country	Location	Time of construction
Mongolia, PR	Ulan Bator	?

Asbestos factory

Country	Location	Time of construction
Albania	Vlora	-1966

Brickworks / Brick and tile factories

Country	Location	Time of construction
Guinea	Kankan	1969-?
Mongolia, PR	?	
Nepal	Lalitpur	1965-1969
Tanzania	Koani (Pemba)	1970-1971 (?)
Uganda	?	1973-

Bamboo processing centre

Country	Location	Time of construction
Guinea	Conakry	1968-1969
Kenya	?	-1966

Bulb factory

Country	Location	Time of construction
Albania	Vlora	-1969

Cable factory

Country	Location	Time of construction
Albania	Shkodra	-1966

Caustic soda factory

Country	Location	Time of construction
Albania	Vlora	-1968

Cement-bag factory

Albania	Shkodra	-1965	

Cement plants

Albania	Elbasan	-1968	
	Fushe-Kruje	1964-1968	
Algeria	Constantine		planned
Burma			planned
Cambodia	Chakrey Ting	-1964	
Guinea	?		planned

Ceramic factory

Algeria	Gelma	1968-1971	

Cigarette (and match) factories

Guinea	near Conakry	1963-1964	
Mali	Bamako	1966-1967	
	Djioliba	1965-1968	
Somalia	Mogadishu	1972-	
Tanzania	Zanzibar		planned

Concrete factory

Albania	Shkodra	-1971 (?)	

Copper refinery

Albania	Rubik	-1968	

Diesel engine and water-pump factory

Burma			planned

Drug factory

Ghana			planned

Farm-tool plant

Guinea	Mamou region		under constr.

Fertilizer plants

Albania	Fieri	1965-1968	
	Lac	-1968	
Cambodia	Kampot	?	
Pakistan	East Pakistan (now Bangladesh)		planned
	near Peshawar		planned

Glass factories

Albania	Kavaja	-1970	
Cambodia	Stung Meanchey	-1968	
	Cholung EK	1966-1968	
Mongolia, PR	?		

Grinding mill

Mali	Sevare	-1972	

Instruments factory

Albania	Korca	-1969	

Lapis lazuli grinding works

Afghanistan	Kabul	1967-1970	

Leather and shoe factories

Burma	Shan state		planned
Nepal	Bansbari	1964-1965	
Tanzania	Maruhubi	1967-1968	

Meat factories (?)

Somalia	Juba region		planned
	Mogadishu		planned

Milk processing factory

Albania	Shkodra	-1970	

Needle-knitting mill

Burma		-1959 (?)	

Newsprint mill

Pakistan	Lower Sind		planned

Oil paint and lacquer factory

Albania	?	1968-?	

Ordnance factory

Pakistan	Gazipur (now Bangladesh)	-1970	

Paint factory

Albania	Tirana	-1969	

Palm-oil refinery

Congo (Brazz.)	?		planned
Guinea	Dabola	1968-1969	
Yemen	?		planned

Paper mills

Albania	Kavaja	-1966	
Burma	Sittang	1965-?	
Cambodia	Chhlong	-1961	
Indonesia	Tjiandju		not completed
Pakistan	Chittagong	1966-1969	

Pencil factory

Ghana	Kumasi		not completed

Plastics factory

Albania	Durres	-1971	
	Lushnje	1972-	

Plywood factories

Burma	Moulwein		planned
	Rangoon		planned
Cambodia	Dey Eth	-1962	
Ghana	?		planned
Mongolia, PR	?		

Porcelain and enamel factory

Ghana			planned

Potato-processinf factory

Mongolia, PR	?		

Printing office

Tanzania	Saateni (Zanzibar	-1967	
	Dares Salam	-1967	

PVC and caustic plant

Albania	Vlora	1971-?	

Refractory project

Pakistan	West Pakistan		planned or und.constr.

Rubberball manufacturing factory

Burma	unknown (1973)		planned

Sand brick factory

Egypt			planned

Salt production

South Yemen	Khormaksar	1971-	

Saw-mills

Albania	Tirana	-1965	
Congo (Brazz.)	?		planned
Tanzania	Zanzibar	-1971 (?)	

Sewing and embroidery factory

Albania	Korca	-1969	

Small-scale industrial plants

Algeria			planned?

Soda ash factory

Albania	Vlora	-1967	

Sugar refineries

Burma	Bilin Thaton distr.	1965-1966	
	Paungde	-1963	
Cambodia	Kompong Tram (?)		
Guinea	Koba	1972 (?)-	
Mali	Dougabougou	-1967	
Pakistan	Hyderabad (?)		planned
	Larkana		planned
Tanzania	Zanzibar		planned

Tannery

Mali	Bamako	-1970	

Tinned fruit and fruit-juice factory

Burma	Rangoon		planned

Tire factory

Burma	Danyingon	1965-	not complete
Cambodia	Takhman	?	

Tractor spare-part factory

Albania	Tirana	1963-1966	

Watch factory

Mali	?		planned

Wood furniture manufacturing factory

Tanzania	Nachingwei	-1972	

TEXTILE MILLS

Afghanistan	Bagrami	1969-1970	
Albania	Berat district	1966-1969	
Burma	Merktila	-1967	
	Thamaing	-1965 (?)	
	unknown (1973)		planned
Cambodia	Kompong Cham	-1960	
	Battambang	-1967	
Congo (Brazz.)	Kinsoundi	1966-1969	
Ghana	Juapong		not completed
Indonesia	Bandjaran		not completed
	Bandung		not completed
	6 more mills		not completed
Iraq	?		und.constr.
Mali	Ségou	1966-1968	
Mongolia, PR	Ulan Bator	1958-1960	
Nepal	?		planned
Pakistan	Tarbela		planned
	Mirpur		planned
South Yemen	Aden (?)	1971-	und.constr.
Sri Lanka	50 small mills	1968-	
	Pugoda		und.constr.?
	Minneriya		planned
Sudan	Hasahisa		under constr.
Syria	Hama	1969-1971	
	Idlib		und.constr.?
	Deir ez-Zor		planned
Tanzania	Ubungo	1966-1968	
	Ruvu	-1972	
Yemen	Sana	1964-1967	

BROADCASTING STATIONS

Albania	?	-1967	
	?	-1967	
Cambodia	Stung Meanchey	-1963	
Congo (Brazz.)	near Brazzaville	-1967	
	Kinkolo	-1970	
Mali	?	-1965 (?)	
	Bamako	-1970	
Tanzania	?	1965-1967	
Zambia	Lusaka	1970-1973	

BUILDINGS

Cinema/Theatre

Guinea	Conakry	-1968	
Mali	Bamako	-1967	

College building

Tanzania	Dares Salam	-1968	

Conference buildings

Guinea	Conakry	1966-1967	
Indonesia	Djakarta		not completed

Conference buildings (cont.)

Somalia	Mogadishu	1966-1967	
Sri Lanka	Colombo	1964-1973	
Sudan	Khartoum		und.constr.

Exhibition and fair buildings

Algeria	Sunawbar al Bahari Palais,near Algiers	1968-1970	
Mali	Bamako	-1968	

Home of Culture

Mauritania	Nouakchott	-1972	

Hotels

Malagasy	Nossi-Bé		und.constr.
Mali	Timbuktu	-1967	
	Bamako		planned
Mongolia, PR	Ulan Bator	-1961	
	Ulan Bator	-1961	
Sudan			planned

House of Youth

Mauritania	Mouakchott	-1970	

Party building

Tanzania	Zanzibar	-1970	

Sanatorium

Mongolia, PR		-1959	

Stores/Warehouses

Mongolia, PR	?	-1961	
Nepal	Kathmandu	1965-1967	
	Birgunj	1965-1967	

Sport stadiums

Mongolia, PR		-1958	
Sierra Leone		1973-	
Syria			planned
Tanzania	Zanzibar	1968-1970	

Sports town

Cambodia	Phnom Penh	1966-1968	

Teachers´training college

Cambodia	Preah Outey	-1962	

Technical and other schools

Algeria	Blida		planned (?)
Cambodia	Stungtrent	-1961	
	Preyvang	-1961	
Congo (Brazz.)	?		planned
Mongolia, PR	Ulan Bator	-1958	
Pakistan	West Pakistan	-1968	
	East Pakistan	-1968	
Tanzania	Zanzibar		planned
Yemen	Sana (?)	1968-1969	

Unknown uses

Cambodia	Svay Rieng	-1961	2 buildings
Mongolia, PR	Ulan Bator	-1958	
Tanzania	Michenzani	-1970 (?)	
	Kilimani	-1970 (?)	

POWER STATIONS

Hydroelectric stations

Albania	Shkodra district	1967-1971	
	Fierze	1971-	
Burma	Kentung		planned
	Kunlong		planned
	Machambaw		planned
	?		planned
Guinea	Kinkon Falls	1964-1967	
	Tinkosso		planned
Mongolia, PR	Suke Bataar	-1958	
	Tolgotin	-1961	
	Aimak Dornod	?	
Nepal	Sunkosi River	1968-1972	

Thermoelectric stations

Albania	Fieri district	1969	
	Korca	-1971	
Burma			planned
Pakistan	Quetta, Baluchistan		planned

ELECTRIFICATION PROJECTS

Albania	countryside	-1970	
Ethiopia	provincial towns		planned
Guinea	Central Guinea	-1970	
Nepal	Sunkosi-Kathmandu	1968-1972 (?)	
	Sunkosi-Chantara		planned
	Sunkosi-Barahbise		planned
Pakistan	Tarbela-Wah		planned

TRANSPORT

Railway-lines

Cambodia	Phnom Penh-Sihanoukville	-1961	traced out
Guinea	Guinea-Mali		planned
	Conakry-Kankan		repairs
Tanzania	Tanzania-Zambia	1970-	

Roads

Burma	Wa state		planned
Equatorial Guinea	Rio Muni province		und.constr.
Ethiopia	?		planned
Laos	China - Phong Saly	1962-1963	
	Phong Saly-Namtha		planned
Mongolia, PR	?	-1958	
	?	-1958	
	?	-1958	
	Ulan Bator	-1960	
	Ulan Bator-Nalaika		
Nepal	Kathmandu-Kodari	1963-1967	

Roads (cont.)			
Nepal (cont.	Kathmandu-Bhaktapur	1968-1970	
	Kathmandu-Pokhara	1965-	
	Pokhara-westward		planned
Pakistan	Halleh Kush-Khunjerab Pass	1966-1971	
Somalia	Belet Wen-Hargeisa		und.constr.(?)
South Yemen	1st Prov.-6th Prov.	1971-	
Sudan	Medani-Gedaref	1972-	
	Nyala-Zalingei		und.constr.
Tanzania	Maziwangombe-Wete	-1964	
Yemen	Hodeida-Sana	1958-1961	
	Sana-Sada	1967-	
Zambia	Lusaka-Mankoya	1970-1972	
	Lusaka-Kaoma	1970-	
Bridges			
Burma	Kunlon district	-1965	
	Takaw, Shan state	1967-	
Mongolia, PR	Ulan Bator	-1958	
	?	-1958	
	Ulan Bator	-1959	
	Bulegan province	-1959	
	Ara Changai prov	-1959	
	Ulan Bator	-1960	
	Ulan Bator	-1960	
	Ulan Bator	-1960	
	Ulan Bator	-1960	
	Selenga province	-1965 (?)	
Sierra Leone	Mange		planned
	Kambia		planned
Sudan	Wad Medani		und.constr.
Miscellaneous			
Airport			
Cambodia	Sien Rap	-1968	
Dockyards			
Congo (Brazz.)		1970-1972	
Malta			planned
Trolley-bus project			
Nepal		1973-	

MEDICAL AID

Medical groups			
Algeria		1963-	
Congo (Brazz.)		1967-1971	
Equatorial Guinea		1971-1973	
Guinea		1968-	
Mali		1968-	
Mauritania		1968-	
Sierra Leone		1973-	
Somalia		1965-	
South Yemen		1970	
Sudan		1971-	
Tanzania	Continent	1968-1972	
	Zanzibar	1966-1973	

Medical groups (cont.)

Tunisia		1973-	
Yemen		1966-	

Hospitals

Afghanistan		1972-	
Cambodia	Siem Reap	-1960	
	Phnom Poreay	?	
	Preakkat Mealea	-1969	
	Takeo Kampot	?	
Congo (Brazz.)	Fort Rousset		und.constr.
Mauritania	Kiffa	-1970	
South Yemen	Aden	-1970	
Tanzania	Mkoani (Pemba)	1969-1970	
Yemen	Taiz	1973	und.constr.

Phármaceutical plants

Tanzania		--1968	
		1969-1971	
		-1973	

AGRICULTURE

Cotton plantations

Congo (Brazz.)	Niary valley		planned
Equatorial Guinea	Micomisseng county		und.constr.
Nepal	Terai	1972-	und.constr.

Fish-breeding stations

Afghanistan	Darunta	1967-1968	
Congo (Brazz.)	Mossaka		planned
	Pointe-Noire		planned
Ghana	?		planned

Fruit plantation

Burma			planned

Poultry farms

Afghanistan	Bagrami	1968-1970	
Burma			planned
Mongolia, PR	Central Aimak	?	

Rice plantations

Guyana	?		planned
Mali	?		
Sierra Leone	Mange Bure		und.constr.
Somalia	Jowkar	1966-1970	
Sudan	Wad Medani		und.constr.
	Gezira area		und.constr.
	Owel		planned
Tanzania	Kilombero (Zanz.)	1966-1969?	
Uganda	Kibimba	1973-	und.constr.

Silkworm cultivation

Afghanistan	?	1967-?	
Burma	?		planned

State experimental farms

Congo (Brazz.)	Kombé	1970-1971	
Ghana	Volta district		not completed
Mauritania	M'pourie plain	1968-	
Tanzania	Ruwu	-1970	
	Upenja (Zanzibar)	1965-1969	
	Mbarali	1970-	

Sugar plantations

Mali	Markala	1962-1965	
Tanzania	Zanzibar		planned

Tea plantations

Afghanistan	Kunar province	1968-?	
Burma	?		planned
Congo (Brazz.)	?		planned
Guinea	Macenta	-1968	
Mali	Balinkoni	-1971	

IRRIGATION AND WATER SUPPLY

Afghanistan	?	1968-?	
	Parwan Province	1968-1971	
Algeria	?		planned
Burma	Yamethin district		planned
Mauritania	Kiffa		und.constr.
Mongolia, PR	Ulan Bator	-1960	
Somalia	Hargeisa		und.constr.
	Belet Wen		planned
	Baidaba		planned
	Galkaayu		planned
South Yemen	Am Ain-Mukalla road		und.constr.
Tanzania	Makundushi (Zanz.)	-1969	
	Chaanion (Zanzibar)	-1969	
	Machui (Pemba)	-1969	
	Douge Mbiji (Zanz.)	-1969	
	unknown		
	Douge (Zanzibar)	-1970 (?)	
Uganda	?	1973-	und.constr.
Yemen	Sana	-1969	

Water supply projects

Congo (Brazz.)			planned
Mauritania	Idini-Nouakchott	1971-1973	

OTHER PROJECTS

Albania	Laboratory for nuclear irradiation Tirana State Univ.	-1970	
	Computer centre, Tirana State Univ.	1971-?	
Burma	Extension of DEMAG-built steel works		planned
Cambodia	12 laboratories and one factory for Royal Royal Compong Cham University	-1968	

Ghana	Grass-plaiting	-1965	
Guinea	Monument	1970-?	
Somalia	Research institute		planned
South Yemen	Wharf for fishing-boats		planned
Sri Lanka	Rolling stock	1962-1966	
	Flood-control scheme		planned
Sudan	Prospecting of chrome deposits		planned